William Henry Paynter, aged 37

THE CORNISH WITCH-FINDER

*William Henry Paynter
and the Witchery, Ghosts,
Charms and Folklore of Cornwall*

Selected and Introduced by
JASON SEMMENS

Foreword by Dr Owen Davies

THE FEDERATION OF OLD CORNWALL SOCIETIES

First published in 2008 by the
Federation of Old Cornwall Societies,
Wingfield, 5 British Road, St Agnes, Cornwall, TR5 0TX

www.oldcornwall.org

Copyright © The Estate of William Henry Paynter
and Jason Semmens, 2008

ISBN 978-0-902660-39-7

All rights reserved. No part of this publication may be
reproduced, stored in a retrieval system, or transmitted in any form
or by any means, electronic, mechanical, photocopying, recording
or otherwise, without the prior permission of the publishers.

Printed and bound in Cornwall by
R Booth Ltd, The Praze, Penryn, Cornwall TR10 8AA

CONTENTS

Acknowledgements		7
Foreword		8
Introduction		10
PART ONE:	W. H. P.	21
Chapter 1:	Life and Background	22
Chapter 2:	"Whyler Pystry"	29
Chapter 3:	"Things that go Bump in the Night"	40
Chapter 4:	Old Cornwall	50
PART TWO:	SELECTIONS	65
Chapter 5:	Witch-Hunting in Cornwall	66
Chapter 6:	Cornish Charms and Cures	98
Chapter 7:	Cornish Ghosts and Haunted Houses	143
Chapter 8:	Cornish Hugger Mugger	178
Chapter 9:	Tales of Mystery and Imagination	194
Appendix A:	Thomas-Paynter Correspondence (1928)	217
Appendix B:	Cornish Witchcraft Queries (1928)	228
Notes and References		231
William Paynter: Select Bibliography		249

Cornish Litany

From ghoulies and ghosties and
long-leggetty beasties, and
things that go bump in the night,
Good Lord Deliver Us.

ACKNOWLEDGEMENTS

Inevitably a work of this kind accrues many debts, some mention of which it is my pleasure to record. The book would not have been possible without the enthusiasm and generous co-operation of Paynter's daughter Anne Tucker and his grandchildren Jane, Nichola and Jeremy. Along with sharing their memories of Bill and his work, as the copyright holders of his works they have granted permission to reprint Paynter's writings and allowed access to the archive of his papers still held by the family. My thanks are also due to Terry Knight, Kim Cooper and staff at the Cornish Studies Library, Redruth; Angela Broome and staff of the Courtney Library, Truro; Ian Criddle and staff at the Local and Naval Studies Library, Plymouth; Heather Medlan and staff at the Liskeard and District Museum, Liskeard; Barbara Birchwood-Harper at the Guildhall Museum, Looe; Dr. Caroline Oates at the Folklore Society Library, London; David Thomas and staff at the Cornwall Record Office, Truro; the staff of the British Library, St. Pancras; the staff of the Hyman Kreitman Research Centre at Tate Britain, London; and the staff of the British Library Newspaper Collection, Colindale. Further thanks are extended to Nik Brooks, Jo Clarke, Dr. Owen Davies, Robert Evans, Ron George, Dr. Amy Hale, Brian Hoggard, Professor Ronald Hutton, the late Robert Lenkiewicz, Richard Paynter, John Rapson and Taraneh Rastan for assistance and support in their various ways. Further gratitude is extended to the Publications Committee of the Federation of Old Cornwall Societies who undertook to publish this book; given that the Old Cornwall movement did so much to stimulate the work in the pages that follow, it is entirely appropriate that it should appear under the Federation's aegis.

Jason Semmens

FOREWORD

I first took notice of William Paynter when I read an article of his in *Old Cornwall* in which he mentioned that he had written but not yet published a book on Cornish witchcraft. After confirming that it had not been published since, I decided to see if I could track down its whereabouts. A few phone calls soon led me to his daughter who very kindly spent an hour on the telephone talking about her father and his work. Sad to say it transpired that his manuscript on witchcraft, for which he had been unable to find sufficient subscribers to raise the print costs, had gone missing in the years since. But I came away with the feeling that this hugely energetic Cornishman had made a big contribution to our knowledge of Cornish culture and its supernatural beliefs. The diffuseness and breadth of his activities, giving many public lectures, writing newspaper articles, running a museum, to name a few, has meant that his overall contribution had not been properly recognized until now. My own research took me off in different directions and I did not follow the Paynter story any further. It was with great pleasure, then, that I received the news that Jason Semmens was engaged in researching his life and putting together a bibliography of his work.

Paynter began writing and researching at a time when traditional beliefs and customs were fast disappearing across the county, as they were elsewhere in the country. The fabric of communities and local economies was being teased apart or transformed under the influence of national and global developments. Local and regional rural identities were diminished in the process. Fewer and fewer people were relying on the supernatural to explain and prevent misfortune and ill health. As Paynter's work shows, after the Second World War some Cornish people continued to resort to charming and charmers for their minor ailments, and ghosts still roamed the countryside, but the world of cunning-folk and witches that he recorded in the 1920s and 1930s was fast vanishing.

It is a shame that Paynter never recorded his considerable knowledge of this changing cultural landscape in a major study of Cornish folklore. As admirable as his public engagement activities were, such an opus would have provided a valuable companion to the earlier studies of the county's popular culture by Robert Hunt, William Bottrell and Margaret Ann Courtney. As it is, we need to piece together the numerous excerpts of his research to get the bigger picture of traditional beliefs in mid-twentieth-century Cornwall. Jason Semmens is to be congratulated for so skillfully taking on this task, giving us a sensitive portrait of an indefatigable and proud Cornishman, and in the process highlighting the contribution he made to the county.

Owen Davies
University of Hertfordshire

Introduction

William Henry Paynter, born in Cornwall at the start of the twentieth century, began his career as a folklorist at a time of particular significance. Belief in witchcraft, ill-wishing and the malignant power of the Evil Eye as an explanation for persistent illness and misfortune amongst humans and domesticated animals had held sway in Western Europe for several centuries. In spite of the spread of materialist philosophies and the "march of intellect" during the seventeenth to nineteenth centuries, witchcraft was still a vital prop in the mental outlook of certain portions of the British population by the early twentieth century.[1] The inter-war years of the 1920s and 1930s saw the effective collapse and near extinction of such beliefs, however, and Paynter's practice as a folklore researcher and fieldworker throughout the South West of England coincided with the period of this decline as he witnessed the steady disappearance of such characters as benign cunning-folk and malevolent witches from the fabric of society. In his own lifetime Paynter was regarded as "the eminent Cornish folklorist" on account of his interest in vernacular Westcountry beliefs, yet posterity has been less mindful of Paynter's work as a regional folklore collector and has overlooked his contribution to the study of the decline of witch-beliefs within a local context.[2]

The nineteenth century is generally reckoned as the 'golden age' of British folklore collecting, when an awareness of the gradual erosion of the country's agrarian economy by the widespread growth of industrialism prompted middle-class collectors to record what were regarded as "the fast-fading relics of the Past which have existed in the forms of legend, tradition and superstition ... through ages innumerable."[3] Folklore collecting was often concentrated in areas perceived as culturally different, and indeed the Cornish folklore collections of Robert Hunt (1807–1887), William Bottrell (1816–1881) and Margaret Ann Courtney (1834–

1920) are still consulted by those seeking a tradition of native, non-English folk culture. Paynter's name is rarely included in the litany of folklorists to have recorded and preserved the oral traditions and folk-practices of Cornwall before the Second World War, after which so many of the old beliefs in "things that go bump in the night" finally faded. The reason for this oversight is not difficult to establish; whereas Hunt, Bottrell and Courtney published their collections of Cornish folklore in books—*The Popular Romances of the West of England* (1865), *Traditions and Hearthside Stories of West Penwith* (1870, 1873 and 1880) and *Cornish Feasts and Folk-lore* (1890) respectively, Paynter's findings were reported in numerous popular articles published by the South West regional newspapers and local history journals, the scattered and ephemeral nature of which has served to obscure Paynter's original contribution. This compendium of Paynter's folklore collections seeks to address the unwarranted obscurity into which Paynter's reputation has subsided since his death in 1976. It presents the most significant part of his published and manuscript works on early to mid twentieth-century Cornish folk practices and beliefs in the supernatural world and offers an alternative perspective to the notion that the spiritual beliefs of the Cornish extended little further than the nearest Methodist chapel.

When Bill Paynter, as he was generally known, began collecting Cornish folklore in the mid 1920s, he found that belief in ghosts, witchcraft, mermaids and fairies was still common and that the resorting to conjurors, gypsies and charmers for cures was prevalent in many districts throughout the Duchy. Such characters were the subject of a steady stream of articles that flowed from Paynter's pen into the late 1930s which, taken together, describe the nature and persistence of supernatural beliefs long after such 'superstitions' were thought to have died out. Paynter was among a number of early twentieth-century folklore enthusiasts dotted around the country engaged in similar fieldwork. Along with contemporaries such as Ethel Rudkin (1893–1985) in Lincolnshire,

Ruth Tongue (1898–1981) in Somerset and Enid Porter (1909–1984) in Cambridgeshire,[4] Paynter researched local folklore as a pastime and while Cornwall remained at the heart of his interest he occasionally strayed across the border as far east as Somerset in search of material. Paynter was by no means alone in his concern to record popular Cornish beliefs as perusal of the early issues of the *Old Cornwall* journal and the various local newspapers from the 1920s and 1930s shows, although the depth and persistence of his research ensured that Paynter was regarded as *the* authority on the supernatural in Cornwall. It is unclear quite how well versed Paynter was with contemporary folklore theory and practice though his success as a folklorist derived from his enthusiasm and dedication and an innate understanding of the reticence of informants to discuss their beliefs; with time and patience Paynter found that he could "get behind the scenes" and in so doing discovered "the pattern of Westcountry and especially Cornish superstitions."[5]

The supernatural world that Paynter uncovered during his research differed little in many respects from that believed in two or three centuries earlier. By the medieval period, ancient practices of sorcery and enchantment had fused with Christian notions of the Devil and of evil, resulting in the widely held belief in the supernatural power of witches to inflict harm and spread disease. It was held possible to be 'overlooked' or 'begrudged' by an ill-wish from a witch with baleful consequences.[6] Known as maleficium, from the Latin word for harm, witchcraft was initially the concern of ecclesiastical courts as a sin against God and a heresy although its nature as a crime against person and property led to its first entry onto the statute books of England in 1542. Henceforth witches could be tried by secular courts and successive acts of Parliament in 1563 and 1604 increased the severity of punishments meted out to malefactors convicted of practising the conjuration of evil spirits, witchcraft, sorcery and enchantment.[7] The path from accusation to eventual trial for witchcraft was a lengthy and uncertain process owing to the number of justices and juries that needed to be convinced of a witch's guilt. The surviving records and descriptions of the Cornwall Assizes indicate that at least three dozen individuals were incarcerated at Launceston during the seventeenth century to stand trial for witchcraft, of which at least eight were found guilty and executed.[8]

A more immediate alternative to the often prolonged legal process was the host of magical practitioners called cunning-folk, or conjurors, who sprang up in towns and villages across the country during the early modern period. They specialised in detecting and countering the effects of witchcraft, with people turning to them when they became ill or had sickly livestock. Cunning-folk offered means of divining the identity of an ill-wisher, often by looking into a reflective surface, and they provided written charms or powders to affect cures. Their prescriptions were drawn from several books of magic published during the mid-seventeenth century, and later, during the occult revival of the early nineteenth century, a host of chap-books and popular manuals of magic were similarly employed. Cunning-folk offered a wide range of occult arts besides witch-detection, such as divination in its various forms—for the finding of lost or stolen goods and discovering the future, and often less preternatural services such as herbalism. Most cunning-folk practiced on a part-time basis, enjoying a modest demand in their localities but are little known today; with skill and business acumen, several conjurors developed their reputations to the point that they could practice full-time, often with enduring fame or even notoriety. Cunning-folk were a staple of British society so long as witches were feared to be present and Paynter was particularly interested in such characters.[9]

At the outset of his research Paynter contended that people had become more superstitious in the years after 1918, in reaction to the horrors of the First World War, and he described the virtue people placed in lucky charms and fortune tellers.[10] He found that belief in ill-wishing was still fairly common in rural communities across Cornwall, both east and west, especially where dairy farming was prevalent. The 1604 Witchcraft Act was repealed in 1735, replaced by another that defined witchcraft as an imposture; with no further recourse allowed to a local justice, many bewitched people of the nineteenth and early twentieth centuries decided to confront those whom they considered ill-wishers directly, to "get their own back" by 'scratching' or assaulting the malefactor to break their curse. Paynter witnessed several examples of people using such 'cures' to combat ill-wishing. During the early modern period the Devil was held to lie behind cases of witchcraft, as either he or his hoards of hellish minions tempted the godly or offered wealth and carnal pleasures to the weak willed, the old and the disenfranchised in return for their fealty. With time Satan seems to have gradually loosened his grip as the consort of witches in the popular mind as by Paynter's day witches were the authors of a range of illnesses visited upon people and cattle by their reliance on the Evil Eye—such individuals betrayed by an inherent quirk or anomalous physical attribute that imbued the owner with baleful capabilities.[11]

Witchcraft was one aspect of a wider milieu of supernatural beliefs, much of which incorporated astrological and Neoplatonic lore, as Paynter came across numerous individuals who conducted their lives according to the phases of the moon or positions of the planets, many of whose practices relied on sympathetic magic and mystical correspondences and antipathies within the natural world. During his fieldwork Paynter also had frequent contact with charmers—specialists in the treatment of skin diseases such as ringworm and shingles, and ailments of an accidental nature: burns, cuts and the like. Unlike cunning-folk, who learned their trade from books, charmers practised a tradition of folk-healing passed down in secret contra-sexually through the generations; they did not diagnose a cause for illness, rather their store of charms were used solely for healing purposes. Along with other folklorists Paynter found considerable difficulty discovering the words charmers used as it was held that once committed to print the virtue of the charm was lost, although he was sometimes able to coax a charmer to talk about his or her practice.[12] Paynter's research on charmers into the 1960s is an indicator of the continued demand for their services, but unlike the Devon folklorist Theo Brown (1914–1993),[13] who published on charmers as late as 1970, Paynter's main publications on the topic all date from the 1930s. Paynter generally referred to all magical practitioners by the mid-nineteenth century west Cornish dialect word 'Peller,' and invariably described them as "white-witches" or "wise-men or women." At lectures Paynter stated that "he would only deal with charmers who, with black and grey witches, were the exponents of the craft."[14] In his blurring of magical practitioners' roles, Paynter followed other English folklorists who similarly failed to differentiate between various types of practitioner, confusing the conceptual differences between them.

Paynter regarded his work "as a social study into folklore," and opined that "So much of it is disappearing as the old folk die. It is so important to record them before they are completely lost."[15] Paynter's inspiration for his folklore recording was the work of the Old Cornwall movement, whose motto, "Gather ye the fragments that are left, that nothing be lost," guided him on his investigations. He was a founder member of the Callington Old Cornwall Society and an early bard of the Cornish Gorsedd. Paynter's folkloric research contributed to the Old Cornwall movement's aim of preserving what were perceived as surviving relics of the 'Celtic' culture of Cornwall, which assumed vital importance in the years following the movement's inception in 1920 as surviving examples of folklore contributed to a sense of cultural difference. Although the contemporary impact of Paynter's researches has faded, his published articles on early twentieth-century Cornish folklore did much to inspire the development of the notion of a uniquely *Cornish* identity. As well as folklorist, Paynter described himself as an antiquary and historian, immersing himself in the rich archaeological and historical heritage of East Cornwall, and he conducted archival research on a variety of Cornish topics upon which he published. As such, Paynter's significance extends beyond folklore studies, and his multi-faceted interests in Cornwall and Cornish life offers insight into the preoccupations of early members of the Old Cornwall movement, their methods of enquiry and the variety of their contacts.

Until the 1970s, with a few notable exceptions, witchcraft and associated supernatural beliefs were not generally studied by professional historians who regarded them as delusional and fringe. The pioneering researches of Keith Thomas and Alan Macfarlane grounded belief in the supernatural within the everyday experience of early modern Western societies, bringing witch beliefs fully within the orbit of academia. In recent years witches and cunning-folk have attracted renewed attention with a series of studies examining their role and function in society and their eventual demise. Whereas the Enlightenment and education were once thought to have banished witch beliefs, recent research has suggested instead that demographic changes, the widespread adoption of personal insurance, the mechanisation of farming and the introduction of the National Health Service all combined to undermine belief in the power of witchcraft,[16] to which may be added the early twentieth-century growth of interest in Spiritualism and the rapid spread of electricity in the domestic sphere during the 1920s and 1930s, so that by the 1950s notions of ill-wishing were increasingly rarely met with. Put simply, witchcraft withered away because it ceased to be a relevant or viable explanation for misfortune.

It is against this background that the field research and publications of eye-witnesses to the decline, such as the work of William Paynter, have assumed a new importance, as Paynter's writings chart the gradual dearth and eventual collapse of witch-beliefs in Cornwall during the critical early to mid decades of the twentieth century. In spite of the occult revival of the mid-twentieth century, which owed much of its popularity to the 1960s counter-culture, in 1969 Paynter could declare that "Witch-belief in its traditional form appears to have gone for ever."[17]

*   *   *

The Cornish Witch-finder builds upon research conducted for a paper on Paynter's life and practice as a folklorist published in the journal *Folklore* in 2005.[18] The bulk of the previous research focused upon Paynter's newspaper contributions supplemented by telephone conversations with Paynter's daughter, Anne Tucker, in July 1998; a visit to the Liskeard Museum at its former site on West Street in June 1999, where a small collection of Paynter's manuscript notes were available to view; and by a visit to the Guildhall Museum, East Looe, where many of the items from Paynter's Cornish Museum ended up, in September 2002. Renewed contact with Paynter's family in July 2005 lead to viewing the remaining archive of his notes in family hands, previously thought lost, and a subsequent visit to the newly relocated and reorganised Liskeard and District Museum brought to light a further cache of manuscript material.

The manuscript notes have enriched the view of Paynter presented in the *Folklore* paper and permit a more detailed understanding of his work as a folklorist and historian. While nothing in the newly discovered notes contradict views previously expressed, a few small matters of fact have been corrected in this volume, as noted by family members and not discernable from the newspaper reports. All of Paynter's manuscript works printed here for the first time derive from either the family or museum archives, denoted as Paynter Archive A and Paynter Archive B respectively. Whereas the *Folklore* paper examined Paynter's position as a regional folklorist and offered some commentary on his findings, the introductory chapters of this volume focus in greater detail on Paynter's experiences during his investigations and discuss the wider concerns surrounding Paynter's fieldwork.

This book is divided into two sections. The first opens with a narrative overview of Paynter's life and interests in East Cornwall followed by two chapters exploring the context of his writings—that is, the scope and concerns of his folkloric researches; the section concludes with an examination of the milieu within which Paynter conducted his researches centred on his membership of the Old Cornwall movement. The second section presents the most significant parts of Paynter's published and unpublished works, bringing together for the first time his collection of Cornish folklore. As intimated above, the compilation and codifying of folklore is often associated with the nineteenth century, with the gathering of the Droll-tellers' fireside yarns, yet Paynter's is as significant a corpus of folklore research as those collected by Hunt, Bottrell and Courtney, as his collections demonstrate the vitality of folk-beliefs in witchcraft, ghosts and the supernatural world into the post-industrial landscape of twentieth-century Cornwall. Paynter's published articles were some of the key texts that Cornish revivalists searching for descriptions of Celtic 'otherness' through folklore drew upon, in spite of their obscurity today; besides all of which, Paynter had many excellent, uncanny tales to tell.

The various newspaper articles included in this volume are presented in their entirety except where Paynter reused material, often whole paragraphs across several contemporaneous pieces. Their provenance is indicated in the 'Notes and References' towards the rear of the book. Abridged sections are indicated thus … The contemporary newspaper practice of inserting single word or phrase paragraph breaks has been dispensed with except in the case of "West Country Folk-medicine" (1929) and in the manuscript article "Ghosts" (1953), where the sense of the paragraphs following require them. Spelling mistakes and infelicities of grammar have also been silently corrected: most are found in the manuscript papers. Occasional words have been inserted where the sense of a passage requires them, indicated by square brackets. As the sole primary source material to survive from Paynter's fieldwork recognizably used as the basis of his writings on witchcraft, the texts of five recently rediscovered letters written to Paynter by the Camborne antiquary Jim Thomas in 1928 are reproduced verbatim in Appendix A.[19] The letters allow comparison between Paynter's source material and his published works on Cornish witches for the first time and they illuminate the manner in which Paynter utilised his sources, sometimes highlighting misreadings and omissions. Appendix B comprises several queries Paynter sent to an anonymous correspondent resident in the locality of Tintagel, dated 27 July 1928.[20] The two-page manuscript consists of a series of typed questions concerning several individuals suspected of witchcraft together with hand-written replies; again, they offer insight into Paynter's research methods. Finally a comprehensive bibliography of Paynter's published works is included, incorporating his monographs, articles, columns and letters.

PART ONE:

W. H. P.

Life and background

William Henry Paynter was born on 3 January 1901 at Callington in East Cornwall.[1] On his father's side he was descended from a family of tenant farmers and small holders originally from the Jacobstow area of North Cornwall, though by the 1870s his grandfather Henry Paynter (1854–1908) had settled further south at St. Dominic.[2] Paynter's mother's ancestors were miners and labourers from Gwennap in West Cornwall.[3] His maternal grandfather James Noble (1848–1928) was the son of a mine captain and educated at the old Truro College. According to Paynter he enjoyed a varied career, by turns salesman for a firm of London goldsmiths, a sportsman, an auctioneers' assistant, and the foreman of a pottery.[4] Noble arrived at Callington about 1870 as landlord of the Sun Inn on Fore Street,[5] where Paynter's mother Elizabeth Bowhay Noble (1873–1946) was born.

Callington was an ancient market town that had depended for centuries on the local agricultural economy. In the late eighteenth century it found new prosperity in the mineral wealth of the area, and the mining of tin, copper, silver and lead saw a number of mines open in the district, centred on Hingston Down, of which Kit Hill forms the summit. The mining boom peaked in the latter half of the nineteenth century and by the early twentieth Callington's mines had largely closed and fallen into disrepair.[6] With this economic decline and the inevitability of farm labouring as an alternative, William Henry Paynter senior (1873–1948) opted for a career with the Royal Navy and was a Leading Stoker aboard HMS Nile about the time of Paynter's birth.[7] Paynter was the eldest of 6 children, born between 1901 and 1915. The family lived at 2, Haye Road throughout Paynter's youth,[8] from where he attended

Callington National School and later Callington County School. Paynter's early aspirations as a writer were encouraged by Lilian Read (1886–1975), one of his teachers at the National School, who "taught him how to put his thoughts upon paper" and with whom he formed a friendship in later life.[9]

From his youth Paynter cultivated a wide set of interests and hobbies, one of the most enduring was the Callington troop of Boy Scouts which he joined on 5 December 1911.[10] The Scouts admitted boys between the ages of 10 and 18, though Paynter maintained his interest in the movement into the 1920s and attended a Scoutmasters' training course at Newquay on 1 April 1920. He was Scoutmaster of the Callington group from 31 October 1921 until his resignation on 21 October 1929, which he said was due to pressure of other commitments.[11] He was persuaded to reorganise the troop in May 1938 and became Acting District Commissioner in 1939.[12] Alongside Scoutmaster, Paynter was also the Royal Society for the Protection of Birds local secretary and organiser of the Royal Society for the Prevention of Cruelty to Animals Callington branch.[13] His keen interest in birds and wildlife took Paynter around East Cornwall and he spent many weekends on the north coast of Cornwall bird-watching. His intimate familiarity with North and East Cornwall was later exploited when he took up folklore collecting. Upon ceasing full-time education in his early teens, Paynter found employment at a local solicitors' firm as a junior clerk, and until his early 50s worked in fairly low-paid clerical positions.[14] He found he could earn extra income as a writer and from 1924 onwards was a regular contributor of articles to local newspapers.

For several years during the 1920s he wrote weekly columns on scouting and wildlife themes for the Tavistock-based *East Cornwall Times* and the Plymouth-based *Western Morning News*. In 1928 he became the Callington correspondent for the Liskeard-based *Cornish Times* and contributed occasional articles and a weekly column under the pseudonym "Kit Hill," under which guise he wrote until March 1940.¹⁵ The columns contained current news and items of interest, such as historical notes, scraps of folklore, and forthcoming events. The newspapers also carried extensive reviews of his many lectures, often quoting him; although

Paynter inspecting the Caradon Meteorite
(Courtesy of John Rapson)

anonymous, it seems likely that Paynter penned these reports himself as a few draft versions exist in the surviving archives of his notes. In the 1920s Paynter became a councillor on the Callington Urban District Council and continued on the local parish council after the former's amalgamation with the St. German's Rural District Council on 1 April 1934.¹⁶ As a councillor, Paynter was involved with the establishment of a road to the summit of Kit Hill, ceremonially opened by the Mayor of Plymouth on 8 September 1928.[17]

It was during the 1920s that Paynter embarked upon a tireless period of folklore research and fieldwork, spanning the later 1920s and 1930s, detailed below in chapters 2 and 3. He travelled over Cornwall in search of tales and surviving examples of witchcraft, ghosts, exorcists, mermaids, and piskies, amongst others. In 1928 he was a founder member of the Callington Old Cornwall Society, involvement in which did much to stimulate his interest in folklore and historical research in Cornwall, as discussed in chapter 4.

Paynter remained single into his early 30s, and as a well-known figure in the town participated in a Callington Women's Institute debate on 5 May 1931 about the married and single states. Paynter "championed the cause of the Bachelor and Spinster" against an advocate for marriage,[18] though shortly afterwards he met Doris Mary Roberts (1907–1990) of Saltash, and they married on 23 June 1932 at St. Stephens by Saltash.[19] The couple honeymooned on the north Cornish coast. Following their marriage, the Paynters moved to 'Heathfield,' Launceston Road, Callington, where their daughter Anne was born in 1934.[20]

Despite his new commitments Paynter maintained his various interests, and from 1939 he found himself in demand as a speaker at the B.B.C. studios at Plymouth, contributing pieces on folklore and items of local interest to various programmes on the regional radio broadcasting service. With the growth of television in the decades following, Paynter was often 'on location' at various events, including the Camborne Show, Guy Fawkes night celebrations, and the Old Cornwall Societies Midsummer bonfire events.[21]

In the autumn of 1939 Paynter developed tuberculosis; the condition forced him to give up his job and in October 1939 he spent the first of several months recuperating at the TB Sanatorium at Tehidy, near Camborne.[22] 'Heathfield' was vacated and Paynter's wife and daughter lodged with a relative at Saltash.[23] In January 1940 Paynter resigned as scout commissioner and tendered his resignation from the council, though initially this was rejected.[24] Prolonged absence from Callington ensured that the resignation was accepted on 18 February 1941.[25] As the Second World War got underway, the onset of tuberculosis thwarted any intention Paynter had regarding military service, though he was able to volunteer with the Army Cadets when he regained his health, in which he rose to the rank of Captain. The Army Cadets formed a kind of home guard and provided initial military-style training for many teenage boys who went on to enlist in the regular army.[26]

Following his return from Tehidy to East Cornwall during late 1940 or early 1941,[27] Paynter found employment at Liskeard as a clerk with the firm Caunter, Venning and Harwood.[28] With this appointment the Paynters left Callington and moved into 18, Castle Street—"a half-hidden cottage, which was once a barn and used as a meeting-house by John Wesley's followers."[29] The building consisted of four rooms, carved out of the two originally used from 1776 to 1800 for preaching, and an old stable underneath formerly for the Methodist ministers' horses.[30] At Liskeard Paynter involved himself in the civic and social life of the town, as he had at Callington. As well as the local Old Cornwall Society, Paynter joined the Liskeard Drama Group and performed in several productions, he also became their secretary and wrote plays for the group.[31] Paynter stood for election onto the town council and in the 1950s was appointed Archivist for the Borough of Liskeard; later, in the mid 1960s, he became Deputy Mayor.[32]

In 1956 Anne Paynter married local businessman Henry Tucker, of 'Roseland,' Menheniot. As one of several interests in Liskeard, Tucker purchased land on the new housing developments at Miners Meadow, Addington, on which he built a bungalow. Paynter, his wife, and sister-in-law Hilda Roberts moved into the house in September 1961.[33] The bungalow was named 'Janola,' taking elements from 'Jane' and 'Nichola'—Paynter's eldest grandchildren, and was his permanent address for the rest of his life. Although Paynter enjoyed a late lucrative career as salesman for the typewriter supplies firm Farquharson Brothers from 1953 onwards,[34] about 1958 Paynter abandoned full-time employment to manage his son-in-law's zoo at East Looe for a year or so before creating his own museum in the town during 1959. 'The Cornish Museum' became Paynter's main concern during his later years and was open to visitors during the summer months, from Easter to October. Paynter rented a flat above the museum for the season to avoid the daily commute from Liskeard, and returned to 'Janola' for the winter.[35]

Paynter outside the Cornish Museum.
(Courtesy of Jeremy Tucker)

During the 1960s and early 1970s Paynter occupied his winters with adult education lectures for the Workers' Educational Association (WEA) and Cornwall Education Committee in Plymouth and East Cornwall. He offered courses on Cornish history, folklore, and the history of Liskeard, delivering as many as eight separate courses concurrently;[36] for many years he was also a popular lecturer and after dinner speaker to various groups and societies around Devon and Cornwall. Paynter maintained an active schedule of lectures, committees' attendance, and television and radio appearances until a couple of weeks before his death. He died at the Passmore Edwards Hospital, Liskeard, on 5 June 1976, of coronary thrombosis and ischaemic heart disease.[37] His funeral service was held on 10 June 1976 at St. Martin's Church, Liskeard, at which his lifelong interests in folklore and historical research were highlighted.[38] Paynter's cremated remains were later scattered at the Cheesewring, the curious granite outcrop on the eastern edge of Bodmin Moor, which had been the focus of his antiquarian interests throughout his life.[3]

A studio portrait of Paynter in 1960 (Courtesy of John Rapson)

"Whyler Pystry"

Paynter's maternal grandfather James Noble was largely responsible for his interest in the supernatural, as the older man regaled Paynter with uncanny tales during his early, impressionable years. After school hours it was his habit to visit his grandparents to do his homework, as Paynter recalled: "It was always a rush to get the homework completed, and then followed the drawing up of the settle to the open-hearth fire to hear about smugglers, highwaymen, witches, ghosts and things that go bump in the night." So lurid were some of the tales that on "many occasions when he was afraid to go home, after hearing many of the old Cornish stories, [he] had to be accompanied by either his grandfather or his grandmother to his own home."[1]

Paynter's adult interest in researching occult beliefs and practices developed in the mid 1920s following a meeting of the nascent Federation of Old Cornwall Societies. Paynter later described how, "While waiting for the meeting to begin, [he] entertained a small audience at the back of the hall with one of his witch stories. It was so interesting that [he] was invited to retell the story from the Platform." Luminaries of the early Old Cornwall movement who heard Paynter speak, including Robert Morton Nance (1873–1959) and A. K. Hamilton Jenkin (1900–1980), encouraged him to venture onto "the highway[s] and byways of Cornwall and collect all the stories he could about witches and wizards, charms and charmers."[2] Thus began Paynter's self-styled "witch hunt." Paynter conceived an ambitious scheme to visit every parish in Cornwall in search of tales of ill-wishing and spell-breaking, seeking specific individuals for interview and taking advantage of chance meetings and leads; he also frequented "old

Cornish Inns, off the beaten track, where aged farmers and clay miners congregate,"[3] and spoke to the "old fisher boys who sit on a bench by the quay and swap tales, or the old woman of the village who doesn't mind talking about her superstitions."[4] The notion of a "witch hunt" recalled the activities of the seventeenth-century 'Witch-finder General' Matthew Hopkins, whom Paynter enjoyed likening himself to at lectures, although he admitted that whereas Hopkins bayed for blood he was content to collect stories only.[5] While many of the folk-tales and experiences Paynter heard were undoubtedly assiduously recorded, none of his field notebooks are known to exist; Paynter was also careful not to betray the confidence that many of his informants placed in him, for fear of embarrassment or ridicule, and as such most of his sources for witch-narratives are anonymous.

One of Paynter's few known contacts, on whom he relied for a considerable quantity of his field-notes for West Cornwall, was the Camborne antiquary Jim Thomas. Thomas *(left; photo courtesy of Jeremy Tucker)*, more properly Frederick James Thomas (1850–1934), was a member of the Camborne Old Cornwall Society and a Fellow of the Geological Society. He was a respected authority on Cornish history and archaeology, including flints and Cornish crosses, and was consulted by the folk-song collector Cecil Sharp.[6] According to Paynter, Thomas knew "every alleged witch and charmer from Truro to the Land's End"[7] and he initially contacted Thomas in early 1928 to ask for information concerning the two nineteenth-century Cornish cunning-folk Thomasine Blight (1793–1856), otherwise known as Tammy Blee, and her second husband James Thomas (1814–1874).[8] The two men began a correspondence that lasted the spring in which Thomas provided Paynter with a considerable quantity of relations and tales, not only of Blight and Thomas but also of other lesser-known conjurors drawn either from personal acquaintance or from that of Thomas's friends.

Paynter also visited Thomas at his home during April 1928. Thomas had what he called "Tammy Blee's Scent Bottle" in his possession—a 300-year old painted glass bottle that was apparently used by Blight to hold love potions. Paynter suggested that Thomas should publish the bottle and the latter arranged for it to be photographed professionally while Paynter wrote the accompanying article, published on 26 April 1928. The bottle was broken sometime after Paynter's visit though Thomas mounted several glass fragments in a wooden surround and presented the relic to Paynter.

In May 1928 Paynter discovered the oil portrait of Thomasine Blight lodged in an attic at Truro. This, along with Thomas's letters, was the basis of his 4 June 1928 article that retold several surviving recollections of Blight by individuals who had known her personally or had heard tales from relatives who had done so. The article and its "Scent Bottle" predecessor illustrate some of the problems Paynter encountered when trying to evaluate the folklore he collected. When publishing the bottle Paynter took the details of Blight's life and the "disgraceful offence" of her husband from Hunt's *Popular Romances* rather than from Thomas's letters.[9] Hunt had reprinted the original 1863 *West Briton* account of James Thomas's attempts to share a bed with a bewitched woman's husband some 13 years previously—the earliest and sole account of the affair.[10] In recounting this, Paynter ignored Thomas's assertion that James Thomas the cunning-man was a native of Wendron (which was the case) in favour of the newspaper correspondent's statement that he was born at Illogan. Evidently Paynter did not verify by research which location was correct and regarded Hunt's printed account as accurate, although he did accept the number of years Thomas alleged the two cunning-folk had been dead, which in both cases was incorrect. The letters also illustrate how far Paynter paraphrased his sources to suit the journalistic nature of his writing and the popular audience his articles were intended for. Furthermore, comparison between the articles and letters reveals that at one point Paynter misread Thomas's notes and that the story told by Paynter of Blight bewitching her unfortunate cobbler in fact referred to another woman reputed in 1870s Camborne to be a witch (and identified as such by James Thomas the cunning-man). Paynter's unidentified "young man," described as leaving the employment of the cobbler for America only to return, may now be identified as Jim Thomas.

In East Cornwall, Paynter had the assistance of Barbara Catherine Spooner (1893–1983), also an Old Cornwall activist, who had independently taken an interest in folklore research and collected witch narratives in the North Hill area where she lived. In 1929 and 1930 Spooner provided Paynter with several sheets of type-written notes recording interviews she had conducted with at least eight individuals who, between them, recalled tales of contemporary charming practices on the north Cornish coast, methods used for unbewitching the ill-wished by two nineteenth-century East Cornwall cunning-men and beliefs concerning witchcraft and the Evil Eye in Egloskerry and North Hill parishes within the previous 50 years.[11]

Alongside interviewing the elderly and gathering narratives from his Old Cornwall acquaintances, Paynter was also witness to a number of cases of alleged witchcraft, as he related at his lectures and in some of his articles during the 1930s. For example, from his youth he could remember "quack pedlars" at local fairs, one of whom was renowned as the "Great White Witch." Paynter recalled that this character was "well versed in witchcraft, and could without apparent difficulty lift and remove evil spells."[12] In 1932 he stated that two people at Liskeard believed themselves

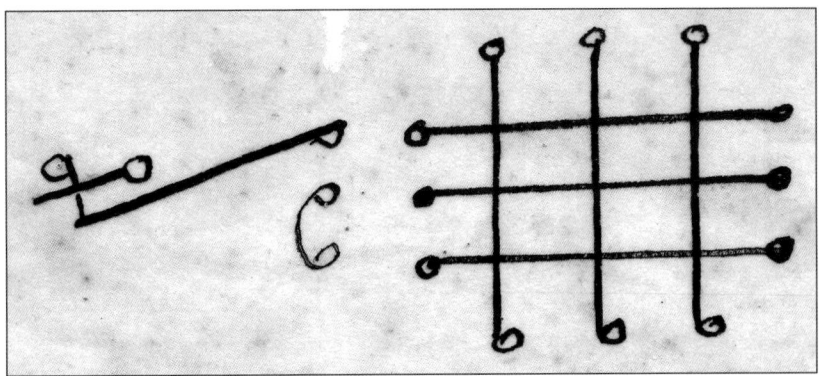

Detail of a charm to expel and drive away flies, to be written on a plate of tin (Courtesy of Jeremy Tucker)

ill-wished after a visitation of body lice: "One man was simply infested, he could do nothing to get rid of them. So he went to a wise woman whose name and address I have, and she told him the only thing to do was to go to the highest field in the parish at sunrise, take off his shirt, 'flink' it three times," and shout out some words she prescribed.[13] Paynter also "spoke of a whole farm near Launceston being bewitched quite recently and the spell was removed by "The great White Witch of Holsworthy.""[14] In his "witch hunt" Paynter also came across numerous instances of the charming of skin diseases and accidental cuts or scalds, and could assert that "there were large numbers of men and women in Cornwall today who can actually charm ... I have seen several people who can stop bleeding, no matter how deep the cut."[15] Despite his interest in actual cases of ill-wishing, Paynter seems not to have investigated the inter-personal conflicts that were the mainstay of witchcraft accusations, presumably out of respect for the participants' privacy.

Paynter regarded his early interest in witchcraft as a literary pursuit, believing that "nothing was too improbable for human credence. Belief in charms, witches, wizards and wise women should have vanished, but it had not, as numerous instances proved." He went on to note that "There were still many people weak enough to put their faith in silly impostors."[16] With time though, as he witnessed a number of curious events, Paynter's opinion gradually changed, and by 1932 he "contended that the many strange and weird happenings he had come across could not be dismissed with a flip of the finger."[17] In his "Witches and Witchcraft" article, Paynter suggested that "There IS something in witchcraft, but what the SOMETHING is I am content to leave for an abler pen than mind to describe,"[18] and despite occasionally glib dismissals,[19] Paynter seems to have remained convinced of witchcraft's intrinsic power. Towards the end of his life Paynter resorted to psychological explanations to demystify the power of witchcraft, as discussed in his 1969 article "Cornish Witchcraft," although in none of his articles did he attempt to explain or articulate his understanding of the philosophical basis of witchcraft. The closest he came was during his WEA lectures in the early 1970s, where he seems to have understood witchcraft practices as the fragmentary remains of a once joyful ancient religion misunderstood as malignant by a hostile Christian church.[20] This interpretation was originally propounded in Margaret Murray's *The Witch Cult in Western Europe* (1921), though it was not until its republication in 1962 that Murray's thesis gained a popular audience, eager for a theory of non-demonic, pre-Christian origins for witchcraft practices. Murray's *Witch Cult* came under sustained attack during the early 1970s, following the publication of Alan Macfarlane's *Witchcraft in Tudor and Stuart England* (1970) and Keith Thomas's *Religion and the Decline of Magic* (1971), neither of which volumes Paynter appears to have been aware of.[21]

On the strength of his research Paynter began giving lectures on witchcraft and the occult from 1929 onwards and spoke to various groups and societies, including the Old Cornwall societies, Women's Institutes and Young Farmers' organisations. Paynter was often popularly referred to as "The Cornish Witch Finder"—the nickname he based his bardic name "Whyler Pystry" upon (meaning "Searcher out of Witchcraft") when he was initiated bard of the Cornish Gorsedd in August 1930. Due to his interest in the supernatural "Whyler Pystry" was often mistaken for a witch; from the late 1920s onwards Paynter received letters from the desperate begging him to use his powers to help them find lost money, rekindle former relationships, charm warts and cure a range of maladies, and this despite his frequent disavowal "I am not a witch, I cannot charm, and I don't believe in fortune telling."[22] Indeed, when asked in 1973 whether he had ever dabbled in witchcraft, Paynter replied, "I have never tried to practice the old spells," adding, "I keep an open mind on the subject. Things do happen sometimes that I cannot explain but it is not up to me to explain them."[23]

Almost as soon as Paynter began writing articles on witchcraft for the popular press he began work on a book detailing his findings. While references to the book in the early 1930s described *Cornish Witchcraft* or *Cornish Witches and Wizards* as its title, the manuscript was eventually completed in February 1939 and entitled *The Confessions of a Westcountry Witch-finder*.[24] The *Confessions* were written with the collaboration of Plymouth schoolteacher Kathleen May Goad (1900–1966),[25] who came to Paynter's attention in 1931 following the publication of her newspaper article on Midsummer customs.[26] The *Confessions* manuscript weighed in at a little over 55,000 words and Paynter found considerable difficulty interesting publishers in what they viewed as a volume of entirely local appeal. For example, Paynter approached London publisher Peter Owen on 8 February 1957 at the suggestion of artist Ithell Colquhoun (1908–1988) whose own

The Living Stones: Cornwall had then been published, though by August following the manuscript had been returned. Paynter was sanguine about the repeated rejections, noting "I am not unduly worried, it is all original research, and one say I shall hit the jackpot!"[27]

In the event the *Confessions* were never published. The personalised title suggests that rather than presenting a general history of witchcraft in Cornwall the book focused on Paynter's experiences and findings while engaged on his "witch hunt" fieldwork. This is consistent with his published articles on witchcraft, that highlighted contemporary beliefs in ill-wishing and the memories of a generation or two earlier.

At no point in his writings did Paynter demonstrate knowledge of historical cases of witchcraft in Cornwall, such as the several Assize court trials of the seventeenth century, and there is little evidence of sustained archival research into nineteenth-century witchcraft beliefs, such as those described in the *West Briton* and *Royal Cornwall Gazette* newspapers. The manuscript is now lost.

Along with folktales and narratives, Paynter collected an assortment of witchcraft-related artefacts on his "witch hunt" that curious visitors to his home might view. His house was a "veritable museum of necromancy" according to A. K. Hamilton Jenkin, who visited Paynter at Callington in 1932.[28] The extensive collection of curios included "amulets of ash twigs to ward off fits; sheep's teeth carried in a bag to ease toothache; a moleskin to resist disease and danger; wish bones from a chicken carried for luck by lovers; various stones for curing warts and bad eyes; a witches crystal and wand, and powdered herbs which have to be dropped into milk to prevent it turning to butter."[29] There was also a "charm box in [the] shape of a coffin; [a] bottle containing hundreds of thousands used as a charm; a charm against the Evil Eye; a "kennin[g]" or Eye stone for charming eye complaints; the famous Abracadabra charm *(pictured opposite)*; a "mommet" *(below [author's photographs])*, small wax or carved image of intended victim ... [and] a Written Charm on parchment for snake bites."[30] On her visit one weekend in 1955, Ithell Colquhoun was shown a carved West African doll that had been used for image magic:

> "Mr. Paynter showed me one carved with fair skill in some black wood, with two nails driven into the heart and one into the left thigh. The agonised grin on the features was realistic, and the whole tiny image exhaled a malign force."[31]

Paynter also possessed some manuscript sigils, employed in ritual magic, apparently taken from Francis Barrett's *The Magus* (1801), and a printed paperback copy of the grimoire *The Sixth and Seventh Books of Moses* (1881).[32] While Paynter relied on donors for the artefacts in his collection, he is also known to have practised more suggestive methods for obtaining those items that he coveted yet were still held to offer protection by their owners. There was an occasion at Penzance when Paynter "had persuaded a householder to part with a charm against misfortunes happening by day only by offering an alternative one which would protect the home both day and night."[33] When he established his Cornish Museum at Looe, Paynter included his occult collection in the exhibition. As the museum just predated the arrival of Cecil Williamson's 'Museum of Witchcraft' in Cornwall, which moved to Boscastle in 1960, it could thereby claim to have been the oldest public display of such material in the Duchy.

As intimated above, Paynter's main period as an active collector of witchcraft narratives spanned the 1920s through until the outbreak of the Second World War, after which such beliefs declined sharply, though Paynter continued to take an interest in the wider milieu of Cornish folk-practices and beliefs into his old age. Despite the continuing interest, Paynter's main articles on such beliefs, like those on witchcraft, all mostly date from the inter-war years. The persistence of charming traditions in the South West proved a particularly fertile field for research, as Paynter noted in the 1950s: "At the moment I am carrying out research into Charms and Charming, a fascinating subject."[34] Of the various letters received by Paynter he always responded to those asking for the charming of warts, usually by promising to pass the request on to charmers he knew, and he asked the sufferers to write back to let him know if this worked—this was one way in which he extended his research. After taking part in the B.B.C. television programme "Have a Go" in 1962, Paynter was surprised at the response to his appearance as he received letters from both Wales and Scotland in addition to those from local addresses. Several were addressed to "The Faith Healer," others to "The Charmer."[35]

Alongside the Cornish Museum, 'Museum Enterprises' was established as a business outlet for charms that Paynter provided to tourists and those who wrote to him. Paynter had long been aware of 'Dragon's Blood' as a charm traditionally used in love magic, and he sold the powder in packets to the lovesick. He provided a covering note describing its origin with exact instructions for its use.[36] The tourist trade in lucky charms was also exploited as

Paynter designed his own talisman, called the "Hap Da"—Cornish for "Good Luck." In the accompanying booklet Paynter described the symbolism present on the talisman, though far from being emblems of good fortune the "Hap Da" bore an engine house, a Cornish cross, a chough, a cromlech and a pilchard. In spite of the dubious apotropaic qualities of the symbols, the talisman apparently sold well.[37]

The novelty of Paynter's research coupled with his heightened media profile from appearances and lectures prompted interest amongst other writers on Cornwall's history. As the recognized authority on the occult in Cornwall there were few books on the subject published during the second and third quarters of the twentieth century that did not mention Paynter. One of the earliest was by A. K. Hamilton Jenkin, who visited him while collecting material for *Cornwall and the Cornish* (1933). Several of the tales Jenkin printed are recognizably Paynter's, and Jenkin included Paynter's photograph of Tammy Blee's portrait among the illustrations. Over 20 years later Ithell Colquhoun devoted a chapter to him in her esoteric pilgrimage around Cornwall, published as *The Living Stones: Cornwall* (1957).[38] From 1929 onwards, journalists from both local and national papers were also eager to hear of surviving beliefs in witches in the Westcountry. The scene that greeted them was described by journalist Russell Hawke, who visited Paynter at 'Janola' in early 1975: "I found him in the attic of his pink-washed bungalow in Miners Meadow on the edge of town. The walls were lined with his work—bookcase after bookcase of heavy volumes on the occult, folders filed across the floor and boxes of tape recordings."[39]

"Things that go bump in the night"

Ghosts and apparitions were another aspect of the supernatural world in which Paynter developed an early interest and he collected Cornish ghost stories and legends while engaged on the "witch hunt." Alongside gathering reports of sightings, Paynter also carried out his own ghost hunts, and his investigations into haunted houses continued long after the hunt for witches had effectively concluded. The ubiquity of ghost stories and sightings intrigued Paynter, as he noted: "The Westcountry has always been famous for its spooks, and there is hardly a village which does not possess a sinister house, haunted road, lane or field." The range of reported apparitions also fascinated him: "ghosts in old-time costume that walk through walls and up and down stairs, ghosts that have hollow mocking laughs, ghosts that grope at one's neck and body with bony fingers and try to strangle, a ghost in the form of a spider, another in the form of a nigger, while at a well-known crossroads the devil can be seen driving a phantom coach across the sky."[1] Paynter began lecturing on Cornish ghosts in the mid 1930s and by then had already conducted a series of ghost hunts at several reputed haunted sites. Later in his career Paynter remarked that "there can be few known haunted houses in East and Central Cornwall which he has not visited in pursuit of ghosts."[2]

Although Paynter denied ever having seen a ghost himself he was prepared to believe that others who claimed they had had at least experienced *something*, and while he was circumspect with divulging his sources for witch-tales, no such reservations attended the naming of his informants for ghosts. This openness reflected a more widespread, general acceptance of the possibility of apparitions entertained by the British public.[3] Paynter's own attitude towards the existence of ghosts was cautious; for example, when asked at a lecture in 1953 whether he believed in ghosts, "he laughed, and stroking his chin he said 'Well, the truth of the matter is I do—and I don't.'"[4] Paynter's ghost hunts were designed to establish the 'truth' of a haunting and demonstrate the objective existence of ghosts by collecting unequivocal, empirical evidence. Paynter's forensic precision reflected the general preoccupations of twentieth-century psychical researchers with proving apparitions by scientific means and he certainly read literature produced by special interest groups involved in such work. What is less clear is whether he paid much attention to the social context of specific apparitions in his investigations, or indeed if Paynter considered the function of such appearances to the witnesses involved. Paynter appears to have restricted his psychical investigations to local ghost stories and possible poltergeist activity; the wider contemporary interest in mediums, séances, clairvoyance and E.S.P. does not seem to have concerned him. If he kept them, no case books recording his vigils survive.[5]

    The earliest investigation known in detail was into the appearance of a phantom 'Black Dog' at Bangor's Hill, Linkinhorne.[6] The 'Black Dog' was a form of ghostly phenomena known from extensive reports and sightings across England during the nineteenth and early twentieth centuries.[7] The apparitions were generally those of either abnormally large dogs or those with unusual or exaggerated features, such as having eyes like saucers or no head altogether. As the name implies, the ghostly dogs were almost always black in colour. In February 1937 several residents of the parish reported seeing a large black dog on the road between Linkinhorne and Rilla Mill after dark that vanished when touched or approached too closely. As news of the apparition spread, further sightings were reported during the daytime. Paynter interviewed several witnesses and described their accounts to the local newspapers, which took an interest in the case, and even supplied a report to the *Daily Mail*.[8] On 19 February 1937 Paynter spent the early evening until 10 p.m. on the road, "in a gale of wind, and with the young moon being continually obscured by heavy black clouds," in hopes of a sighting, though the two young men from Liskeard who succeeded him on his vigil until midnight also failed to see the dog. Apparently Paynter determined to lay the ghost if it appeared to him and reckoned that he had the requisite formula for so doing: "It is to assume first that the manifestations are signs of the presence of a tormented soul; that the disturbance is a call from the dead. Then find out what is the nightmare from which the dead is suffering, dissipate it, and with the nightmare the ghost will go."[9] Despite the fear that surrounded the Linkinhorne Black Dog, an explanation came eventually in the shape of "a grey farm dog with a long chain which has been straying in the parish," whose capture brought an end to the sightings.[10]

Over several years during the late 1930s and early 1940s, Paynter often took his young daughter with him on his ghost hunts, who assisted him by sprinkling talcum powder on floors and placing cotton on doorways to detect any interference from this world or beyond,[11] though despite frequent strange and unsettling sensations Paynter reported that "ghosts were very elusive, and [I have] not had the pleasure of meeting one face to face!"[12] Paynter was also accompanied on his otherwise lonely vigils by Prince Birabongse Bhanubandh (1914–1985), cousin of Prince Chula Chakrabongse (1908–1964), the English-educated heir to the throne of Siam. Paynter met Prince Chula during the early 1940s at an Army Cadet training camp, in whose activities Chakrabongse was involved, and the two men formed a firm friendship. Chakrabongse purchased Tredethy House, near Bodmin, in 1945 and Paynter was a frequent and welcome guest at Tredethy.[13] While Bira and Chakrabongse both had a passion for motor car racing, Birabongse had leanings towards the occult and took especial interest in Paynter's investigations.

Their most extensively described ghost hunt took place on the evening of 15 December 1947, when Bira accompanied Paynter and Henry Maxwell the barrister to Madford House, near Launceston, which was the reputed haunt of a "ghost which was said to cause the sound of hollow footsteps, occurring first in the cellar and them moving slowly up two flights of stairs, to fade away into a wall at the end of a corridor." The B.B.C. had originally intended to send a van to record any strange happenings, though subsequently abandoned the plan. As the arrangements were already fixed, the 3 men pressed on with the watch regardless. Paynter recounted the events of the night at the September 1953 meeting of the Tavistock Young Farmers' Club:

> "[T]he Prince and I laid our traps. We put powder on the staircase where the ghost was supposed to have been seen. You can guess what it was for.
>
> "We cottoned the doors and I held one position and Prince Bira the other. We were in touch with each other by means of the cotton. But it was a cold job sitting there in the dark waiting, waiting, waiting … for what?
>
> "Nothing happened. No ghost appeared, until it got to be midnight when I was so bitterly cold in that freezing staircase that I determined to give up the quest.
>
> "I told the Prince and we agreed to come away, when all at once there was a strange sound. The Prince and I asked each other the same question: "Did you hear what I heard?"
>
> "The quest was on again. Soon that strange, haunting eerie sound came again. It was like a sigh and a groan in one. It chilled the spine. Then we heard a chain rattle slightly. But it was unmistakably a rattle.
>
> "The quest was on in earnest.

"Then the Prince and I agreed the sound came from a certain room off the staircase. Quietly we opened the door wondering what the room on the other side had to reveal. The Prince flashed on his torch ... We gasped."[14]

As with the 1937 Linkinhorne Black Dog haunting, the cause of the strange noises was a perfectly live dog, in this case a Great Dane left in the house on guard duty by its owners.

Alongside his ghost hunts, Paynter conducted archival research to determine any factual, historical basis for ghostly traditions. The apparition of the '6-foot Negro' said to haunt old Whiteford House near Stoke Climsland came to Paynter's attention around 1950 after the editor of a national newspaper contacted him, asking him to investigate. Paynter spoke to several people who claimed to have seen the apparition, reputed to be the ghost of a black man brought to Cornwall when Sir John Cale, M.P. for Callington in 1790, returned from his travels in the East. A bloodstain was rumoured to appear on the anniversary of the Negro's death, killed after murdering Sir John's wife with his connivance. Paynter contacted the British Museum, and "After a lot of trouble I got ... a photograph of the beautiful old house as it was in those days." He also visited the parish church to inspect the registers: "Believe it or not I found an entry ... under 'Burials,' in the time of Sir John's occupation of the old house. You see the date and the following entry—'A man of colour was buried in the churchyard.'"[15]

Despite his own lack of success in ghost hunting, Paynter collected Cornish ghost stories over many years from those who claimed they had seen apparitions, 'percipients' as he called them, which collection he framed into a book during the late 1940s with the collaboration of Muriel Hawkey (1915–1993), editor of *A Cornish Chorus* (1948). Originally entitled *Cornish Ghosts and Haunted Houses*, the book was later renamed *Cornish Ghosts and Other Strange Happenings in Cornwall* to take account of a widening of its scope. Hawkey and Paynter's book enjoyed a fate similar to the *Confessions* in that Paynter spent several years trying, unsuccessfully, to find a publisher for it. *Cornish Ghosts* was apparently being considered for publication in November 1949; later, in September 1953, it was 'about' to be published though failed to appear.[16]

The surviving manuscript consists of an introduction, a preface by John Courtenay Trewin (1908–1990), a 3-page contents list and 5 complete chapters: 'The Murder of Charlotte Dymond and Subsequent Appearance of her Ghost,' 'A Midnight Apparition,' 'The Mysterious Visitor,' 'Haunted House near St. Ives' and 'The Phantom Hound of Linkinhorne.'[17] It seems likely that the manuscript represents as much of the book as Hawkey and Paynter prepared—the introduction, contents, and sample chapters—to interest potential publishers, with the intention of writing the rest of the book once a publishing deal was secured.[18] Two further chapters, 'The Dream of Mr. Williams of Scorrier House' and 'The Botathen Ghost,' were also sketched, and consist only of short introductions to *The Times* report of 16 August 1868 and the account of the seventeenth-century cleric Parson Rudall respectively. From the contents list and the surviving chapters, the projected extent and tenor of the book may be gauged.

Hawkey and Paynter appear to have intended to retell ghost stories as related to them or to quote their percipients verbatim, and claimed to have included "only true accounts, that is to say, true in the sense that the people who experienced them really believed they happened." From the surviving portions there appears have been little or no exposition on the history or nature of ghosts with the narratives presented to readers either to form their own opinions concerning the existence of ghosts or merely to titillate. As Hawkey and Paynter noted in their introduction, the book would have contained other tales besides ghosts and covered prophetic dreams, glimpses into the future and miracles. The miraculous tales included the story of "the donkey which returned to St. Hilary for Christmas"—evidently taken from Bernard

Walke's *Twenty Years at St. Hilary* (1935). Alongside contemporary, or near contemporary accounts of hauntings, Hawkey and Paynter intended that selections from the work of Robert Hunt and William Bottrell would be included under the heading 'Legendary Ghost Stories of Cornwall.' While none of these chapters exist in manuscript, the contents pages indicate which tales Hawkey and Paynter had in mind.

Aside from the *Cornish Ghosts* book, Paynter wrote at least one other work on ghosts intended for publication, in 1953, though this was also rejected; as such, the only material on ghosts published in his lifetime are the various newspaper reports of his lectures on ghosts that he probably wrote himself. Notwithstanding the lack of a publication record on apparitions, Paynter developed a considerable reputation as an authority on ghosts, and as with witches this led to his home being an essential stopping point on the itineraries of other writers treating of the same theme. While researching the chapter 'A West Country Ghost Hunt' for his book *Haunted Houses* (1956), Joseph Braddock (1902–1986) called on Paynter in 1955 and found him "as hospitable as he was interesting." The two men "talked in his home until the small hours about all sorts of subjects,"[19] and Paynter supplied Braddock with several uncanny tales, including two from personal experience—one a prophetic dream (possibly the same as the chapter 'A Cornishman's Dream' listed in the *Cornish Ghosts* manuscript), the other an account of an uncomfortable, restless night spent at Tregantle Fort, the site of Army Cadet activities during the early 1940s.[20] Paynter related how he was sent to sleep in a room in which an unlucky soldier some years earlier had cheated at cards and as punishment was forced to strip off his clothes and spend the night naked outside. He was found dead from exposure the next morning. It was only after the sleepless night that Paynter learned of the room's dread reputation. In places in his text, Braddock evidently owed more to Paynter than he acknowledged, as a comparison between his chapter introduction and Paynter's 1953 article "Ghosts" demonstrates.

Short fiction was another aspect of his work as an author that Paynter began to explore more fully from the 1930s onwards, and his knowledge of Westcountry ghost lore served as inspiration for various rum tales that Paynter generally submitted for publication to newspapers as Christmas ghost stories, often referring to them as 'Tales of Mystery and Imagination.' The earliest of these, "The Mysterious Visitor," was published in the *Cornish Times* on 24 December 1937, and aside from alteration into a first person narrative it is identical to the chapter of the same title in the later *Cornish Ghosts* manuscript. Further stories in successive years revolved around nightmares, uncanny coincidences, communication with the dead, and threatening ghostly apparitions—many of which reworked or combined tales intended for the *Cornish Ghosts* book.

The folklore associated with ghosts was also explored in at least one broadcast for B.B.C. radio in the mid-1950s, taking as its introduction beliefs in premonitory apparitions upon St. Mark's Eve. The theme of St. Mark's Eve was also the basis of Paynter's two-act play of that title, started about the same time as his radio script though never apparently completed or performed.[21] The first act involved discussion of superstitions and 'primitive' beliefs against the claims of Christianity and rationalism; the second saw the character of the Vicar, Henry Burngullon, enter a graveyard about midnight on April 24th, when ghostly projections of those of the parish who were to die during the following year would appear. In view of his fieldwork on both ghosts and witches, something of Paynter's own views towards the beliefs he spent his life researching may be detected in the following exchange between the Vicar and the character Miss Venton Vane:

> VICAR   Good heavens woman, you and your superstitions drive me mad. One would think we were living in the middle ages. What a

burden you make of life Miss Vane. You bow to this and that, you spit and mumble at that which you do not like and of which you are afraid. You wear and carry charms and talismans for every complaint, ailment and trouble under the sun. In fact your very existence is controlled by the stars whose influences good or bad are dictated to you by the daily and Sunday newspapers. Isn't it time you dropped those primitive beliefs and practices? Surely Miss Venton Vane, with the free education of today, a National Health Scheme shared by all comers, roving evangelists and the ever on tap wireless and television it's about time you grew up.

MISS VANE   (Annoyed and agitated). No Vicar, in spite of what you say there are more things...

VICAR   In heaven and earth than are dreamt of in our philosophy. Such stuff and nonsense.

MISS VANE   No it's not stuff and nonsense. Pause. After all Vicar, what's the difference in the stuff and nonsense you've been preaching for so many years?

VICAR   (Surprised). Me?

MISS VANE   Yes, you and your so-called faith and religion is not a wit better. You chant mumbo jumbo exactly like the witch-doctor. You distribute charms and passports for this world and the next and when we poor deluded souls question their worth or value you damn us for ever.

The ghosts in Paynter's folklore collections reflected the popular belief in apparitions as the souls of the dead returning from an undefined spirit realm on specific errands—often unfinished business or as witness to a violent end, and were generally associated with specific places or localities. This notion contained echoes of the Catholic doctrine of Purgatory that the Protestant Reformation was never wholly able to erase.[22] Paynter's research revealed how far supernatural beliefs in the early twentieth century were indelibly part of the mental outlook of the Cornish, just as they had been in the eighteenth and nineteenth centuries when the Cornish acceptance and adoption of Wesley's evangelism had been predicated on a common belief in ghosts and witches.[23] While Paynter was unable to prove the existence of the spirit world from his vigils, his collection of ghost stories and witness accounts demonstrated unequivocally that beliefs in the intervention of spiritual agencies had lost none of their potency and had survived the influences of 'modernity' into the present, ready to be exploited as curious 'survivals' in Cornwall's resurgent interest in its own past.

Old Cornwall

Paynter's interest in folklore collecting was intimately connected with his participation in the activities of the early Old Cornwall movement, and it remains to describe this involvement and examine the wider scope of Paynter's studies in Cornish history. The Old Cornwall movement had its roots in the late nineteenth century, in the desire to see Cornwall recognized as a Celtic nation and member of the Celtic Association, something it achieved following the publication of Henry Jenner's (1848–1934) *Handbook of the Cornish Language* in 1904.[1] Calls during the first decade of the twentieth century for the preservation and revival of Cornwall's Celtic heritage reached fruition following the founding of the first Old Cornwall Society at St. Ives in 1920.[2] The Society's stated aim for the recording and preservation of Cornish culture "embrace[d] the antiquities, dialect, folklore, the ancient Cornish language, and other things relating to the history and traditions of the county of Cornwall,"[3] and was later adopted by the Federation of Old Cornwall Societies when further societies were established in West Cornwall during the early 1920s. Robert Morton Nance later elaborated that such "fragments" should be collected "not as dead stuff to be learnedly discussed nor as merely amusing trifles," but rather understood as "the Living Tradition of the Cornish People."[4]

The emphasis upon antiquities, language and folklore reflected late eighteenth and nineteenth-century assumptions about the shared cultural identities of the 'Celtic fringe' territories of Western Europe. Folklore and folk-practices especially were seen in terms of 'survivals' from the pre-modern, pre-industrial past, and

William Henry Paynter in 1930 (Courtesy of Jeremy Tucker)

therefore understood as authentic examples of Celtic culture and belief. It has been suggested that "Folklore collecting and the rise of cultural nationalism are intimately related,"[5] and the nineteenth-century folklore collections of Robert Hunt, William Bottrell and Margaret Courtney helped to define the early Cornish-Celtic movement's sense of its own traditions and Celticity. After Henry Jenner's support from the Cornwall Education Committee for his scheme to collect Cornish folklore in the early 1900s, it followed that folklore collecting should have been recommended to Old Cornwall Society members, for the recovery of the contemporary, living 'Celtic' culture of Cornwall to bolster the sense of a Cornish national identity into the twentieth century.[6]

Paynter attended early Old Cornwall Federation meetings during the 1920s, of necessity held in West Cornwall, and he felt the need for a society local to East Cornwall. The possibility of a Callington Old Cornwall Society was discussed with friends such as Lawrence Maker (1902–1972), who was also involved with the Scouts, and Paynter contacted Henry Jenner and Robert Morton Nance with a view to affiliating the prospective Callington Society to the Federation. The formation of the Society was announced in Paynter's "Kit Hill" column on 5 October 1928:

> *I sincerely hope that all lovers of Cornwall will make a special point of being present at the public meeting to be held this (Friday) evening, to discuss the proposed formation of an Old Cornwall Society in the town.*
>
> *As a contributor pointed out in last week's "Cornish Times," local patriotism is a virtue to be commended, and we are in danger of losing it in these days of flux and change.*
>
> *With the stimulus which an Old Cornwall Society would supply, much priceless local interest might be preserved. Certainly if such a society was formed it would call attention to the collection of historic survivals which exist in and around the town ... It is with these aims in view that the starting of such a*

Society is contemplated, and, I hope, will become a familiar feature of Callington life.[7]

At the inaugural meeting a constitution for the Society was adopted, based on the pattern already developed by the existing societies, and its key officers appointed. Paynter took the position of the Society's 'Recorder,' whose responsibility it was to receive items of local interest and history from members and to record them for posterity in notebooks. Such a position assisted Paynter in his personal collecting of local folklore and history, though to what degree is uncertain as the Callington Society's notebook is not now known to exist. While Paynter's earliest newspaper articles, published from 1924 onwards, reflected his youthful interests in wildlife and the Boy Scout movement, the change of focus onto Cornish topics from 1927 onwards suggests his deepening identification with the aims of the Old Cornwall movement at this time.

Liskeard Old Cornwall Society's Programme of Events for St. John's Eve, 1948. (Courtesy of Jeremy Tucker)

Liskeard Old Cornwall Society.

Kyntelleugh an brewyon es gesys, na vo kellys travyth.
(Gather ye up the fragments that are left, that nothing be lost).

St. John's Eve Celebrations, St. Cleer Downs,
Near Liskeard, Cornwall.   23rd June, 1948.

PROGRAMME

8 p.m.	Flora Dance through the village of St. Cleer.
8 to 9 p.m.	Maypole and Folk Dancing by the School Children.
9 p.m.	Welcome to ONE AND ALL by Mr. A. H. Philp, President of Liskeard Old Cornwall Society.
9 to 10 p.m.	Reading of the COLLECT for the Benediction of the Fire of St. John from the "Ritual of Montauban" in France (printed in 1785) and a short address by Rev. A. Lane-Davies, Vicar of St. Cleer.
	A Short Description of the ancient Customs and Superstitions connected with St. John's Eve by Mr. William H. Paynter.
	Songs in Cornish.
	BRO GOTH AGAN TASOW (*Land of our Fathers*)
	ARTA EF A-DHE (*He shall come again*) School Children.
10 p.m.	The Bonfire will be lighted by Mrs. W. H. H. Huddy, President of Liskeard Women's Institute
	When the fire is well alight, Mr. Edwin Chirgwin will throw on the flames a garland of emblematic plants and weeds with the cry in Cornish: " Ny a-wra kepar del o gwres gans agan kendasow yn dedhyow solabrys", meaning "We do as our fathers did in the days that are long past".
10.30 p.m.	Hand-in-hand Dance round the Bonfire.
11 p.m.	Singing of the National Anthem.

The Hon. Secretary, Mr. Kenneth Oates, will be happy to give any information as to membership of the Society.

The recovery of Cornwall's Celtic culture by the Old Cornwall movement extended beyond the recording and preservation of the Duchy's immediate past, as, along with the ancient Cornish Language, several members called for the revival of extinct customs that were perceived as Celtic traditions, with a view to assimilating them into contemporary culture. For example, in 1919 Nance suggested the revival of Christmas guising at St. Ives,[8] elements of which, he believed, were Celtic, such as the 'Penglaze' hobby horse that once accompanied the guisers in nineteenth-century Penzance.[9] Later, the eighteenth-century Cornish antiquary William Borlase's (1695–1772) account of a chain of beacons on the hilltops between Land's End and the Tamar was similarly cited as evidence for the survival of an ancient Druidic practice until relatively recent times. The first suggestion for the revival of the Midsummer bonfires was aired by A. K. Hamilton Jenkin at a general gathering of Old Cornwall Societies held at Penzance on 4 January 1929.[10] Paynter took up Jenkin's call and was instrumental in the Callington Society's participation that summer of the 'Revival of Ancient Midsummer Customs,' which culminated in the lighting of a beacon on the summit of Kit Hill on 24 June 1929.[11] Prior to the ignition of the bonfire, Paynter gave a short description of the many customs associated with the Midsummer fires, starting a tradition of his speaking at the Callington, and later Liskeard, Old Cornwall Society's Midsummer events that lasted many years. The sole version of his speech to survive dates from 1948, at St. Cleer Downs, and while probably typical of his earlier talks, it owes a considerable debt to the newspaper article on Midsummer customs published in 1930 by the otherwise anonymous "J. F."[12]

Paynter's activism within the Old Cornwall movement and his prolific media profile ensured his early membership of the Cornish Gorsedd, which first met at Boscawen-Un in 1928. Paynter was initiated at the Gorsedd held at The Hurlers stone circles on Bodmin Moor on 29 August 1930. Paynter took as his bardic name "Whyler Pystry," in recognition of his research

*Paynter leading the Furry Dance at St. Cleer, 1948.
(Courtesy of John Rapson)*

into witchcraft. At the ceremony, Henry Jenner, himself the first Grand Bard of the Gorsedd, described how "Mr. Paynter had done, and would do a great deal more excellent work in the investigation of witchcraft and the supernatural in Cornwall. He had done a tremendous lot in regard to other aspects of Old Cornwall, and, being young, they hoped he would do a great deal more."[13] One of Paynter's "witch hunt"

Paynter watches the Gorsedd proceedings (Courtesy of John Rapson)

contacts, Barbara Spooner, was initiated at the same time, mainly for her own work on Cornish folklore. The Callington Old Cornwall Society did much to stimulate Paynter's research, although active interest in the Society began to wane in the early 1930s, prompting an emergency meeting in January 1933 to decide whether to keep the Society going.[14] Paynter spoke in favour of continuing the Society's activities, though the decline of interest proved inexorable and the Society was suspended in May 1933.[15] Despite the lack of local focus during the mid to late 1930s, Paynter maintained his links with the Old Cornwall movement, as, for example, he gave a tour of Callington to the Looe Society members in 1935,[16] and upon his arrival at Liskeard he joined the Society there.

While witchcraft and folklore remained as Paynter's core research topics, from 1927 onwards he published a considerable quantity of articles on antiquarian and historical subjects, several of which were later reprinted in pamphlet form.[17] Articles on Cornish epitaphs, the histories of various churches, tin and copper mining, the antiquities of East Cornwall, and memoirs of Cornishmen and women of note were among the subjects he covered.[18] Paynter's publications were not intended for academic audiences and he appears never to have submitted a paper to a peer-reviewed journal, unlike several of his folklorist contemporaries;[19] his articles were written solely for the popular press, and it seems probable that the need for remuneration precluded submission to journals outside *Old Cornwall*. Of his monographs, several were self-published in later life, largely for tourist consumption, including *Trelawne and Bishop Trelawny* (1962), *Our Old Cornish Mines: East Cornwall* (1964), and *Looe—A History & Guide* (1970).[20] Each had a print run of 3000 copies save for Paynter's edition of John Wesley's *Primitive Physic* (1958), which proved so popular that it ran to

*Above: Paynter in the Gorsedd procession behind Grand Bard
G Pawley White, Liskeard, 1969.   Below: Paynter (left) in full bardic robes
(Both courtesy of John Rapson)*

several editions.[21] As Borough Archivist, Paynter was commissioned by Liskeard Borough Council to produce a second edition of John Allen's *History of the Borough of Liskeard* in 1967, a volume that had grown scarce since its first publication in 1856. As editor, Paynter was initially unsure what to excise and what to retain, but upon consultation found "that the great majority wanted a repeat of Allen in its entirety with additional notes," and this is what he endeavoured to do.[22] As he earned money from his pen, Paynter was a regional correspondent for the Westcountry Writers' Association, and also, apparently, a member of the Society of Authors.

Due to his publications, Paynter attracted attention from and collaborated with several Cornish historians during his life. For example, one of his earliest memoirs, on the Cornish 'Cave-man Mathematician' Daniel Gumb, resulted in a short-lived association with the antiquary Dr. Thomas Dexter (1860–1933) in 1932. In a series of books during the 1920s, Dexter drew attention to the pagan heritage of Cornwall, charting with increasing zeal across successive publications the debt Christianity in Cornwall owed to the earlier pagan gods. Dexter's *Cornwall: Land of the Gods* (1933) was the most fulsome statement of his assertion that many aspects of Cornwall's contemporary culture were survivals from its neglected pagan past. While 'Celtic' was respectable amongst the early revivalists, being redolent of early Christianity or even Anglo-Catholicism, paganism in the 1930s was still associated with heathenism, and few in the early Old Cornwall movement were so radical as to make such a link explicit. On 30 April and 7 May 1932, Dexter led study groups across the eastern parts of Bodmin Moor surrounding the Cheesewring to examine the ancient monuments of the area in support of his thesis. Paynter seems not to have participated in the debate on Dexter's ideas, neither was he involved with the Ancient Egyptian-based theories for Cornish monuments propounded by Edwin Chirgwin of St. Cleer, rather he

Paynter inspecting the remains of Daniel Gumb's House, Bodmin Moor, 1956. (Courtesy of John Rapson).

accompanied the groups to offer antiquarian remarks concerning Gumb's life and the remains of his house close to the Cheesewring.[23]

With his interest in contemporary folk-beliefs, one of Paynter's chief attractions was as a source for those mid twentieth-century Cornish historians who were constructing a history of Cornwall based on cultural and linguistic difference, such as the work of A. K. Hamilton Jenkin. Rather than rely on the nineteenth-century folklore collections, Jenkin was able to tap Paynter for current examples of Cornish folk-belief as evidence of Cornwall's continuing Celtic 'otherness,' although Cornish witch and ghost beliefs differed little in substance from those prevailing elsewhere in the country. The intensive folklore-collecting programme advocated and encouraged by the Old Cornwall movement itself contributed to Cornwall's reputation as a particularly 'folky' or 'witchy' place, where the uncanny was part of everyday life, and was something that also attracted writers from outside Cornwall, such Joseph Braddock, who communicated and further emphasised this sense of difference to their non-Cornish readership. Paynter's work was also acknowledged by Cornish institutions and the wider Cornish 'diaspora.' As a collector of artefacts, Paynter was invited to participate in the "Cornish Treasures and Antiques" open day held at Liskeard on 22 February 1969, in aid of the Cornwall County Museum's 150th Anniversary Appeal.[24] In common with other active Old Cornwall Society members, Paynter was a popular figure on the Cornish lecture circuit throughout his life, and received invitations to address Cornish groups across the country, including the Cardiff Cornwall Association,[25] the London Cornish Association,[26] and a gathering of Cornish "exiles" organised by the Merseyside Cornish Association,[27] amongst others.

Paynter's interest in Cornish history effectively culminated in 1959 with the creation of the privately run 'Cornish Museum,' housed in an old fish cellar on Lower Street, East Looe. The museum opened on 18 June 1959 and displayed exhibitions on "charms, early lighting devices, a section on early transport, another on John Wesley, relics of Cornish mining, a china clay exhibit, a section of an old Cornish kitchen, and many others illustrating how people lived in past generations."[28] Paynter advertised the museum as "representing the life and culture of Cornwall" and it was ideally situated to appeal to the burgeoning tourist trade of the later 1950s and 1960s, spurred on by the post-war spread of motor car ownership.[29]

The Cornish Museum embodied the desire articulated by Robert Morton Nance at the outset of the Old Cornwall movement that "It would be very interesting and of great permanent value to establish a museum for housing the collection of old implements and methods of working them. Records should be gathered of fishing, farming and mining of the olden days, together with particulars of local trades."[30] From a museological perspective the exhibition was on a par with others of its time, with the objects for the most part arranged thematically case by case behind glass, with illustrations and pictures hung on the walls behind the table-top cases, though the kitchen hearth display at the far end was open.

The kitchen display at the Cornish Museum (Courtesy of Jeremy Tucker)

While most objects were labelled individually, there does not appear to have been much textual narrative to link them, thus visitors were expected to make connections between objects by their juxtaposition. This aspect of the displays was acknowledged by journalist David Truen:

> *Like a jigsaw puzzle, a host of individual items mould together to give the inquisitive visitors—whose numbers reach well into the thousands each summer—an almost three-dimensional picture of Cornish heritage, the way the people lived, their work & play, people and events which affected their lives, and the side not often seen, their belief in things supernatural.*[31]

The various items Paynter collected during his "witch hunt" were also displayed at the museum—"a unique collection of relics dealing with Cornish witchcraft, charms and superstitions"—and included the mounted fragments of "Tammy Blee's Scent Bottle," amongst other artefacts already described. The scope of the exhibition widened over successive years as Paynter acquired new artefacts or accepted loans to the collection. For example, a newly discovered witch-bottle from Killigarth Manor House was donated by its discoverer, Mr. G. K. Roberts, in 1959.[32] Visitors to the museum were often given guided tours by Paynter, who regaled them with Cornish stories and was known to pretend to charm warts;[33] the museum also became a backdrop for many of Paynter's television appearances, where he was filmed seated before the Cornish kitchen display.[34]

Paynter may well have been following Nance in deed as well as word in setting up the Cornish Museum, as Nance was the inspiration behind the St. Ives Museum, which opened in 1951 as a collaborative venture by the St. Ives Old Cornwall Society,[35]although Paynter's museum embraced the whole of Cornwall rather than just one town or area. Paynter's Museum was unique amongst the Old Cornwall membership as being the work of one collector and was a literal fulfilment of the Federation's aims of collecting and preserving the "fragments," in this case the material culture of old Cornwall. Paynter created a vision of bygone years in line with the aspirations articulated by Henry Jenner in 1904. While Paynter was predominantly interested in antiquarian research and not given to radical political activism, the Cornish Museum does seem to have been in part a response to the growing sense of Cornish nationalism in the 1950s and 1960s, as the museum was a visible meditation on contemporary Cornwall's sense of itself, its traditions and its distinctiveness, for itself and for the many visitors from 'up-country' who flowed through its door during the summer months. If Paynter's folklore collections gave the early Old Cornwall movement a sense of surviving traditions and a basis for its desire for 'Celtic' otherness, his museum offered the more radicalised mid-century movement a definition of what Cornish culture was once like and, arguably, still continued to be.

A view from the entrance

A view back to the entrance

*Illustration of a Flying Witch, 1931 - used by Paynter in his displays
(Courtesy of Jeremy Tucker)*

PART TWO:

SELECTIONS

Witch-hunting in Cornwall

The articles presented in this chapter include Paynter's entire published output on Cornish witch beliefs and are based on his findings during the "witch hunt" of the 1920s and 1930s, from which period all but one derive. The articles describe surviving examples of witchcraft and cunning-folk during the opening decades of the twentieth century and record the memories of the elderly, who participated in such beliefs during the latter half of the nineteenth century. While they no longer offered services of unbewitching, Paynter recognized that fortune tellers still carried on aspects of the trade previously offered by cunning-folk, and described his visit to one in 1934. While his "witch hunt" effectively concluded with the outbreak of World War II, Paynter wrote a retrospective of his fieldwork on witchcraft in 1969, which concludes the chapter. In the article he contrasted the traditional witch beliefs he found evidence of many years before with the practices of the mid twentieth-century occult revival, which he was generally dismissive of, recognizing the distinctive differences between them.

WITCHCRAFT
[1928][1]

A Glance into the Past

The inhabitants of a little Devon town have been completely bewildered by the strange happenings in an old-world cottage in their midst. Showers of twigs have fallen upon the floor from apparently nowhere; quantities of kidney beans have struck the occupants, and have been found in covered pans of milk, while household and dairy utensils have moved themselves in a mysterious fashion.

Many strange tales are being circulated, and it is said, that there is a great deal of superstition amongst the residents in this district, many of whom think that the happenings are the result of witchcraft. It was in 1541 that witchcraft was first denounced by the law in England. For some time this law was not very actively enforced, though no one denied the existence of such criminal power, and a certain bishop used, we are told, constantly to conclude his sermons with a prayer that her Majesty might be preserved from witches.

In Scotland, the belief and consequent persecution was somewhat more active, and it is supposed that in less than forty years as many as 17,000 persons suffered. The accession of James awakened in England a like active spirit of persecution.

The last judicial murder in England was in 1716, when a mother and her daughter, the latter of tender years, were hanged at Huntingdon for selling their souls to the devil and raising a storm by pulling off their stockings, and making lather of soap. In 1736 the statute was repealed. Amongst the mysterious fraternity of witches and wizards who haunted the Westcountry, the pellar took the foremost place and could only evolve from reasonably prolific families as a pellar had to be a seventh son or daughter of a seventh daughter born with magical inclinations. Other persons who practised the black art were "black witches," the difference being that a white witch could remove spells and a black witch could cast them.

Anyone, however, might become a "wise woman" or wizard who either (1) touched a logan rock (a large stone balanced so as to be easily moved at midnight), or (2) received instruction in the mystic art from a wise woman or wizard of the opposite sex. A wise woman could not instruct a woman, but could teach a man her trade, and a woman would have to be instructed by a male wizard.

The writer, who has collected a considerable amount of reliable information concerning these strange beliefs, finds that it was a valued profession in certain Westcountry circles, as when proficient in the art, one could cure diseases, "over-look" an enemy, "ill-wish" a rival, utter incantations, raise a storm, cast spells, use the witch's bowl, charm various ailments including warts and burns, the latter with almost immediate results, staunch the flow of blood, find water and minerals by divining or "dowsing," and cultivate the evil eye.

To this day there are many who believe in the power of Old-Mother-so-and-so, to over-look and ill-wish their cattle and even themselves, and that witchcraft is at the bottom of every mischance.

WITCH OF THE WEST
[1928][2]

Tammy Blee and Her Scent Bottle

Mr. W. H. Paynter, Callington, who is preparing a work on "Cornish Witches and Wizards," and who has recently visited the west of the county and interviewed a number of people concerning the mysterious fraternity, sends a photograph ... of "Tammy Blee's" scent bottle.

Tammy Blee, more often called "The Witch of the West," lived at Helston, and carried on as a fortune teller. She married "Jimmy," the wizard, whose real name was James Thomas, a native of the parish of Illogan, and an engine driver by trade. On account of a warrant being issued for his apprehension by the magistrates of St. Ives for attempting to take a spell from a local woman, his wife parted from him, and was not seen or heard of for about two years, when he again appeared in the West. During his absence his wife stated that the virtue was in her and not in him; that she was of the real "Pellar" blood; and that he could do nothing but through her. Together they were responsible for many mysterious happenings in the West, and it is stated that they caused a great disturbance in many quarters, especially amongst neighbours, by charging some with having bewitched others. Tammy Blee died about 68 years ago, and on the day of her burial it is said that the

The remains of 'Tammy Blee's scent bottle.' The inscription on the reverse reads "Pieces of glass which / was part of / Tammey Blees Sent Bottle / Yours Sincerely / Jim Thomas." (Author's photograph)

district was visited by a severe thunderstorm, for which the Devil was popularly held responsible. Jimmy, her husband, died about 35 years ago. Although he was described as a "drunken, disgraceful, beastly fellow," he was respected by many, especially by those who went to him to be relieved of spells, under the influence of which either they or their cattle were supposed to be suffering.

The bottle was discovered in the possession of Mr. Jim Thomas, the Camborne antiquary. Mr. Thomas, who is 80 years of age, is as the Old Cornwall Federation described him, "a priceless bit of Old Cornwall." He corresponded with Sir John Evans about flints, and some of his finds are in the British Museum; he helped A. G. Langdon to collect material about old Cornish crosses, and Cecil Sharp acknowledged him as a colleague in collecting folk-songs, while Vulliamy has published character sketch of him. He is, too, a noted raconteur.

Mr. Thomas stated that he secured the bottle after considerable difficulty, the woman in whose possession it was stating that it could not be parted with until she was dead. When this happened, the husband sold it to Mr. Thomas for 2s.

It is described as a Spanish scent bottle about 300 years old; hand-painted with a flower and leaf design. It holds about one pint. Unfortunately the neck of the bottle is missing.

A HELSTON WITCH

[1928][3]

Oil Painting Found and New Stories Related

Since my recent notes on Cornish witches, I have discovered in the possession of a lady residing at Truro a portrait in oils of "Tamson Blight, the Helston Witch," more commonly known as "Tammy Blee." The portrait is about 3 feet by 2 feet, and was purchased at an auction sale at Penzance about 34 to 36 years ago. At the time of the sale there was some controversy as to the artist whose work it was; some suggested it was by John Opie, the Cornish artist, while others contended it was the work of his brother, Edward Opie, who resided at Plymouth. Unfortunately it is unsigned. It is well painted, set in an elaborate and costly frame, and represents a dignified-looking old lady. The inscription under the portrait is as follows: "Tamson Blight, the Helston Witch."

Tales of the witch and her clients include the following:–

About 70 years ago a woman living near Helston had a child affected with a mysterious sickness, to cure which medical aid had

*The portrait of Thomasine Blight (1793-1856).
(© RIC Royal Cornwall Museum [Pblight01])*

been in vain tried. As it was generally believed in the neighbourhood that the child was "ill-wished," the woman was advised to go into Helston and see Tamson Blight, the witch, who, it was said, had the power of discovering who had bewitched it, and of compelling them to remove their influence.

A visit was accordingly made, and the woman demanded of Tamson the name of the ill-wisher. This she refused to do, but she described the ill-wisher in such clear detail that the woman "immediately named the sorcerer," and returned home resolved to "bring blood from her." Some days afterwards the reputed witch passed her door, so she laid violent hands upon her and scratched her arm, drawing blood. The story told was that from that hour the child began to get well, and was soon able to leave her bed and play with the other children, free from all disease.

"My mother," said my informant, "lived beside a woman who was very ill, and none seemed to know what was the matter with her, except that she was supposed to be ill-wished.

"Two neighbours one morning left the sick woman in bed and visited the witch to enquire what was the matter with the unfortunate woman and if there was any hope of her recovery. 'Give me sixpence' said Tamson, 'and I will tell you all about it.' 'We have no money,' replied one of the women. 'Oh, yes you have!' said the witch; 'put your hand into your pocket,' and on doing so the woman discovered a sixpence, which she had placed there some time ago and forgotten; it was given her to go to Copperhouse Fair.

"Handing the coin to Tamson, the latter said 'Go home, my dears, your neighbour is all right; and by the time you reach home she will have baked a "heavy cake" for your tea.' On their arrival, they stated, they found the sick woman in the kitchen quite well, and cutting a heavy cake which she had made and baked during their absence."

A woman living at Breage (near Helston) suffered from a severe sickness, being unable to move her limbs, and as a result she was compelled to sit in one position by day and night. A neighbour one day informed her that very likely she had been ill-wished, and the best thing she could do was to go into Helston and see the witch. Being unable to undertake such a journey on foot, it was decided that the preacher (meaning the rector of the parish) be asked if he would take her in his dogcart.

At first he refused, stating that he did not believe in such rubbish, but later he consented, and together they went into Helston. After certain incantations had been used Tamson informed the woman that as soon as she arrived home the one who had ill-wished her would come to the door and say, "Is my little black cat here?" The homeward journey was continued, and on reaching the house "an old woman hobbled in and asked if they had seen her little black cat! Whereupon the sick woman got up from her chair and, taking two pitchers, went to the well and drew water, much to the amazement of the preacher, who departed mystified and upset."

A man living in Camborne tells me that recently he met a woman who knew Tamson Blight well; in fact, her husband, when a child, used to be put to bed with her, while his mother went about her business. He relates that before she died she was confined to her bed for a considerable time. Sometimes people were brought on stretchers and laid by Tamson's bedside entirely helpless, and "they were known to rise up and go down over the stairs perfectly well."

The following was related to me by an old lady over 80 years of ages, who was well acquainted with the witch. In fact, she remarked that Tamson told her fortune when she was a young woman, and even described her husband before she had met him.

"When I was a young girl," said the old lady, "my master suffered many losses, which he attributed to the malign influences of some evil-disposed person. Tamson's help was sought, and she advised as follows: 'Go home, catch the cock, put him under the brandis (an iron tripod in common use with fires over the hearth for supporting crock and kettle), and cover him over with a red cloth. Then call together all your friends and neighbours and give them plenty to eat, and before their departure let each one stroke the brandis, and the cock will crow over the one who stole.' Returning home, the farmer did as directed, and each one in turn was requested to go through the ordeal. Now it happened that one old woman present refused, but the farmer, not wishing to be outdone, forced her, and immediately she neared the brandis the cock crew, and she thereupon made a confession, in which she stated that she alone was responsible for the ill-luck he had had."

A shoemaker living in Camborne used to make and mend the witch's shoes; but, alas, she was such a bad payer, he informed her that in future she must get her work done elsewhere. "You'll be sorry for this," said the enraged Tamson, "and I will see that in a short time you will have no work to do." Then she left him muttering. At that time four men were employed in the shop, including my informant, who, some time later, went to America and remained away about four years. On his returning again to the West he visited his old employer and found him packing up his few remaining goods prior to leaving the country. On being asked for an explanation, he said that his work began to fall off after Tamson had ill-wished him, so it was no good staying any longer; he had lost practically everything he possessed.

A farmer who possessed many acres, and was in many respects a sensible man, was greatly annoyed to find that his cattle became diseased in the spring. Nothing could satisfy him but they were ill-wished, and he resolved to find out the person who had cast the evil eye on them. A visit was paid to Tamson, who advised him to confine his cattle until the next moon was as old as the present one. This, she explained, tamed the devils within them, and sent them to a far-away place, where she would lock them up forever. He did as commanded, "and the spell was removed."

Tamson advised another farmer to go home and take the heart of one of the animals which had met with a mysterious disease and burn it with fire in one of his fields at midnight, at the same time uttering some strange words which she gave him.

TALES OF CORNISH WITCHES

[1929][4]

Few Cornish people, probably, are aware how widespread was the belief only a few years ago in charms and charmers, and all other superstitions; or that there were witches in almost every village, shunned and dreaded by some, who feared their supposed power to ill wish those who offended them and sought out by others, who wanted by their aid to avert the evil eye, or by their magic to remove spells already cast on them or their cattle by an ill wisher who had overlooked them.

The following is a selection from the many witch tales I have collected during the past six months in various parts of the Duchy.

THE BEWITCHED COW.— A farmer living not far from Launceston had a cow which was suddenly taken ill with a mysterious sickness. A cow-doctor was sent for, but was unable to do anything for the suffering animal. At length the farmer was advised to visit an old man in the district who was known to be well versed in witchcraft. He did so, when on payment of certain fees the witch visited the farm, and after inspecting the animal came to the conclusion that it was bewitched. "Well," said the farmer, "what can I do about it?" "I'll tell you," replied the wise man; "take a handful of salt, and go at sunrise to the cowhouse and sprinkle it about the building. Cast what remains over the door of the house, turning east while you are so doing, but be very careful with the salt; on no account let any of it fall into the hands of your enemy (meaning the person who had ill-wished him), for with it a lot more harm could be done." The farmer did as directed, and within a few days the cow was in perfect health again.

WHOLE FARM BEWITCHED.— A large farm in the Tintagel district was some years ago bewitched on an extensive scale. Everything went wrong; day after day the cattle died; the cows would give no milk; the crops were a failure, and even the butter would not turn. Hearing of a celebrated "White Witch," residing at Plymouth, the farmer and his wife undertook the journey to seek his aid. The witch, it appears, was a man of wonderful gifts, and showed a most uncanny knowledge of the farmer's affairs before any information had been imparted to him. This so impressed the farmer that he at once engaged him to visit his farm and remove the evil spell. The witch duly arrived, and after great preparations ordered all of the household, including the farm hands, to prepare themselves with lighted candles and lanterns. At midnight they assembled and commenced to perambulate the farm; every field, stable, linhay and house was visited—the witch walking in front "saying words" and reading something out of a book with the result that the evil spell was removed and the cattle and crops again flourished. This reminds one of the medieval way of exorcising, by the priest, with bell, book, and candle; but as far as I can gather no bell was used in this curious ceremony.

A DELABOLE WITCH.— A neighbour of mine, said a lady near Tintagel, once had an attack of what is locally called "wildfire" (meaning shingles). For days she suffered much pain, and was at least advised to visit "Old Ann," the witch of Delabole. Being unable to undertake the journey, she sent an aunt, who took with her three handkerchiefs. One of these Ann charmed by putting her hand on it and uttering some incantation. She then commenced the homeward journey, just over five miles, and on arriving placed the handkerchief on the affected part; but the curious thing was, the sufferer was already better before she arrived, for she began to improve at the very time the spell was laid, though she had no idea of the hour when her aunt was going to the witch.

This old dame, I find, was consulted by many people in the Delabole district, including an old woman living at Trewarmett, who suffered from a sore leg. The same method was employed, namely the charmed handkerchief. In the directions given, the handkerchief had to be placed on the affected spot from above downwards, that is, striking it towards the toes; the evil would then ooze out from the feet instead of being driven higher up the body.

TWO CALLINGTON FARMERS BEWITCHED.— During a recent lecture at Callington the following stories were related to me, showing how two local farmers were bewitched, and how the spells were successfully removed after a visit to the great White Witch at Plymouth. In the first case the farmer, who had his farm stock ill-wished, was ordered to take the heart of one of the animals which had met with a mysterious death, stick it full of pins and needles, and burn it in the centre of one of his fields at midnight, at the same time uttering some strange words which the white witch enunciated. This he did, and the spell was immediately removed. In the second instance the witch produced in some mysterious way the photograph of the ill-wisher, and the farmer was requested to strike the unfortunate woman whom it happened to portray on any part of her body, but not with intent to kill. He struck the portrait, as requested, across the leg, and was told after paying the usual fee that on his homeward journey he would find her lying by the roadside with her leg broken. Sure enough, he did, just outside the town, and the spell was at once removed, or at least it was said he suffered no further losses!

THE ILL-WISHED COWS.— A farmer of Saint Mellion had three dairy-cows to let, and an old woman, who was known as a witch, living near, offered to take them. As the farmer did not like her, he would not make a bargain with her, but agreed with another neighbour for the dairy. When the woman heard who had been preferred, she informed everyone she met that old "so-and-so," the man who had taken the cows, should rue the day that he ventured to cross her path. "I will lay such a spell," said she, "that he will wish he had never seen the cows." After a few days, the new owner and his wife came to the farmer one night and said how they believed the cows must be ill-wished, for the milk daily went to curds. The farmer was greatly puzzled when he heard this news, for it was early spring; however, he exchanged them for three others, but, alas, the milk of these also "runned." Things then began to go wrong with him and his family, till at last he was obliged to take back his cows because they had, as he stated, "no profit in them." Meanwhile the old witch who had coveted them bragged how she had served him, and stated how she had been on her knees under a white-thorn tree growing by the cross-roads; and there, for the best part of the night, had called on "the powers" till they had helped her to cast the spell that had turned the cows' milk into junket (One is tempted to wonder why this witch, who was very proud to be known as such, chose the cross-road thorn as a suitable place for her evil work. Was it because such trees were said to have sprung from stakes driven into suicides' graves?).

A HELSTON WITCH.— About seventy years ago, a woman living near Helston had a child affected with a mysterious sickness, to cure which medical aid had been in vain tried. As it was generally believed in the neighbourhood that the child was "ill-wished" the woman was advised to go into Helston and see Tamson Blight, the witch, who it was said had the power of discovering who had bewitched it, and of compelling them to remove their influence. A visit was accordingly made, and the woman demanded of Tamson the name of the ill-wisher. This she refused to give, but she described the ill-wisher in such clear detail that the woman immediately named the sorcerer, and returned home resolved to "bring blood from her." Some days afterwards the reputed witch passed her door, so she laid violent hands upon her and scratched her arm, drawing blood. Strange to relate, from that hour the child began to get well, and was soon able to leave her bed and play with the other children, free from all disease.

Here, again, it is interesting to note that the drawing of a witch's blood was mentioned in the twelfth century by Glanvil, who relates that when Jane Brooks, known as the "demon of

Tedworth," bewitched a boy, his father scratched her face and drew blood, whereupon the boy instantly exclaimed that he was well. Shakespeare also alludes to the same practice in "Henry VI.," Pt. I., Act I., sc. v., where Lord Talbot says to Joan of Arc, "Blood will I draw on thee, thou art a witch." …

THE WIZARD OF THE WEST.— While discussing the mysterious fraternity of wizards and witches with an old man well over eighty, he informed me that about forty-five years ago he attended the Assizes at Bodmin, and after the necessary business had been got through a dinner was held, at which all the chief of the county were assembled, including many prominent farmers. Just before the dinner was timed to commence a strange individual, dressed in a long white shirt, entered the room. He was at once hailed by the farmers present as the "Wizard of the West," and each in turn paid him a sum of money to keep "witchcraft" off their farms during the ensuing twelve months. Later in the evening, says my informant, the wizard was discovered drunk, and certain members, who during the year had been "over-looked" or "ill-wished" in spite of having bought his protection, tried to set a light to his shirt, but he escaped, and was not seen again until the following year, when he once more appeared to collect his dues.

THE EVIL EYE
[1929][5]

Quaint Belief That Persists in Cornwall Today

During a recent visit to a village not far from Callington, I was informed by a mason that while preparing an old fireplace he discovered a bottle of pins and needles, which had been placed there by a previous occupant as a talisman to preserve him and his family from the effects of the Evil Eye.

Belief in the Evil Eye has inspired fear from the darkest ages, far beyond chronicles and history. Science, religion, and law have combined against it without a shadow of success. Believers in the Evil Eye have included all sorts and conditions of men. Solomon, in the Book of Wisdom, speaks seriously of it; also St. Paul, while Virgil, Luther, Aristotle, Pliny, Plato, Bacon, and a host of other authorities have dealt with what our modern scientists denounce as a vulgar superstition. It is interesting to observe that even today the Egyptian mother ascribes the sickness of her children to the Evil Eye, while the Arabs and Scotch Highlanders alike resort to charms against it.

In Cornwall I have discovered numerous examples of the belief in the malignant influence of the human eye. Robert Stephen Hawker, the parson-poet of Morwenstow, for instance, whenever he came across anyone with a peculiar eye-ball, sometimes bright and clear and at others obscured by a film or with a double pupil, would hold this thumb, fore and middle fingers in the peculiar position which the superstitions of Eastern Europe had taught him would ward off the ill-effects of the Evil Eye.

According to a Cornish dame, well-versed in witchcraft, the following may be recognized as possessors of the Evil Eye: Those with a double pupil or a pupil that contains the figure of some animal, usually a horse; lean bodies and melancholy temperaments; squints, hollow eyes, hook noses, broad overhanging eyebrows; while there is said to be always a strange glare in the eye of a person who can "over-look" and the eyelids are always red.

Apart from the deliberately wicked fascinators, the Evil Eye has been at times attributed to apparently innocent and even benevolent persons—dear old men and women of small stature. "Luckless, indeed," says one writer, "is he who has the misfortune to possess, or the reputation of possessing, this fatal power. From that time forward the world flees him. A curse is on him, and from the very terror at seeing him accidents are most likely to follow. Keep him from your children, or they will break their legs, arms, or necks. Invite him not to dinner, or your mushrooms will poison you and your fish will smell."

Of the many safeguards which have been used against the Evil Eye in Cornwall, the following are just a few: Red coral, if tied round the neck of an infant, will protect it against witchcraft and those possessed of the Evil Eye. Tying red worsted threads round the horns or tails of cattle before turning then out for the first time in the season to grass will protect them from all evil. Milk is also said to be safe from witchcraft and the Evil Eye if covered with red cloth.

If a farmer's cows were affected by 'milk produce,' it was the custom when one of his cows calved, to take away the calf immediately, before it drew mile from its dam, then to take a bottle and draw milk from the four teats into the bottle, the person so doing being on his knees and saying certain prayers in which God was asked to bless his cattle, folds, crops, etc. The bottle was then tightly corked and hidden in a safe place. This was considered a magic way of retaining the whole by keeping part.

In some parts of the county, farmers still refuse to be present during churning operations, as their glance would prevent the butter coming, while I have known a farmer's wife make the sign of the cross over the contents of the tub during butter-making. The repeating of certain charms and prayers has also been resorted to when any difficulty has arisen in turning the cream.

It is also the custom in some Cornish villages not to praise your friend's cattle, as the act of praising might lead accidentally to the Evil Eye, or wounding of the cattle. As a preventative, it was customary to say to the person making the complimentary remarks, "Wet your eye." This wetting of the eye is generally performed by moistening the tip of the finger with saliva and moistening the eye with it thereafter. Another preventative was to take a bundle of thatch from the threshold of the suspected person and burn it beneath a churn.

Garlic is a potent charm against the Evil Eye, while burnt sulphur, laurel leaves, and green frog's bones have also been held in high esteem. It may also be warded off by wearing certain charms, and afterwards burning them, at the same time uttering strange words. To draw blood from the ill-wisher has been strongly recommended, and the sticking of pins into either an apple, potato, or bullock's or sheep's heart. According to an authority, when such sticking of pins is carried out, the ill-wisher will feel a stab for every pin put in, and in self-defence will take off the curse.

An interesting proof of this belief recently appeared in a Westcountry newspaper. A smallholder was convicted for assaulting a woman neighbour, whom he accused of having cast the evil eye on him and his pigs. The assault consisted of attacking the unfortunate woman with a pin, and a plea of "not guilty" was entered. Obviously the man was of the opinion that, instead of punishing him, the magistrates should have laid hands upon the "witch." And, although the magistrates tried to persuade him that there was no such thing as witchcraft, he persisted in his belief. In rural England this belief is as prevalent as ever, and rustic opinion will be wholly with this man, for did he not do exactly as tradition enjoins in order to get the spell lifted from him? Having discovered the witch, he "drew blood on her with a pin," and that, as any Cornishman will tell you, is the only way to make a witch powerless to harm you further.

Of all the safeguards used, however, none has been more generally trusted than spitting. To spit three times in the face of a person with the Evil Eye is said to counteract its influence at once. According to Pliny, we obtain the indulgence of the gods for any audacious expression of hope by spitting on our bosoms, and spitting into the right shoe before it is put on is also an amulet against fascination.

WITCHES AND WITCHCRAFT
[1932][6]

Superstition in the Westcountry

The recent case of the witness at Wolverhampton Police Court who refused to give evidence because a woman in the case was a "witch" and if he spoke of what he had seen she would have put him under a spell draws attention to the survival of a superstition which has existed since the dawn of history. When Paul addressed his audience at Athens he began by saying, "Ye men of Athens, I perceive that in all things ye are too superstitious." Today when we are told that the witch tribe is by no means extinct we are led to think, and very naturally too, that men have indeed altered little in their superstitions.

Were it not that dogs and horses have frequently been observed to express their fear of ghosts an apt definition for man would be "the superstitious animal." Certainly no human feeling is more universal or more enduring, for deep down in each of our hearts there dwells an amount of peculiar beliefs, and whatever colour our skin be we are all in some measure superstitious.

The Wolverhampton man's statement that the "witch" uttered incantations over bowls of violet-coloured water reduced the Court to uproarious laughter. "What rubbish! Fancy witches still existing in 20th century England!"

It is easy to say with glib tongue, "Oh, it's all humbug," but such sweeping assertion can hardly be substantiated; in fact, there seems much to controvert it. I have to admit that much, very much, is just pure unadulterated fraud; but when one looks at the matter from a sane and reasonable standpoint it will be discovered that there is a certain modicum of truth in it.

For some years now I have devoted much time and attention to the investigation of the subject, particularly in Devon and Cornwall, where in spite of motor omnibuses—which now link up the once isolated villages—compulsory education, and advancing knowledge, people still believe in charms and charmers, the power of the evil eye, as well as in ghosts, pixies, and the fairy folk.

Witches are looked up to and feared by the native population, who believe that can work terrible vengeance if offended. On the other hand, country people often go to wise women for help in times of trouble and sickness, and very often they are benefited. The wise woman differs considerably from the witch, for the witch "ill-wishes," while the wise woman breaks the evil spell.

Witches, however, are not only found in the West of England; they exist in our towns and cities throughout the country. Every day a great number of people flock to fortune-tellers. So popular, indeed, are they becoming that their number is increasing. There are astrologers, crystal-gazers, palmists; there are soothsayers and others who veil their profession under abstruse and elaborate names.

That these are not merely common superstitions to which only the poor and uneducated are prone is evidenced by the fact that high and low, rich and poor, educated and ignorant are all eager, anxious, and willing to wear a mascot or charm and to "have their fortunes told."

On several occasions, especially at our celebrated Westcountry fairs, I have myself paid a shilling or two with the greatest of willingness, and have been strongly reminded after the "telling" that the modern witch is not a whit behind her mediæval predecessor in these qualities which led her to so high a place in public estimation.

When I first took up the study of witchcraft I, too, regarded it with cynical contempt, but after a number of personal experiences I have altered my point of view on the whole question. There IS something in witchcraft, but what the SOMETHING is I am content to leave for an abler pen than mind to describe. It is a great consolation to know that I am not alone in this belief, for I am in the company of many others, among whom may be included some of the leading scientists of the day.

I can instance literally hundreds of examples where people, cattle, crops, and even machinery have been "ill-wished," and where these evil spells have been successfully "lifted." In addition to a collection of charms which I have collected from various parts of the country I have a portfolio of letters which I have received from people who believe that because I have made and incursion into the world of magic I can help them.

Here are just a few extracts from the letters which have reached me:

"My husband has been ill-wished with fits," writes a woman. "Can you charm him or send me the name and address of someone who can?"

"I am troubled with warts, and I shall be grateful if you can give me a charm. My mother was charmed some years ago for the ague, so I know it can be done."

"Are you the gentleman that charms diseases? If so I should like to go and see you, as I have been troubled with epilepsy."

"I saw in the paper that you cure people that are 'ill-wished.' Will you cure me of rheumatism? I will pay you well for it, if you can cure me," wrote a woman residing in Somerset.

"I would be grateful if you could send me the address of someone who can lift 'evil spells,'" writes another correspondent, from Manchester.

Another unfortunate woman writes from Chesterfield, "I am madly in love with a man in a good position, but he does not return my love. Will you kindly tell me how I can draw him to me and keep him. It can be done by the power of 'Dragon's blood,' but

I do not know how to use it. Please help me, as I love this man better than anything else in the world."

The substance this woman refers to is a gum resin obtained from Pterocarpus indicus, a tree indigenous to the East Indies. In early times it had some repute in medicine for its astringent properties and also as an emmenagogue, but it has gone out of use and is now employed as a colouring agent for varnishes and stains. Three hundred years ago it is said to have been used by goldsmiths and painters in glass, by the former as a base for enamel, and by the latter to strike a crimson for stained windows.

Its use, however, as a magical charm has survived to the present day, and it is still employed as a love-charm in some parts of the country. A great deal of mystery surrounds its employment for this purpose, and it is only with difficulty that I have obtained details. For the benefit of those who may be tempted to write me for this or any other charm let me say that I am neither a witch nor a charmer, and I cannot "lift" evil spells or charm various ailments.

I have instanced these few examples of my personal knowledge of witches and witchcraft to show that their belief in the craft, under one form or other, is as widely prevalent in the modern civilized world as ever it was, and it is likely to remain.

I HAVE MY FORTUNE TOLD
[1934][7]

"It is astonishing and tragic that there are people to-day who can still be influenced by the mumbo-jumbo of necromancers. Women have been driven to suicide, have broken off their betrothals, or become estranged from their families through believing in the prophesies of some alleged seer. Itinerant soothsayers, like truculent hawkers, are often a menace to women who are too credulous or too frightened to show them the door."

The above is an extract from a leading article in the "Daily Mail" last week, and it is really astounding the number of people who flock to fortune tellers. So popular, indeed, are they becoming that their number is increasing. There are astrologers, crystal gazers, palmists; there are soothsayers and others, who veil their profession under more abstruse and elaborate names.

That these are not merely common superstitions to which only the poor and uneducated are prone is evidenced by the fact that high and low, rich and poor, educated and ignorant, are all eager, anxious and willing to wear a mascot or charm and to "have their fortunes told."

One of the strongest allies to superstition is the memory of man. We remember when things go wrong and forget when things go merrily. We remember the day and even the hour when the arrow of adversity hits but we forget the many happy days and hours when it goes wide of the mark.

For example, should we happen to walk under a ladder and immediately suffer some misfortune, we dwell on the fact that we did walk under the ladder. But if on the other hand we walk under a ladder many times a day and nothing eventful happens, then we forget ever having done so. This is how superstition grows and memory is its life blood. What thousands of men and women go about in fear and trembling! We do not stop to consider that there is such a thing as coincidence in the world.

With these and kindred thoughts in mind, I decided to visit one of these "miraculous and gifted" beings, and selected Madame X, who had set up her den at one of our local fairs. My choice, by the way, was not the only "Dark Esmeralda" present, but I selected her because she claimed not only to be a palmist, but also a clairvoyant.

She received me with flattering cordiality, and after I had been securely landed, asked if I would like the 1s. 6d., or 2s. 6d. reading. The 1s, I gathered, was rather limited, as also was the 1s.

6d., but for 2s. 6d. I could have an extended reading and character delineation. Anxious to hear the worst whilst hoping for the best, I selected the extended policy, and thrust my palm into her anxious hands.

"You are a gentleman," she began, "born under a very lucky sign," which sign, I may mention, she did not seem to know. However, that was just as well as she might have been upset if she had realised that the month she predicted was a long way adrift from my real birthday.

"You are instinctively active and determined, easily led but never driven. Like travel and change, not easily deceived, sociable and friendly, good natured and free with money" (Quite true, if I was not I should not pay 2s. 6. to hear such mumbo-jumbo).

A short pause.

"You have recently placed a ring on a lady's finger, and you are naturally very happy." Seeing I did this over two years ago, I was not impressed with this bit of information.

The next prognostication concerned how I earned my daily bread. The lines of my hands in this respect must have been rather fogged or crossed, as I was placed among the building fraternity.

I had a number of kind friends and acquaintances. I was to beware of a snake in the grass—"jealousy." "Guard against it and all will be well," she warned.

Within the next six weeks a stranger was going to cross my path and I was to get a handsome present. The stranger (and his gift, I hope) are to meet me on or near a flight of stairs.

1935 was to be my great year, and about the third month I should be called upon to make an important decision.

"Do not worry," continued the seer, "your decision will be a wise one and you will leave your present surroundings."

Another dip into the witch's brew and out came more concerning my character. A little did apply, but the remainder I am strongly convinced must have belonged to someone born under another sign. "The Goat" I should imagine.

And so the teller rambled on, every now and them remarking that she hoped I should not be annoyed if what she saw in my palm was told.

At length she came to a sudden stop, as if the lines had run out, and produced a character chart, which she deftly marked with pencil ticks. Handing this to me, she remarked that I was only to read where the chart was marked, as the other information did not apply to my case. "Your money returned if not satisfied," I read at the foot of the chart, and "For amusement only."

I certainly had been amused and as I crawled from the web 2s. 6d. poorer in cash, I was strongly reminded that the modern witch is not a whit behind her mediæval predecessor in those qualities which led her to so high a place in public estimation.

We all have a streak of superstition, but unless we temper it with a sense of humour we had better steer clear of fortune-tellers.

THE HORSESHOE
[1935][8]

Deep Rooted Beliefs as Luck Bringer

"The virtue ascribed to the horseshoe is of very ancient date, and the causes at first assigned for its especial service against the attacks of evil spirits is now lost among the rubbish of past ages," says a recent writer.

In spite of this, however, no doubt remains that whatever may have been the cause, its virtues for many ages seem to have been universally acknowledged, and in many parts at the present day it still holds a high place among the amulets for the averting of misfortune and protecting the individual from the spells of witches, and of securing a successful issue to any dangerous enterprise or speculation.

Some writers trace the pedigree of the horseshoe back to the horns symbolic of the Egyptian cow-goddess Hathor, and even beyond that to the worship of the crescent moon, whose emblem protected her devotees from the forces of evil.

Others ascribe the virtue of the horseshoe to the rule of contraries, and maintain it was first used as an amulet in virtue of the undivided hoof to which it was once attached, in contradistinction to the cloven foot which forms one of the distinctive marks by which to discover the Devil who, whatever shape he may assume, cannot conceal or disguise the cloven foot, the barbed tail, and asinine ears.

Another folklorist assigns the horseshoe's virtue to its rude resemblance to the halo, or rays of glory, which in ancient pictures the painters have made to surround the heads of saints and of angels, while others, with more propriety, assign its virtues to the cure of horses that had been vicious or afflicted by any ailment which village farriery did not understand.

Diseases of animals were in olden times nearly always attributed to witchcraft and the mode of cure seems to imply the belief in the imperfect purification by fire of the shoes which the animal wore, but afforded an inlet to the malevolent influences. It is interesting to recall the method by which the cure was affected. The horse was led to the smithy, the doors of which were securely closed and barred. Following the placing of the animal in a certain position, the shoes were taken from its feet and placed in the fire. While the shoes were in the fire, the ill-wisher was supposed to suffer terrible tortures, and be freed under such influence, thus removing the spell under which the animal suffered.

That the efficacy of the fire constituted a part of the virtue inherent in the horseshoe is further proved, says a writer in 1839, by the manner in which it is used for reclaiming witched milk, that is, by first submitting it to red heat, and, unknowingly to the person carrying the pail, suddenly plunging it into the milk contained in it.

In Cornwall, and especially in the eastern part, the horseshoe is frequently seen attached to the threshold of doors, especially those of cow-houses as a security against the entrance of witches and those with the evil-eye. In the fixing of these amulets it is important to note that the horns of the shoe must point upwards, not only because the luck will run out if it is the other way, but because, if the points hang downwards, it will not represent the symbol of Diana, the Moon Goddess.

During the writer's investigation of the subject of witchcraft in the Westcountry, he has discovered many cases in which horseshoes have been hung up to prevent "witch-riding," or as it was called many years ago, "nightmare." The witches and "little people" are said to ride the horses in the fields at night and keep them in a sweat, but if a horseshoe is hung over their stables it protects them.

It is related that a farmer in the St. Austell district, having suspected an old woman living near of ill-wishing his cattle went to her cottage with a horseshoe in his hand, and on threatening to draw blood from the woman with it, she removed the evil spell and the cattle recovered.

Other Cornish beliefs concerning the horseshoe are the carrying of a piece of horseshoe in the pocket of a new suit to ensure good luck, including in the wedding bouquet a cast horseshoe, or a horseshoe nail, while it is considered great luck to find a horseshoe but in order to keep the luck, the finder must spit on it three times and then throw it over his left shoulder.

In parts of Devon it is affirmed that the luck lies in the first shoe cast by any particular horse, not only does it protect one from witches by drives away fairies and elves, and destroys their power.

Being creatures of the ancient stone age, the new metal is hateful and harmful to them.

Quite recently a Cornish fisherman told the writer that iron, if thrown overboard, enables mariners to land on a rocky coast with safety, even in rough weather.

These are just a few of the many beliefs and superstitions concerning the horseshoe, which can still be found in our midst.

CORNISH WITCHCRAFT
[1969][9]

Many years ago, I set myself the task of collecting the superstitions and folklore associated with Cornwall. I realised that with the present generation probably all these relics of the past will disappear. I therefore set out on my so-called witch hunt.

It was not an easy task, however, for I soon discovered the difficulty in getting behind the scenes in order to find out as there appeared a subconsciousness that such dealings are unorthodox, and again there was the fear of ridicule.

Spells and magic, evil wishes and sudden cures are very near and potent things and to question their existence would be flying in the face of providence. Again, I frequently met with the remark that the Bible denounces witches, "Thou shalt not suffer a witch to live" says *Exodus* 22, 18, and time and time again, I was reminded of this by people who, to use their own words, "wish to get their own back" after being bewitched or over-looked!

Others again reminded me that preacher John Wesley was a firm believer in ghosts and witches and insisted upon it years after all laws upon the subject had been repealed in this country.

It is interesting to note that although John Wesley's views on familiar spirits have been frequently alluded to, as far as I am able to ascertain, no convincing statement has been published to show his actual attitude towards the question of witchcraft.

Doubtless the Bible text, as well as convincing John Wesley served as the basis for many a witch hunt and bitter prosecution in the past.

Probably few people are aware how widespread was the belief, not a great many years ago, in charms and charmers and other superstitions or that there were witches in almost every villages, shunned and dreaded by some who fears their supposed power to ill-wish those who offended them and sought out by others who wanted their aid to avert the evil eye or by their magic to removed spells already cast on them or their cattle by an ill-wisher who had over-looked them.

In my witch hunt, I covered the whole of Cornwall, visiting parish by parish and came across numerous cases of witchcraft—generally ill-wishing or bewitching, alleged power to remove spells, which were sometimes a form of blackmail. Today witchcraft is not so common as it was, the scientists' wand is dissolving many things with the result that the old tales and legends are fading from the memories of the country folk. Witch-belief in its traditional form appears to have gone for ever.

It is natural, says a well-known authority on the subject, to think that magic is a thing of the past, which must have withered to dust under the hard light of modern science and scepticism, but this he maintains is not the case. Magical thinking is still deeply embedded in the human mentality and even today it attracts interest and support.

There is certainly a curious revival of interest in witchcraft, black magic and the like, probably because things occult are so widely discussed nowadays, though witchcraft and black magic do not touch the finer issues of the occult. Cornish wise men and women once got a good living out of practising their so-called witchcraft. They could be consulted for casting and removing spells and curses. One famous Cornish wizard, as he called himself, attended the Law Courts at Bodmin, and undertook to keep witchcraft off farms for a shilling a year and in addition could guarantee no further trouble.

Another could not only remove spells cast on man and beast, but could looking into the future and predict things to come with uncanny accuracy. Others again could charm snakes, and moles, stop or staunch the flow of blood, charm burns and scalds, take away ringworms and vermin and even find water and buried treasure.

Their sometimes roguish skill they pitted against the simple countryman and woman, "but after all" said a Cornish farmer to me, "who could resist the lifting of a spell from cattle or milk for a few shillings."

The ailments of animals and their care are important to farming folk and the help of a charmer or even a gypsy is well worth the trouble.

In my search I discovered there were men and women in our Cornish villages and moorland areas who believed in witches and the power of the evil eye as well as in the fairy folk.

They were known as the "Devil's" agents, and consisted of black, grey, and white. The black variety were believed to have unlimited power of doing evil and were usually malicious, cunning thieves, and afflictors of children, cattle and crops. The grey witches were a mixture of good and bad; they could cast a spell on one hand, and for a further consideration, remove it with the other; while the white variety, the "do-gooders," were known in Cornwall as Pellars, they had the power to help but not to harm. The magic they used was for healing the sick or curing disease and various ailments, through the medium of charms.

It is curious to observe how many of the beliefs of our fathers and fore-fathers thrown aside long ago as mere old wives' tales reappear as real and well attested phenomena.

The miraculous cures and equally miraculous curses, which were believed to have been the effect of words, charms, spells, or incantations, in which—and here lies the secret of their power—the person affected had implicit belief.

It has seemed absurd to our modern minds that the mere recitation of a sentence, or even a meaningless jargon of words, or the wearing of a charm, should be able to cause such material results as the cure of apparent paralysis, the complete removal of warts, the production of skin eruptions, fits, the symptoms of definite disease, and even death, but with the new light which the study of psychology has thrown upon the working of the nervous centres such occurrences are not only well attested but scientifically explained.

It is, indeed, now an accepted scientific fact that the effect of the action of the brain on the material substance of the body is most powerful.

The real secret of witch-belief lies in the nature of the mind itself and the whole problem of what psychologists call projection.

Although the so-called black witches are not now so common in Cornwall, like Devon we still have our folk medicine, which includes charms, incantations, and the traditional habits and customs relative to the preservation of health and the cure of disease. It is amazing that there are still a large number of people who hold in great reverence many herbs which they use to cure divers diseases, often accompanying their application as did the Druids with sundry mystical charms.

These charms are held in high estimation and are carefully handed down from one generation to another; there are some families in Cornwall who have been charmers for generations, thus they are preserved to their full efficiency.

Here again in seeking out, I have experienced great difficulty in obtaining the words of many of the charms used for the efficacy of many of them are destroyed as soon as they are told or recorded in print.

Yes, there are still people who can successfully charm warts and burns and scalds, stop the flow of blood, charm various complaints of the eyes, relieve and cure various skin complaints, charm snake bites and even charm snakes themselves. I have actually seen a snake charmed, have witnessed the stopping of blood from a badly cut and bleeding wrist, and been present when an old lady successfully charmed a badly scalded leg.

In a recent talk on Cornish Charms and Charmers to the members of a Cornish Young Farmers' Club, no less than five young farmers told me their respective fathers or grandfathers could charm ringworms in humans and cattle and it was not always necessary for the cattle or the patient to be seen by the charmer, they could be charmed over the telephone. The same applied to the charming of warts, and in the case of burns and scalds sometimes the charmer saw the sufferer, in others all that was required was a garment or some possession of the sufferer. This was charmed, returned to the patient, and placed on the burn or scald.

Quite recently I was intrigued to see a number of black slugs impaled on a thorn tree in a cottage garden. Enquiries revealed it was a cure for warts.

"Get" said the charmer, "a black slug and slit it open to show the white inside, and rub this over the wart, then pin the still live slug to a thorn tree during the new moon, or the waning of the moon, which ever happens to be. As the slug dried up the wart will fall off and be gone by the full moon."

The belief that warts can be charmed by sending the number to a charmer was illustrated to me when I was shown a postcard to the wart charmer which read, "I have 18 warts on my hand. Yours obediently."

"Let us laugh at the folly of our forefathers by all means," was a remark made to me by a person who had been successfully charmed, "but it does not therefore follow that our means to an end are more efficacious though being presumably more sensible."

Strange and curious things still happen in the country and as a Devonshire writer on Folklore says the outstanding point about black witchcraft lies not in its practice, but in the lingering belief that it can still operate. Much has been written of late on the subject of the black arts and of alleged existence and practice in the Westcountry, but as far as I am concerned, I have found no evidence of this. The supposed witchcraft signs and symbols I have inspected in churchyards and desolate and derelict buildings have never been authentic, just rubbish scribblings and oddments as pranks and jokes by young people out for kicks.

The following is an example. Quite recently a university student came with her friend to see me to say she had been threatened with dreadful happenings if she did not join a Black Magic session. So persistent was the dabbler in the diabolical practices that he handed the young woman a piece of paper on which was written sundry mystical signs and told her that if she did not join the session on her return to college dire consequences would follow.

The young woman was naturally upset but I was able to assure her that the supposed curse on her piece of paper was complete rubbish, and the person who had written it and indeed, threatened her, was a swindler of the first order who was attempting to practice the most contemptible form of deception.

To laugh at the folly of witchcraft is the only way of being [un]influenced by it, is the advice I offer.

Cornish Charms & Cures

As discussed in chapter 2, Paynter did not limit himself solely to the study of witchcraft and his research took account of the wider context of Cornish folk-practices and beliefs. In every part of Cornwall he visited Paynter recorded the popular customs of the locality, though many of the articles reprinted in this chapter focus on the lore associated with East Cornwall. The various healing charms and actions of charmers also fascinated Paynter, and many of his articles on Westcountry folk-customs recorded his encounters with them. Paynter followed up his interest in ornithology by recording the various superstitions associated with birds, including the magpie and the cuckoo—the subjects of two articles. This chapter concludes with an account of a walking tour Paynter took on the North Cornish coast in 1965 in search of folklore, following the route he took as a convalescent 25 years earlier.

EAST CORNWALL BABY-LORE
[1929][1]

The following baby superstitions were very common in the Callington district a few years ago:–

1. Never wash the right hand of a baby until it is a year old; to clean it deprives the poor child of riches.

2. Never cut a baby's nails for the first few months after its birth; they must be bitten short by the teeth, otherwise baby will grow up to be a thief and rogue.

3. Never rock an empty cradle, for it leads to an over-large family.

4. Never measure or weigh a baby until it can "run away" (meaning to walk).

5. Never give a child a mirror, or allow it to look at its reflection; this is considered most unlucky.

6. Should a child break one of its teeth, or have a tooth pulled out, it should be burnt at once; for it was believed that if a dog got hold of it, dog's fangs would grow in its place.

7. A necklet of blue beads or coral worn round the neck, was said to protect a child against bronchitis, while red beads or flannel averted sore throats.

8. If a small bag containing a tooth was placed in a bag and tied around the neck of an infant, it would prevent teething convulsions.

9. Not only was it considered unlucky for a child to be born in May, but May kittens ("May chats" as they are called) were by the superstitious drowned, as to keep one would inevitably bring sorrow and bad luck to the house.

10. Only a short time ago it was deemed fortunate for a still-born baby to be buried in a newly-made grave, as the next person buried therein would assuredly go to heaven.

CURIOUS EAST CORNWALL CURES
[1929][2]

The following remarkable recipes, which have been given to me as cures for the thrush and whooping-cough, illustrate the widespread belief in superstitions that existed in East Cornwall only a few years ago. A cure for the thrush (a disease of the mouth and throat):– Procure six thread of cotton, pass them separately through a cat's mouth, and then through the mouth of the sufferer;

after so doing, throw the threads into a stream, and as the current bears them away, so will the complaint disappear. Now three cures for whooping-cough:– Cut two hairs from the shoulder of a donkey, put them in a little bag and fasten the bag around the child's neck.—Gather nine spar-stones from a stream that divides two parishes, taking care not to interrupt the free passage of the water in so doing. Then dip a quart of water from the stream, which must be taken in the direction in which the stream runs; by no means must the vessels be dipped against the stream. Then make the nine stones red-hot, and throw them into the quart of water. Bottle this prepared water, and give the affected child a wine-glass of it for nine mornings following, and the cough will entirely disappear.

Take a hair from the patient's head and place it between two slices of bread-and-butter and give it to a dog to eat, if he (the dog) in eating it coughs, then will the whooping-cough be transferred to it, and the child will get well.

KING'S EVIL
[1929][3]

About twenty years ago, said my informant, a man living near Callington suffered from swellings in the neck and shoulder, which were thought to be King's Evil. Various remedies were tried, but without success. At last he was advised to visit a local White Witch, who was noted for curing complaints by the touch of a hangman's rope. He accordingly went, and described how the witch first muttered some strange words and then stroked the affected part with a piece of rope, with which he said a man had been hanged, and strange to say, within a short space of time the disease completely disappeared.

Knowing the son of this old man, I made a number of enquiries, and discovered that the valuable relic had been in the possession of the family for a great number of years, and was secured at Launceston after a public execution.

It was not difficult of course to procure such rope in the good old days, when sheep-stealers, and even others guilty of lesser offences, were publicly hanged.

A RINGWORM CURE
[1929][4]

About eighty years ago there lived at Saint Mellion, near Callington, a dear old dame, by name Ann ____, who was noted far and wide for her curative powers. According to those who remember her, she made a celebrated ointment, consisting of chopped pennyroyal and lard, with which she could cure ringworm. Only three applications were needed to effect a perfect cure. On her death, I find she passed on her secrets, as she called them, to her son, who later sold them to various persons in East Cornwall, including a well-known veterinary surgeon.

In writing of ringworm, I am reminded of a so-called "Pellar," at present residing at Callington. In a recent conversation he informed me that he could cure and transfer ringworm, both in humans and cattle, but he refused to give me any particulars of his methods, except to say that he had cured scores of sufferers in the district, who, it appears, had to visit him three times on three successive evenings for an effective cure.

Although he is not a Pellar by birth, he claims to have been instructed in the "magic arts" by a witch, in return for a bag of potatoes.

WESTCOUNTRY FOLK MEDICINE
[1929][5]

Strange Superstitions

With the advance of education many old superstitions regarding cures for all sorts of ailments are dying, but some still linger and here and there people who still have faith in them may still be found. In this article Mr. William Paynter, Recorder of Callington Old Cornwall Society, has collated a number of these so-called "cures," some of them being of a somewhat revolting nature.

"Folk-medicine includes charms, incantations, and traditional habits, and customs relative to the preservation of health and the cure of disease, practised now or formerly at home or abroad."

The people of Devon and Cornwall held in great reverence many herbs, which they used to cure divers diseases, often accompanying their applications, even as did the Druids, with sundry mystical charms. These charms were held in high estimation, and were carefully handed down from one generation to another. Women communicated the secret of these mysteries to men, and vice versa, whilst occasionally it happened that the secret was told to one of their own sex; thus they were preserved to their full efficacy.

Right down through the ages certain individuals have been credited with peculiar gifts, all of which to the average person are incapable of a really satisfactory explanation owing to the fact that such phenomena are apparently at the edge of the occult. It is interesting to note that there are still families in the Westcountry who are reputed by tradition to have had dealings with evil spirits, and who are said to possess to this day peculiar virtues as charmers.

The Sennen Charmers.

Many years ago a forefather of a certain family living at Sennen found washed in on the Gwenver Sand a very old man, almost dead, whom he took to his house and had well cared for, so that he soon recovered and prepared to depart. Before leaving, however, the old man told his host that he had neither gold nor silver to pay him for his hospitality, yet he would bestow on him and his [posterity] what would be of more value, and imparted to the man of Sennen a large number of charms, which a descendant of the family could use. If they were written down they were useless, and the giver of a written charm would henceforth lose the power to cure by charming.

Although many of the old charms and customs have now become obsolete, yet more survive than the average person would believe, and it is an amazing fact that such beliefs as "ill-wishing," "overlooking," and the charming of diseases have survived until our times, and are practised still in remote districts.

The following are a number of charms and quaint cures which the writer has collected in various parts of Devon and Cornwall during the past few months:–

Cures for Warts.

Steal from a butcher's block a piece of beef and rub the warts with it, then cut a slit in the bark of an ash tree and place the beef under the bark; as the meat decays so will the warts, and instead of appearing again on the hands they will make their appearance on the tree as rough excrescences. The ash, it must be remembered, was always considered more or less sacred, and should one find an even ash leaf, it was a sure sign of good luck. When such a leaf was found, the following charm was said over it:–

> Even Ash, I thee do pluck
> Hoping thus to meet good luck;

> If no luck I get from thee
> I shall wish thee on the tree.

The bark of the ash was also used for curing warts, and it is recorded that a person living in the Helston district suffering from warts visited an old woman, reputed to be a witch, and well known for curing many diseases. She, it is said, would place a table knife lightly over the warts, and, after muttering an incantation, would hobble to an ash tree in her garden and cut from it a small strip of the bark. This she presented to the sufferer, again muttering strange words, and assuring her that as the strip of bark withered, so would the warts.

A cure recommended to the writer by an old lady residing in the Camborne district was to rub each wart with a "churk" (meaning a cinder), and this tie up in paper; drop where four roads meet, and the warts will be transferred to whoever opens the parcel.

Another mode of transferring warts is to touch each one with a pebble and place the pebbles in a bag, which should be lost on the way to church; whoever finds the bag gets the warts.

Still another cure was to proceed to a point where four roads meet, lift a stone, rub the warts with the dust from below the stone, and repeat the following nine times:–

> I am one, the warts' two,
> The first one to come by
> Takes the warts away.

Another remedy was to cover the warts with fasting-spittle at early dawn, whilst swine's blood has also been held in high esteem, and said to be a sure cure. The finding of a bottle of pins in a field near Callington some 45 years ago accounted for the curious custom of burying pins which have touched warts.

Gruesome Cure for Quinsy.

Catch a live toad and tie a string around its throat, and hang it up to a rafter to die. When at last the body of the animal has decomposed and dropped from the head, so freeing the cord, take the cord which had thus acquired virtue and tie it round the patient's neck, where it would have to remain until his or her 50th birthday. Another curious method of getting clear of various diseases was by forcing them in some manner upon a dead person; for example, following a corpse and saying as it was laid to rest: "My ailment goes with you." A cure is sure to follow.

Epilepsy.

Against epilepsy a patient was ordered to catch a toad and cut off one of its legs and wear it round the neck in a bag. If, however, she was unable to procure a toad, she might take a black cock without a white feather and bury it on the spot where she had her first fit. A special modification was the taking of the parings of the nails of the fingers and toes, binding them, with a sixpence, with hemp in a piece of paper, on which was written the names of the Father, the Son, and the Holy Ghost. The parcel was then taken, tied under the wing of a black cock, and buried in a hole dug at the spot where the first fit occurred by the oldest God-fearing man of the district, who must watch and pray all night by the fire, which must not be let out. Surely this is a relic of a sacrificial offering to an evil spirit.

Chilblains and Corns.

A cure connected with the Nature worship of Pagan Cornwall was to wash the hands under the direct rays of the moon in a dry metal basin, and at the same time repeating the following:–

> I wash my hands in this thy dish.
> O Man in the Moon do grant my wish
> And come and take away this.

The moon was also invoked to cure corns in a similar way, only the feet this time had to be washed in a dry basin and the following repeated nine times to be effective:–

>Come down here.
>No corns up there.

The forefinger being pointed first to the ground and then to the sky, while the sufferer repeats these words, the corns will disappear.

A Charm for a Scald.

The following charm was given to the writer for scalds:– The person to be charmed gathers nine bramble leaves, which are put into a vessel of spring water; then each leaf is passed over and from the diseased part, whilst he repeats three times to each leaf:–

>Three ladies came from the East,
>One with fire, and two with frost;
>Out with thee fire, and in with thee frost,
>In the name of the Father, Son, and Holy Ghost.

A stick of fire is then taken from the hearth and passed over and around the diseased part, whilst the above is again repeated nine times.

The Cramp.

The hare, which shares with the cat the reputation of being the familiar of witches, has naturally some virtues attributed to it. To carry one of its fore-feet in the pocket will infallibly ward off rheumatism, while its ankle-bone has been said to be good against the cramp. A friend of the writer, on being suddenly seized with the cramp, was heard to repeat the following, which appeared to restore the use of his limb at once:–

>O cramp, O cramp, why crampest thou me,
>Go to the wood and cramp a tree.
>God the Father, God the Son, God the Holy Ghost, help me.

It must not be thought that these passages were repeated irreverently, for it was believed the repetition of the phrases would really effect a perfect cure.

Toothache.

"Let him that suffers from toothache," said an old dame to the writer, "catch a frog and spit into its mouth, and request it to make off with the pain and it surely will." According to an old lady residing in East Cornwall, toothache can be cured by repeating slowly and reverently the following charm:–

> Our Lord passed by His brother's door,
> Saw His brother lying on the floor.
> What aileth thee, brother?
> Pain in the teeth?
> Thy teeth shall pain thee no more,
> In the name of the Father, Son, and Holy Ghost.

Toothache can also be cured, say the superstitious, by biting from the ground the first fern that appears in spring, and this will also prevent the person so doing from suffering from this pain during the year ...

Snakes and Snake Bites.

A former vicar of Bolventor records that charms against snake bites are still used on the Bodmin moors. On one occasion a dog had been bitten by a viper and its head was swollen to the size of a football. This charm was repeated over it, and immediately the swelling diminished, and the dog recovered. The words used were an adaptation of the 68th Psalm, "Let God arise and let His enemies be scattered. Let them that hate Him flee before Him. Like as the smoke vanisheth so shall thou drive them away, and like the wax that melteth at the fire so let this poison perish at the presence of God. In the name of the Father, and of the Son, and of the Holy Ghost. Amen.

The practice of charming was much resorted to one the moors, and when anything happened the wise woman was always sent for. In many cases she was preferred to a doctor or veterinary surgeon; and often long distances were undertaken for a charmer of special ability.

CURIOUS WESTCOUNTRY CURES
[1931][6]

How People of another Generation Banished Warts with Snails and Moon-Magic

In remote villages of Devon and Cornwall, especially on the moors, a great deal of superstition and folklore still lingers amongst the old inhabitants; but the difficulty is to get behind the scenes in order to find it out, as there appears to be a sub-consciousness that such dealings are unorthodox, and possibly some fear of ridicule. Some years ago I set myself the interesting task of trying to gather up the fragments that remain; the superstitions and arts that still exist as quaint and interesting remnants of the past, but of which the next generation will probably be ignorant, unless some record is made of them.

The following are just a few of the many curious cures for warts which I have been able to glean ... While snailing in my garden the other evening a passer-by informed me that my catch was worth a great deal, as it contained several dew-snails (anglice, black slug). "But what are they good for?" I asked. "Why, warts," he replied. "Get a large one and slit it open to show the white inside, and rub this on the wart, then pin the still live animal to a thorn tree during the new moon, or the waning of the moon, whichever happens to be. As the slug dries up the wart will fall off and be gone by the full moon."

Later, while using soot, I was reminded of the "churk" (cinder) cure. Rub each wart with a churk, and this tie up in paper;

drop where four roads meet and the warts will be transferred to whoever opens the parcel, or, better still, touch each wart with a pebble and place the pebbles in a white bag, which must be lost on the way to church; again, whoever finds the bag gets the warts … A member of our Old Cornwall Society told me that as a boy, he remembered walking through Callington Fore-street with a small linen bag about six inches by two inches suspended on his shoulder with a piece of cord, and that he had to drop as he walked along. If he dropped it unconsciously he would lose the warts which were a great disfigurement on his hands in those days. On my inquiring what the bag contained, he said "black pins which had pricked each wart." Another method was to bury the pins which had touched warts in a newly-made grave. This remedy, said my informant, is considered infallible.

An old dame I met in Devonshire recommended the eating of large quantities of watercress to cure warts, while another said they could be successfully cured by giving the patient nine leaves of dandelion or heart-fever grass, as she called it, and directing them to be eaten, three leaves on three successive mornings, after which, they will have disappeared.

Find a young ash tree in the hedge, then walk backwards to the tree, and pick a branch over your left shoulder. Bite it in half, and rub the wart with it. Then throw the branch away over your left shoulder and tell no one. This is similar to the blackberry cure; rub your warts with the first blackberry you pick, thrown it over your head and as it rots so will your warts …

One of the most remarkable narrative charms is that for warts. It is to be sung first into the left ear, then into the right ear, then above the patient's poll (head), then "let one who is a maiden go to him and hang it upon his neck, do so for three days, and it will soon be well with him."

> Here came entering
> A spider wight,

> He had his hands upon his hams;
> He quoth that thou, his hackney wert,
> Lay thee against his neck.
> They began to sail off the land-
> As soon as they off the land came, then
> Began they to cool.
> Then came in a wild beast's sister,
> Then she ended.
> And oaths she swore that never could
> This harm the sick, nor him who could get at
> This charm, nor him who had skill to sing this charm.
> Amen.

Another cure well known to Westcountry farmers is to take a nat of a reed and strike the wart downwards three times, then bury the reed, while smearing the hands with the blood of either a mole, pig, or hedgehog will effect a perfect cure.

It is interesting to note that there are still families in the Westcountry who possess peculiar virtues as charmers. Even in Callington two are to be found, one can charm burns and scalds and the other warts.

Some time ago a wart appeared on my hand and I went with all speed to a chemist. He gave me a small bottle of "trade" (Cornish for medicine or lotion) and I painted my wart for several days, but without any effect except that it got larger. A friend advised me to visit our local charmer. I did so, and, taking my right hand, he passed his over it seven times, at the same time muttering something, and within a fortnight the wart had entirely disappeared. This same man has charmed many wart sufferers, and in every case it has been successful. So successful, in fact, are his cures that he has a great reputation in all the countryside.

CORNISH CHARMS AND CURES
[1931][7]
How a Dead Person's Hand Proves a Gruesome Remedy

"I am a great believer in charms and charmers," wrote a "Western Evening Herald" reader, "and if you are ever in this district (near Bodmin) will you come and see me, as I can give you a number of interesting recipes?" During the past weekend I happened to be in this particular area and with the help of my new acquaintance was able to add the following to my ever-growing list of remarkable Westcountry cures:

"Callington is not the only place that can boast of a blood charmer," said my friend. "I can charm myself, and I know it works all right. Only the other evening I was called into a hayfield to stop a flow of blood. It was a very bad cut, you know; youngsters meddling with things what don't concern 'em. However I soon put the boy comfortable, and I hope 'twill be a lesson to him not to play with paring hooks again."

"Most interesting," I remarked, "but what about nose bleeding?" "Yes," he replied, "I have stopped hundreds, but usually folk who suffer from nose bleeding wear a little bag around their necks containing five pieces of red silk. It's a sure preventative."

It is interesting to observe that binding on with red wool is a very ancient and widespread custom. An early writer considers the use of red to be an imitation of blood. In the "Grete Herball" of 1526 we read "opium is good for lunatyke Folke if it be bounde to the pacyentes heed with a lynen clothe dyed reed," &c. Red, it will be remembered, was the colour sacred to Thor, and it was also the colour abhorred not only by witches but by all the powers of darkness and evil.

"Some women can also charm," continued my friend. "I once saw an old woman known to be a witch, use the blood charm on a farmer she did not like. He was killing pigs at the time, and after he had cut a pig's throat in the usual way she stopped the blood and the poor old pig didn't die. Observing the woman standing in the doorway of her cottage, the farmer at once realized what she had done and, rushing toward her with his pig-sticking knife, he threatened to cut her throat if she did not undo the spell. She did so, whereupon the blood again flowed and the unfortunate pig was soon dead."

According to my friend the efficacy of all charms is destroyed when they are recorded in print. However, the string of rhymes to stop an effusion of blood is so barbarous that it is worth the risk:

"Our Lord was born in Bethlehem,
Baptized in River Jordan, when
The water was wild in the wood,
The person was just and good;
God spake, and the water stood;
And so shall now thy blood—
In the name of the Father," &c.

"Talking of pigs," said a farmer we met during the afternoon, "on my inquiring how a neighbour's fared he told me that at times some of them got crippled with rheumatism."

"Well, what do you do?" I asked. "Do?" said he. "Why, the only cure is to cut off the tip of their tails. It's a bit of a mess as they bleed so, but it's a sure cure, as it draws the blood away from their heads, and that's what does the good.

We next discussed boils, and I was able to record the following: "Find a place where you can cover seven or nine daisies with your left foot, then pick and eat them; or if you cannot manage that apply salt bacon to the body and the boils will disappear."

A lady writing from Delabole told me that a charm for the cure of boils was confided by a Tintagel wise woman to the district nurse when she was very ill. It consisted of reciting the following over the patient, using his or her own name:

> "Mary Brown, three angels came from the West,
> One had fire, the others water and frost.
> Out fire. In water and frost.
> In the name of the Father," &c.

"A few years ago," said my friend, "there was a strong belief in this district that if a person afflicted with any cutaneous disease was secretly taken to a corpse and the following gruesome ritual carried out he would be cured. First pass the hand of the corpse over the parts affected; then take a piece of linen the patient has worn and cover the sores, which must be afterwards dropped upon the coffin during the reading of the burial service, and a perfect cure will result."

This reminded me of a story I gleaned at Penzance. A lady who was staying in that district and was present at a funeral observed that when the clergyman came to the words "Earth to earth" a woman made her way to the edge of the grave and dropped a cloth upon the coffin, closed her eyes, and apparently said a prayer. On the lady making inquiries as to the reason of this extraordinary proceeding she was informed of the superstition just recorded.

Some years ago the following curious paragraph relative to charming for burns and scalds appeared in a London newspaper:

"The child of a Devonshire labourer died from scalds caused by its turning over a saucepan. At the inquest the following strange evidence was given by one Ann Manley, a witness: 'I am the wife of James Manley, labourer. I met Sarah Shepherd about nine o'clock on Thursday coming on the road with her child in her arms wrapt in the tail of her frock. She said her child was scalded; then I charmed it as I charmed it before, when a stone hopped out of the fire last Honiton Fair and scalded its eye. I charmed it in the road; I charmed it by saying to myself, "There was (sic) two angels come from the North, one of them being fire, and the other frost. In frost, out fire," etc. I repeat this three times. This is good for a scald. I can't say it is good for anything else. Old John Sparway told me this charm many years ago. A man may tell a woman the charm, or a woman may tell a man; but if a woman tells a woman, or a man a man, I consider it won't do any good at all."

CURES FOR TOOTHACHE
[1932][8]

Curious Superstitions in Devon and Cornwall

"The management of the Windmill Theatre, Great Windmill Street, London, have decided to insure the teeth of the "Windmill Girls" for £100,000."

They are marvellous, these teeth of ours! To many people they are just things placed in the mouth for chewing and masticating, and to generally aid digestion of food, but let us look abroad.

In the Congo, men and women have their teeth filed to sharp points to resemble those of the cat; in the Harz, the most northerly chain in Germany, teeth of the dead are used to cure headache; very frequently, too, teeth of animals are used both as drugs and as health protecting amulets, while people have been known to remove an evil spell cast on them by fumigating themselves by pulverised human teeth.

There are many curious superstitions concerning teeth to be found in this country, and especially in Devon and Cornwall, and if, by disclosing the following sovereign cures, I bring to ruin any member of the dental profession, I tender my humble apologies and regrets!

"There was never yet a philosopher that could endure toothache patiently," said Shakespeare. Here then is good news for those who suffer from this common and distracting complaint:—Repeat, slowly and reverently the following charm: St. Peter sat at the gate of the Temple and our Lord said unto him, "What aileth thee?" Peter said "Oh, my tooth." Our Lord said unto Peter, "Arise and follow Me, and thou shalt not feel the toothache again."

At a recent Cornish fair, a farmer showed the writer a double hazle-nut threaded on a silver chain, which, he said, if worn round the neck not only prevented toothache, but also kept the wearer free from pain. He had worn the nut over 30 years and had never been troubled.

According to another Westcountry authority, if a tooth is extracted from an old skull found in a churchyard and kept in the pocket all the year round, the possessor would never have pain in the teeth or gums.

The mole, which figures in the practice of divination in Brittany and in other parts of France, is also highly esteemed in Cornwall. Apply a piece of mole's skin to the aching tooth and the pain will immediately stop, while the mole's teeth are good for the gout.

A quaint old soul living on the famous Bodmin Moors, told the writer that if you did not care to repeat the verses concerning the blind beggar (St. John IX, v. 9, or Exodus, c. XII), where it is written that no bone of the Passover shall be broken, you can visit the parish church, and placing your finger on the fifth nail from the handle of the door, say the Apostle's Creed three times.

A Devonshire farmer who had suffered great pain from his teeth, was advised by a "charmer" to go to a young oak tree, place his arms around it, and mark the place where his fingers met; then make a slit in the bark with a knife, put his left hand behind his right ear, and pull out seven hairs; place them in the slit in the bark, and he could never have toothache again. This cure is considered by many to be better that carrying a sheep's tooth in a bag, biting from the ground a first fern that appears in spring, or catching a frog and spitting into its mouth, and requesting him to make off with the pain.

Of the many baby superstitions to be met with frequently in the Westcountry, the following concerning the teeth and teething are highly recommended.

If a small bag containing a tooth is tied around the neck of an infant, it will prevent teething convulsions, as also will the wearing of a necklace made from either peony roots, the stems of nightshade, or pieces of mistletoe.

A bag containing mole claws worn by an infant will facilitate teething, while the youngster's teeth can be protected from all evils by cleaning with the ash obtained after burning rosemary wood. Should a child break one of its teeth, or have a tooth pulled out, it should be burnt at once, says a Cornish mother, for if a dog should eat it, dog's fangs will grow in its place, while under no circumstances let your children touch the teeth of a whale, for doing so might make them unhappy for the remainder of their lives.

In other parts of England it is considered unlucky to count the number of teeth in a comb, as it means you are numbering the days of your life. It is not right to take fire out of a house where there is a child who has not got teeth yet, as it is said that the child will never get teeth if the fire be taken away, while in East Invernesshire it is still held that water drunk from the skull of a suicide will bring good luck and be a cure for toothache.

WESTCOUNTRY BIRD LORE
[1933][9]

Some Remarkable Superstitions and Strange Beliefs

It seems almost incredible that even today there are people who still regard certain species of birds with a feeling of awe and prejudice, firmly believing the old superstitions concerning them. The much-maligned raven with its hoarse, uncanny croak has ever been regarded as being supreme in malignant crime. It is supposed to be fatally ominous, and even today it is spoken of in certain parts of Devon and Cornwall as "death's messenger." Robins, too, are considered unlucky, and many a Westcountry housewife, on observing the bird tapping on her window or entering her house, considers him a warning of evil to come.

The magpie is another that has long been associated with quaint superstitions. Magpie lore is somewhat extensive and country folk generally have some queer belief with regard to its being either a bird that brings good luck or bad luck.

An old gamekeeper of my acquaintance always associates the magpie with ill-luck, and on his seeing a single bird religiously spits three times over his left shoulder. Another acquaintance always raises his hat to the bird, while a third, after repeating:

> "One for sorrow, two for mirth,
> Three for a wedding, four for a birth,
> Five for a sickness, six for a death,
> And seven's the Devil himself."

politely bows. It is interesting to recall the legend concerning the magpie. According to the story told, when the birds were ordered to take their allotted places in the Ark the magpie did not obey Noah's voice, but perched on the roof and jabbered at him; wherefore to this day the magpie lies under Noah's curse.

It is also interesting to observe that the bird is not at all popular in sunny Spain, for he is believed to be the bull-fighter's bird of ill-omen. Even skilful, heroic matadors, we are told, shake in their shoes if they meet a magpie on their way to the arena.

"No, I won't have peacock's feathers brought into this house," I heard a Cornishwoman exclaim to her child, who had arrived with a fine bunch of peacock's feathers. "They are unlucky."

Like Westcountry folk, the Arabs also consider the peacock an unlucky bird and declare that it was the cause of the entrance of the Devil ("Old Sir Nick" as we know him in Cornwall) into Paradise and the expulsion of Adam and Eve.

They also relate that the devil watered the vine with the blood of four creatures—with that of the peacock, and when it began to put forth leaves with the blood of an ape; then, when the grapes began to appear, with that of a lion, and lastly, when they were quite ripe, with the blood of a hog; which is the reason, say they, that a wine-bibber is at first elated and struts like a peacock, then begins to dance, play, and make grimaces like an ape; he then rages like a lion and, lastly, settled down on any dunghill like a hog.

During the recent spell of wintry weather a large number of curlew have been driven inland. These birds are considered by many to be birds of ill-omen. According to one legend they are supposed to be lost souls tossed hither and thither by the winds. The Arabs say that the cry of the bird, which they call "harawan," has a solemn meaning when translated into human language.

Impressed with a due sense of the power and majesty of the Creator, this bird in its solitary flight among the rocks thus addresses the Deity: "To Thee, to Thee, to Thee belongs the sovereignty of the world, without partner or companion."

Probably their mournful cries give rise to this ancient belief.

Another member of the crow family that ought to be mentioned, a bird of whom every Cornishman should be proud—the Chough. It was the noble chough, with its sable plumage and scarlet beak and legs, which was chosen for the home of the soul of the mighty King Arthur, and that is the reason why the chough loves the wild Cornish coast where Arthur's Castle of Tintagel stood.

Not all birds, however, are regarded with disfavour; many are believed to be beneficial in the cure of various ailments. Among these can be mentioned the swallow, whose burnt body will cure quinsy; its heart, epilepsy and ague; and its blood, especially that drawn from beneath the right wing, is good for defective eyesight.

A small bone found in the stomach of young birds, tied to the arm or hung around the neck, is said to be a sovereign remedy for children's fits; but this must be sought in the eldest of the brood before the August moon is full.

Of the owl, the "fatal bell-man," we learn that the ashes of its eyes is a cure for imperfect sight; and those of the head a remedy for disorders of the spleen. The feet, burnt with herbs, is a charm against snakes; and the eggs and nestlings' blood make the hair curl!

TALES AND SUPERSTITIONS ABOUT THE CUCKOO
[1933][10]
Old Saws & Sayings in the Westcountry

There are many strange tales and superstitions in the Westcountry concerning the cuckoo, whose familiar cry, from early morn to dewy eve, we hope soon to be hearing. He is regarded with mixed feelings, for although the old assertion that

> "He sucks little birds' eggs
> To make his voice clear."

was always open to doubt, its parasitic habits and well known destruction of the eggs and young of other birds have taken away much of its charm.

Many country folk consider the cuckoo a bird of omen, and believe that he is connected with the Other World, to which he migrates after the summer solstice. The cuckoo's note was hailed by the British priesthood as the harbinger of the sacrifices of Mayday Eve.

With the Devonians he is still an ominous bird, since to hear him for the first time on the left hand is considered a sign of great ill luck.

In Germany he is taken as an omen of good weather, and German children, on hearing him for the first time cry, "Cuckoo, how long am I to live?" Then they count the cuckoo's cries, by the number of which they judge of the years yet to be allowed to them.

A similar question used to be addressed to the bird by the old folk of Cornwall, who used to go into the woods and ask: "Cuckoo, cuckoo, when shall I be relieved from this world's cares?" Maidens, too, used to ask the bird when they would be married. To all these questions the cuckoo answered "Cuckoo" as many times as years would elapse before the wish would come true.

Some old people live till they are very old indeed, and some maidens live unmarried till they are very old, and so the cuckoo had to say "Cuckoo! Cuckoo!" so many times that she spent her days in doing nothing else, and had no time, so the legend tells us, to make a nest for herself. That is why cuckoos lay their eggs in the nests of other birds.

The so-called "Cuckoo-spit," "Frog-spit," or "Froth-spit," the name popularly given to the spittle-like secretion found in summer time on many of our wild flowers, and is produced by an insect, the frog hopper, or froth-fly, as a protective covering for its larvae, was by our ancestors believed to be the origin from which cuckoos grow, while ancient writers tell us that the bird changed during the winter months into a merlin.

Of the many rhymes concerning the bird, the following is still very common in parts of Devon and Cornwall:

> "The cuckoo is a bonny bird,
> He sings as he flies;
> He brings us good tidings;
> He tells us no lies.
> He sucks little birds' eggs
> To keep his voice clear;
> And he'll come again
> In the spring of the year."

In the following quaint lines, the whole history of the bird from the time of his arrival until his departure is given:

> "In the month of April
> The cuckoo shows his bill;
> In the month of May
> He sings all day;
> In the month of June
> He alters his tune;
> In the month of July
> He prepares to fly;
> Come August
> Go he must."

"Early lambs are never reared on Dartmoor, on account of the coldness of the air," writes a Devonshire folklorist. "Those that come late, however, are considered to do well there. These are called 'Cuckoo lambs,' as being contemporary with the appearance of that bird."

It is very unlucky to hear the cuckoo after June 24, an old Devonshire dame told the writer; while a Northcountry acquaintance, in a letter describing the habits of the bird, says that he remembered that during his youth boys on first hearing the cuckoo would take out of their pocket the money lying there and spit on it for good luck. This is very similar to our Westcountry custom of showing or "turning" our money when we first see the new moon.

It is said that if a cuckoo's body is wrapped in a hare's skin and applied to insomnia cases, it will induce sound sleep, while portions of its entrails render the bearer proof against the bite of a mad dog.

The following amusing story is related concerning the cuckoo in Cornwall. In consequence of the wet and marshy condition of a certain Cornish parish, the good folks residing there began to think of some way of putting a stop to it. A meeting was therefore held, but after a long discussion the only way they could see out of the difficulty was to hold on to summer when it turned up, and so get rid of winter altogether!

This, they discovered later, was easier said than done, so another conference was held at which an old ancient exclaimed that he had got a solution. "Good folks," said he, "if you want to hold on to summer there's only one way, and that it is to hedge the 'gookoo': when the old bird do go, summer do go after him."

Upon this point they all agreed, and thought if they could keep the "gookoo" summer was sure to stay. So they found out the bird and gathered round it with hurdles and sticks and a whole gallery of things to fence him in with.

The cuckoo watched the strange proceedings with much interest, but, at last, growing tired, took wing and flew away, whereat they all dropped their tools and looked at one another open-mouthed with wonder. "Co!" they said, "what a pity! A voot higher an' we should ha' had 'en!"

LOVE AND MAGIC
[1933][11]

Some Curious Superstitions and Their Origin

It seems natural to suppose that the aid of the practitioners of magic should be sought in connection with the "malady" of love—common to mankind from the time of the creation. Love, like death, is a mysterious and unreasonable thing, and it is because it is such a gamble that men and women are superstitious about it.

In love and marriage the ardent and romantic person stakes his (or her) life, and his very self. Is it any wonder then that the bride hesitates to wear a certain colour, as for example green; or to be married on a Friday, during the season of Lent, or on the thirteenth of the month! The old shoe, the showering of rice, the horse shoe, and all the rest of it, she has not even an idea of what they all mean, but is glad to see them. The old shoe is a symbol of the authority of her husband, and in bygone days the father gave a shoe to the bridegroom as a sign that it was the latter's privilege to keep his wife in order.

According to folklorists, the custom is a remnant of something which came from the Egyptians, or some other ancient nation with which the Jews came in contact, though investigations show that it was never confined to any one race. We are all obsessed by that craving to see into the future, and perhaps love stirs us to superstition more surely than anything else.

Superstition has ever held a mysterious power over men's actions, and few, even at the present day, can positively assert that they are entirely free from its baneful influence. We find superstitions mingling in the most common affairs of life, and though unacknowledged, they are yet observed with the most scrupulous attention, which shows the powerful influence they still maintain over the minds of even the most intelligent classes of men. At the hour of birth we are ushered into an atmosphere of superstitious prejudice—our bridal path is traced through its many windings, and we are laid in the grave, like a hunted fugitive, with all the formulae of long established and deep-rooted superstitions.

In love the practitioner's help is still sought by both sexes who desire to obtain the object of their affections or assistance in the pursuit of their amours. In mythology, the media employed usually consisted of philtres or potions of magical herbs and plants, charms to be worked, or rites to be performed, in order to obtain the desired end.

Gipsies still continue to sell love potions for your sweethearts. The writer met one of these only some days ago, and she informed him that she "was a sister of the black arts," and could "raise up and lay down on a bed of sickness," as well as being able to look into the future.

The supernatural has a certain fascination, even over the severest sceptics, and there are times when we secretly wonder, though few of us admit it, "Is there really anything in it after all." In my investigation of the subject of witchcraft, I have gleaned much information about charms, etc., from various manuscripts, and from village folk, especially in the isolated districts of Somerset, Devonshire and Cornwall.

The association of apples with love enchantments goes back to an early date, and the following selection applies to the rites and customs of Halloween.

Write on an apple, Raguell, Lucifer, Satanus, and say, "I conjure thee apple by these three names, written on thee, that whosoever shall eat thee may burn in my love." Or, write on an apple these three names, Coamer, Synady, Heupide, and give it to eat to any man that you wouldst have, and he shall do as thou wilt. Or, cut an apple at midnight, and make your wish, then count the number of seeds that have been cut in two. If one seed is cut, it is hard luck; if two, it means a disappointment; if three, a happy marriage; if four, an unexpected legacy; if five, great wealth; if six, political fame; if seven, travel is in store; if you count as many as eight seeds, your wish is granted.

Of plants and herbs the vervian (verbena officinal is a weedy plant of the verbena family) plays a prominent part, owing to its association with witchcraft. In the time of the Druids it was worn as a charm against evil and for good luck.

To gain the love of a man or woman, it is necessary to go to this herb when it is in flower, near the full moon, and say to it the Lord's Prayer. Then say, "In the name of the Father, Son and Holy Ghost, I have looked for thee. I have found thee, I charge thee Vervian by the Holy names of God, Helion, Adonay, when I carry thee in my mouth that whosoever I shall love or touch, that thou make them obedient unto me and to do my will in all things. Fiat, Faith, Fiat.—Amen."

In addition to its power as a charm for love, the vervian has been used to bring quarrels to an end, and as a charm to catch fish, hive bees, and keep the traveller from becoming footsore. Other curious love charms which the writer has collected consist of taking the tongue of a sparrow and placing it in virgin wax under your clothes for three days. At the end of that period it must be placed in your mouth under your tongue, and the woman you kiss will be

Copy of a love charm found in mid-Cornwall (Courtesy of Jeremy Tucker)

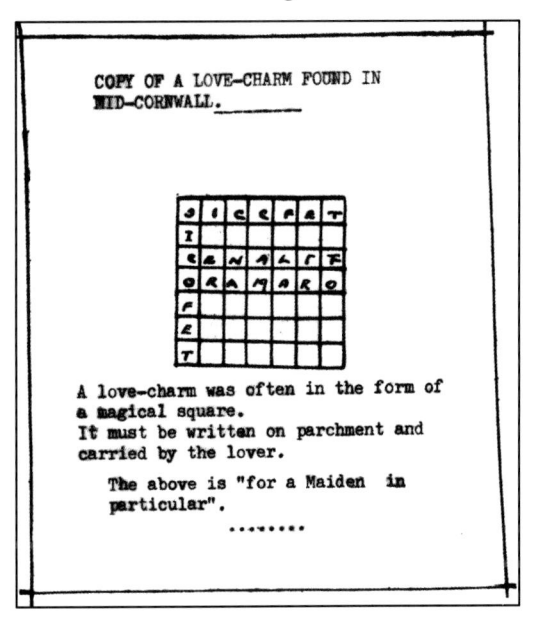

COPY OF A LOVE-CHARM FOUND IN MID-CORNWALL.

A love-charm was often in the form of a magical square.
It must be written on parchment and carried by the lover.

The above is "for a Maiden in particular".

125

the woman you love. Garters are also very popular, and many young Cornish girls, on going to bed at midnight, place a garter (upon which three knots have been tied), under their pillow. They will then dream of their future lover, but much depends on the manner of his dress. If he is in green his love will be visible in the dream; if he is in grey his love will be far away, while if he is in blue, his love will be true. Another celebrated Cornish rite is of cutting a cabbage at midnight, and the maiden who sleeps with a slice under her pillow will dream of her future lover …

It is to be wondered at that men are still superstitious about this amazing, magical, dangerous thing called love!

MOST COMMON SUPERSTITIONS
[1933][12]

I am repeatedly asked by visitors, and school children who have to prepare essays on local history, what are the most prominent superstitions still current among Westcountry people.

According to my own investigations I would say they may be placed under the following heads: Those regarding the fairy folk, mermaids, witchcraft, the evil eye, remedies for ailments of man and beast, old customs and games. The belief in fairies is still prevalent, while the idea that the sea has its human or humanlike inhabitants as well as the land has been common amongst insular populations in various parts of the world.

Quite recently a Cornish fisherman told me that the mermaids had the power by putting on a seal's skin of actually changing themselves into these animals, and that it was only in that shape that they had the faculty of moving through the waters. The belief in mermen and mermaids assumed at one time a singular form amongst the West Highlanders, who identified these watermen and women with the seals which frequent their rocky shores.

A legend was long current of an ancient Highland chief who accidentally surprised a mermaid asleep on a rock, and got possession of the seal's skin which lay beside her, thereby depriving her of the power of returning to the water. The hopeless mermaid was obliged to submit to her captor, who took her to his castle and married her. The clan of Macphies, the former possessors of the Isle of Colonsay, were said to be the descendants of this marriage. There is still a common saying among the Isles that the Macphies, or, as some have it, the Macleans, are blood relations to the seals.

Sir John Rhys in his "Celtic Folklore" refers to the old belief that the kelpie, or spirit or god of the water, must once a year be given a life and quotes rhymes upon Scotch rivers that seem to embody such an idea. The rhyme concerning the river Dart each year claiming a heart is a well-known Westcountry example.

There is a very ancient "religious" belief, found still among certain primitive people who depend on the water for a living—the Eskimo, for instance—that a fisherman must not interfere to save the life of a drowning companion. The sea-god claims a life in return for the fish that he provides and if he is defrauded of his victim, he may be expected not only to take a yet greater toll than a single life, even to cutting off the supply of fish altogether.

Another Celtic superstition is that concerning witchcraft. Many people believe, as most uneducated people did at one time, that certain individuals acquire, by a direct compact with an evil spirit, a certain amount of supernatural power, which is in general, though not always, employed to the prejudice of their neighbours or others who have incurred their displeasure.

Many stories can be related of the casting and removing of evil spells and of the power of white witches or charmers. It is not always by a compact with the powers of evil that a supernatural power of inflicting injury on others is obtained. There are individuals in Devon and Cornwall who are supposed to possess such a power involuntarily, or even against their will; this power is known by a name equivalent to the Evil Eye. Singularly enough, too, it is supposed to be exercised by the very act of praising or complimenting the person or thing to be injured; so that it is, in every respect, the exact counterpart of the Evil Eye which is so much feared by the Greeks and other races of the south-west of Europe. Country folk still wear charms, etc., against the Evil Eye, and farmers have been known to cover their milk with red cloths and tie red rag on their farm animals to keep off the mischief of the Evil Eye.

Dreams, which can also be included in the list, are everywhere a fertile source of superstitious belief. Among Westcountry folk they are regarded as generally either foreshadowings of the future or warnings to be acted upon. The idea of luck, good or bad fortune, attached permanently to particular times, things and persons, exercises a powerful influence on the minds of many people. If an individual has experienced a remarkable run of good or bad fortune, he will imagine the day of the week on which it occurred as peculiarly favourable or otherwise to him throughout the rest of his life. But in particular, things or actions, generally of a very trivial character, are supposed to influence luck in particular circumstances. Again, it is believed by many that luck accompanies certain persons in whatever circumstances they may be placed.

As regards the superstitions relating to the ailments of human beings and animals and their cure, I have already dealt with these in previous articles in "The Cornish Times." Many of them give the reader an idea of the psychological condition of mind of those who imagine themselves subject to spells.

The collecting and arranging of old village jokes, games and sayings is a fascinating hobby. In many cases a saying or joke will only drop out when it just illustrates the circumstance. Recently a farmer illustrated something to me by an old "saying." Shortly afterwards I asked him to repeat it while I wrote it down, but for the life of him he could not do so. It flowed out naturally enough in its right place.

Realising that with the present generation probably all these relics of the past will disappear, and that with education and a wealth of books and newspapers and improved locomotion, the time is gone for ever when the children sat around the cottage hearth and heard from their fathers and mothers the doings and sayings of grandfathers and grandmothers; every help and encouragement should be given, especially to the younger generation to "Kyntelleurgh an Brewyon es gesys na vo kellys Travyth"—"Gather ye the fragments that are left, that nothing be lost."

WITCHCRAFT TREES AND FLOWERS
[1934][13]

It is not surprising that members of the toadstool-mushroom clan have long suggested magic in men's minds, for the amazingly rapid growth and the curious shapes of the fungi, which cop up in such unexpected places, are as fantastic as any beanstalk of fairy-lore.

The toad has an evil reputation and, according to some legends is the very devil himself. His venom is indeed no myth, for both birds and beasts shun it on account of his power of secreting a virulent fluid that burns and blisters sensitive skins. Toads seem to have been associated with witches owing to the repugnance they generally excite, and in some districts in the Westcountry it is a common superstition that those whom they regard fixedly will be seized with palpitations, spasms, convulsions, and swoons.

It is incorrect, however, to say that all fungi with a popular name suggesting black magic are poisonous, for the common puff-balls are know as "Devil's Snuff-boxes," and they are not dangerous. The writer has heard of cases in which dried puff-balls have been successfully used to stop bleeding, and the fungus has astringent properties; while the flesh of the giant puff-ball, which is firm and white before it turns to the mass of spores that make the "snuff," is edible. Even the "snuff" has its uses, since the fumes from its burning are said to stupefy swarming bees.

By those who visit the woods during the winter months, large masses of a yellow jelly-like substance is often seen on dead branches and rotting trees. This fungus is known as "Witches' Butter," while another fungus, or sometimes a small insect, is responsible for "Witches' Brooms." At this season of the year these untidy bundles of black sticks are sometimes mistaken for birds' nests, but on closer examination they are discovered growing out of the branch.

It is on these brooms, or "besoms," that the witches are supposed to take their flights. In Cornwall, however, the Rag-wort is used by the witches when making their midnight journeys. Although connected with witches a broom was sometimes used to drive them away, and in some parts of Germany it is customary to lay a broom inside the threshold of a house to keep them from entering the dwelling.

Among trees especially obnoxious to witches there was none that they feared more than the Mountain Ash or Rowan-tree. Probably on account of its connection with Druidical ceremonies, it was accounted as the greatest protection against witchcraft—hence the saying: "Rowan tree and red thread put the witches to their speed."

Even a small twig carried in the pocket was believed to ensure immunity from evil charms, for says the old ballad:

> "Witches have no power,
> Where there is row'n tree wood."

Throughout Europe the Mountain Ash is in equal repute, and in Norway, Denmark, and Germany it is customary to place branches over the stable door to keep the witches from entering.

Beneath the shelter of the walnut tree the Neopolitan witches are said to hold their midnight meetings, while the elder tree has also a great deal of witch-lore attached to it.

In the Westcountry, a well known eyewash is made from elder flowers, which is also used as a lotion for the skin and for fomentations. Wine is made from its berries, ointment from its leaves, tea from its flowers, and the strong smell of the leaves is supposed to keep away insects from plants, and flies from a dwelling.

The list of flowers associated with witchcraft is a long one. The Deadly-Nightshade, or "Devil's Berry." The Hemlock, which has had an evil reputation from a period of great antiquity. It is always associated with witches' potions, etc., though in medicine it is beneficial in some diseases when properly administered.

The Henbane is another plant of ill-omen, and was anciently used at funerals and scattered on burial places.

Foxgloves, though believed by some to be the bell which adorns the fairies or "little people," are by others called "Witches' Bells," as they are said to decorate their fingers with the cup-like flower.

Then again there is the Clematis, or the "Devil's Thread"; the Yellow Toadflax, the "Devil's Ribbon"; the House-leek, the "Devil's bread"; Tritoma, the "Devil's Poker"; and the Mandrake; all these find a usefulness in the witches' pharmacopoeia.

A number of plants and trees were used in exorcism, and among them may be mentioned the tamarisk. The magician always carried some in his hand, probably because it was believed to contain the emanation of the tree-spirit which was supposed to live in the sacred tamarisk tree. It was believed to be all powerful over the evil demons that lived in trees, as the following text shows:

"These evil ones will be put to flight,
The tamarisk the powerful weapon of ANU,
In my hands I hold."

It was cut like mistletoe, with a golden axe and silver knife, with certain ceremonies. According to a Babylonian incantation:

> "Let a wise an cunning coppersmith
> Take an axe of gold and a silver pruning knife unto a grove undefiled;
> Let him carve a hulduppi of tamarisk
> Touch it with the axe."

The St. John's Wort was likewise reputed to possess magical properties, and among others that of compelling love. A necklace, or girdle, anointed with the oil of this plant and given to a maiden to wear was said to make her love the giver.

It is also said to have the property of driving witches away and is known in some districts as the "Devil-chaser."

FOR "WHOOPEN COUGH"
[1935][14]

"Witch Remedies" of Our Forefathers

Having heard that East Cornwall is being visited with a severe epidemic of whooping cough and that all manner of remedies are being tried, I was reminded of the great deal of superstition and folk-lore that still lingers amongst the old inhabitants. But the difficulty is to get behind the scenes in order to find it out, as there appears to be a subconscious feeling that such dealings are unorthodox, and, possibly, some fear of ridicule.

There is, I find, a curious belief that if a child is put crosswise over a donkey's back and led round a field while the Lord's Prayer is repeated, he can never have the "whoopen" cough. An old man, living not far from Callington, in reply to a question as to the best cure for the complaint, replied with no uncertain voice, "The 'chin cough' can be cured by drawing the sufferer naked nine times over a donkey's back and nine times under its belly." "Then," he said, "three spoonfuls of milk must be drawn from the teats of the animal, and three hairs cut from its back and three from its belly, and placed in milk and given to the child in three doses." If this ceremony is repeated three mornings running, he assured me that whooping cough will disappear.

In parts of West Cornwall country folk believe that the cough can be cured by cutting six hairs on the cross off a he-donkey's back, placing them in a silk bag, and directing the sufferer to wear it round his neck. A mother, who had tried it with much success, averred: "As our Lord rode into Jerusalem on the back of an ass he made it holy, and if the hair is cut from the cross on its back, it will cure all ailments."

An old shepherd friend of my acquaintance recommends taking the patient into a field where unshorn sheep are kept. His instructions are to find a sheep lying down, stir it up, and immediately place the face of the sufferer where it had been lying. He maintained that anyone suffering from a cough could get rid of it by being with sheep. "Your complaint," he added "goes into the wool." …

Other cures which I have gleaned include the frying of black spiders which have been gathered at sunrise and inhaling the fumes; catching a mouse "kill 'un, put 'un in the oven and roast 'un till he's burnt to a cinder, taake 'un out and pound 'un to a powder in a basin of milk and give et to a cheeld to drink." Wearing a muslin bag of spiders round the neck day and night until the cough disappears; swallowing wood-lice alive, in a spoonful of jam or treacle to stop the "whoop," and wearing on the chest a piece of mole's skin.

From a collection of recipes dated 1755, which I was permitted to inspect, I found the following under the heading of "Chin Cough or Hooping Cough." "Use a cold bath daily; or rub the feet thoroughly with hoggs' lard before the fire at going to bed, and keep the child warm there; or, rub the back at lying down with old rum. It seldom fails, or, give a spoonful of juice of Penny-royal mixed with brown sugar-candy, twice a day; or, half a pint of milk warm from the cow with the quantity of a nutmeg of conserve of roses dissolved in it every morning."

I am tempted to wonder if any of these curious old remedies are worth trying, especially the latter ones, but as an old writer wrote many years ago, "It is best in uncommon and complicated ailments, or where life is more immediately in danger, to apply without delay to a physician that fears God."

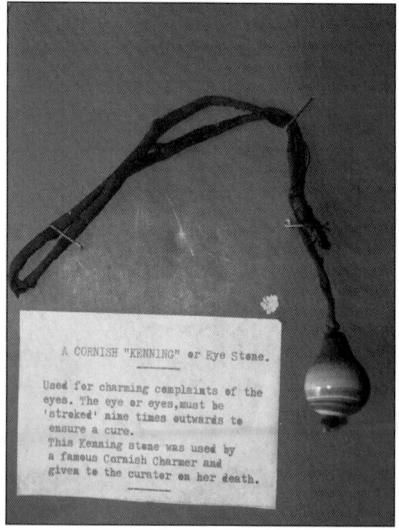

A copy of a charm found near Helston (left) inscribed "Whoso beareth this signe about him, let him feare no fo, but feare GOD." (Courtesy of Jeremy Tucker); and a Cornish 'Kenning' or Eye Stone charm (right) with caption "Used for charming complaints of the eyes. The eye or eyes must be 'stroked' nine times outwards to ensure a cure. This kenning stone was used by a famous Cornish Charmer and given to the Curator on her death." [i.e. of the Cornish Museum] (Author's Photograph)

IN SEARCH OF THE ODD ON THE NORTH CORNISH COAST
[1966][15]

Twenty-five years ago I spent some time on the north coast of Cornwall in search of material for a book I was then writing on Cornish superstitions and customs; now, after a quarter of a century, I have again been exploring the rugged grandeur of one of the wildest stretches of our Cornish seaboard. It was my intention to follow the cliff-tops and coastguard paths and, here and there, to visit the many quaint hamlets and villages en route. I carried all my bits and pieces in a rucksack and relied solely on getting meals and a night's shelter in the wayside cottages and farmhouses.

In my ramble, I discovered that many of the coastguard paths still existed but some of them were difficult to find; gorse, bracken and tangled undergrowth had covered them. The guardians of our coasts no longer walk these paths as they did in days past; today they have a far more convenient method of travelling. For long stretches of the coast I met few travellers; I was indeed an explorer and it was an adventure.

Leaving Bude, I was reminded of a fellow-traveller who, many years ago, in describing what he termed the *village* of Bude, wrote, "little can be said about it. It is in a chrysalis state and will want a lot of improving before it emerges as a butterfly." At that time it had no railway and no crowded promenade. Fashion had not then introduced its fooleries, but it boasted of few bathing-machines; and carts, then, like the lorries of today, carried away the sand as manure. Times, indeed, have changed.

Close to Bude is Stratton which, as my old pocket guide of a century ago told me, was celebrated for the garlic which grew in the vicinity. I was reminded of this later, for I came across a large patch of wild onions growing right on the cliff's edge, between Tintagel and Trebarwith. A quarryman told me that he remembered them growing there over forty years ago; "In fact, they are a relic," he said, "of a wreck in that part of the coast." The onions were washed in with the wreckage, took root and have been there ever since. His companion added to the onion story by telling me that the crew of the boat lived on onions—it was their only food for several days.

At one point along the coast, after having watched for some time a herd of seals with their young, I was caught in a downpour and, as luck would have it, saw a small cottage which I made for with all haste. I had no intention, if I could possibly help it, of getting as "wet as a shag," being as cold as a "quilkin" or looking as "wisht as a winnard." A charming old lady gave me shelter and wanted to make me a cup of elder tea, "to save me," as she explained, "from taking cold." A bag of elder flowers hung from the beam of her kitchen and she told me, "if brewed and drunk like tea, elder flowers will cure any feverish cold." Mugwort was another of her remedies. It was infused in the same way, sweetened with honey or treacle and drunk very hot. After assuring her that I was not very wet and admiring her kitchen dresser filled with clome of all shapes and sizes, I retraced my steps to the thyme-covered cliffs.

Nature has been very generous to north Cornwall in her gift of flowers. Although I was too late to see them in all their Spring glory. I did come across many hardly plants. The Samphire, the Sea Spleenwort, the Sea Holly, Sea Kale, and Sea Cabbage were to be found, and I was still able to gather the last of the pink and white Thrift; also I came across the Woadwaxen or Dyer's Green Weed. This low, bushy shrub of the bean family is a native of Central and Southern Europe. It is common in parts of this country and has become naturalised in the United States. It yields a yellow dye but, by a mordant, becomes a permanent green. It is interesting to recall that it was originally used by the Flemish weavers who settled in Kendal in Westmorland, hence the name, "Kendal Green" by which it is known to many. My greatest joy, however, was the occasional patch of maidenhair fern growing on the steep face of the cliffs. This delicate fern, known on the north coast, so a quarryman told me, as the "Rock Maidenhair," was very common along the coast some years ago. Quarrymen, in the early days of this century, used to gather the fern in large quantities between Tintagel and Trebarwith, plant it in small pots or strawberry punnets and sell it to visitors as a souvenir. The gathering of the fern became a serious matter and the plant was eventually protected.

That reminds me of a story I gleaned. The old-time policeman at Boscastle warned a noted fern-collector in the area that if he caught him red-handed he would "take him before his betters." The following night, the constable seeing the man coming over the cliffs with a well-filled sack, stopped him and demanded to know what the sack contained. "You find out; if you think 'tis fern, open up and find out," said the man. The officer of the law untied the sack and thrust both his hands into it, only to find that he had grasped handfuls of nettles. But to return to the maidenhair proper, on my last visit to the coast I knew of a particular cave, around the edges of which the fern flourished. After much rock climbing I found the cave but, owing to a large fall of cliff, the fern had been completely destroyed. A little further along the coast I found a large patch and rejoiced to know that after twenty years it was still to be found.

After this I spotted what I thought, in the distance, to be a pair of Cornish choughs, but alas, they were a couple of chattering jackdaws. Some twenty years ago, I knew of a spot where four pair of choughs could be seen, but now they have all but gone. From numerous enquiries I learned that only one pair are known to exist. Of a party of schoolboys I met on the way to the beach for a dip, only one had actually seen a chough and that in a museum. The others had seen pictures, and one of the youngsters said he had heard his grandfather say that, many years ago, a pair of tame choughs could be seen on the green patch in front of one of the Tintagel hotels.

It was nearing "crib" time and, as I settled to eat my pasty, I realised how very quiet everything was; then, suddenly, a mother raven sailed out of a cleft in the cliffs, calling frantically to her mate who, following, gave out his harsh double note. How grave and stately they looked, turning their heads to look backwards as though pursued by an evil conscience. They are frequently described as birds of the night, of doom and of all kinds of dreariness and, if half the stories that are told about them are true, they must possess intuitive knowledge of things terrestrial and celestial, greater even than any witch that ever flew over a broomstick. As I watched them, now flying at great height and striking and cuffing each other on the wing, I was reminded that they are becoming scarce, except where they can nest in places inaccessible to mankind.

During my walk, I came across an old man repairing a stone hedge and, as he lifted the heavy stones into position with apparent ease, I asked him if he had ever heard of Anthony Payne, the Cornish Giant. "I didn't knaw him, sir," he replied, "but I've heard tell of him; he was long before my time." He did confirm, however, that this famous Cornish giant was born at the Tree Inn up to Stratton and was a kind of servant to one of the Grenvilles of Stowe. As I left the man I made a note in my diary to visit the Royal Institution Museum at Truro and see again the portrait of Anthony Payne, painted by Godfrey Kneller, hanging there. It was at Tintagel that I met the descendants of another of Cornwall's authentic giants, one Charles Chilcott. I was told that an ordinary man could stand underneath his outstretched arms. He was six feet nine inches tall, six feet round the chest and weighed four hundred and sixty pounds. What a blessing he is not alive today, for his weekly allowance of tobacco, smoked in a giant pipe, was three pounds! I must not forget to mention his stockings—you could put six gallons of wheat into them with little trouble. He died at

Bosinney in 1815, in his 60th year and left many descendants who still live in and around Tintagel.

On my last visit to Tintagel Castle, now many years ago, the famous Florence or, to give her her full name, Florence Nightingale Richards, was the custodian. I well recall her sack-like dress and tea-cosy hat. Yes, Florence made tea; the cosy kept the tea warm but, when she was on the Castle, it kept her head nice and warm, too. On rare occasions when she had her hair cut she wore the tea-cosy, and the barber had to trim her tangled locks around her strange head-dress; on no account would she remove it. Florence not only acted as keeper of the keys to the Castle but also as guide. I recall, on one visit, listening when she conducted a party of visitors over the ruins. "And this," she said, "is Merlin's Cave." (Voice). "And who is Merlin?" "Merlin, my dear," she replied, "he was a wizard and this is his cave. It's a kind of souptureen passage where he used to come up and down." Florence continued as custodian of the Castle until she was eighty-five and died some ten years later.

I stayed until the Castle was locked up for the night and, as I walked away, I asked the keeper if it was by any chance haunted. "I've never seen a ghost," he replied, "but on many occasions I've heard people talking. Often, during the winter months, when the place is completely deserted and not a visitor about, I have heard voices and snatches of conversation but, on leaving my hut to investigate, I have seen no-one. They are not human voices but voices from the past."

Although I am a "collector" of ghosts I did not see any on my coast walk, but I was reliably informed that there is a house in the district which is still haunted by a figure of a man. In another, the ghost objects to the installation of electricity and plays all sorts of tricks with the switches. On occasions a hanging light in one of the bedrooms swings to and fro like a pendulum; but, immediately the electricity is switched off, it ceases. The occupants of the house say there is really no peace in the place until it is in darkness. Then there is the phantom coach which haunts a certain road not far from the cliffs; in one of the coves something white appears at intervals and, in a small cottage built many years ago from a wreck, footsteps can be heard.

To the "foreigner," the word "wrecking" conjures up pictures of ships lured on to the rocks and the carrying away of valuables; but, today, wrecking amounts to no more than collecting driftwood brought in by the tides. I saw one of these wreckers patiently waiting for a baulk of timber to wash in. Over a cigarette he told me that the best time was after a good sou'wester has been blowing. "'Tis the early bird wot catches the worm, or rather plank." I told him I had come across several small piles of driftwood, all neatly bundled, but there appeared to be no owner in sight. "Them's all right," was his reply, "provided the visitors don't interfere with them. You see, the cliffs be pretty steep and sometimes it takes a couple or three evenings to get the load from the sea floor to the top of the cliff. This we do in stages and there is an understanding among us wreckers, you never touch another man's pile."

I was sorry I could not visit the famous Delabole quarry, but the slate fences, headstones, fireplaces, pavements, window-boxes, clothes poles and posts all were there to remind me of it. I saw a housewife using a slate rolling-pin and, when I remarked about it, she told me that once a woman has used this type of rolling-pin she will never use any other kind. "It's always cool; you must get one for your wife," she said. I'm afraid I had other ideas about the use to which the rolling-pin could be put, and decided that my wife's wooden one served its purpose.

My grandchildren were anxious to hear if I had come across any tales of the giant Tregeagle. I found that stories are still told about him round the fireside, and, here and there, I was shown caves in which his restless spirit carried out its unending tasks. In the church of St. Breock, among the old slate slabs, one finds one inscribed, "Here lieth buried John Tregeagle of Treworder, Esq.

1679." Another is Jobber Mail, the noted cattle-dealer and black wizard. He lived in the St. Teath area and made a fortune, so the stories tell, by unfair dealings. Long before his death he was regarded by his neighbours as a notoriously wicked man. After he died, his spirit troubled the neighbourhood and the clergyman said he was earth-bound. He haunted the place in the form of a huge calf or yearling, making the most uncanny sounds. Eventually seven persons assembled to exorcise the spirit and they succeeded in driving it to Trebarwith Strand, where it was bound for ever and a day, like Tregeagle's, to make beams or ropes of sand.

Thunder in the distance and a flash of lightning prompted me to take cover in a disused slate quarry. While I sheltered I thought of the unfortunate Thomas Hemings who, in 1702, was killed by lightning and buried in the churchyard at Tintagel. When the storm had ceased I made for the church and enquired of a man cutting the grass if he could tell me where I could find the burial place of poor Hemings. It stood near the south doorway of the church. His epitaph reads:

> "The body that heere buried lyes
> By lightning fell, death's sacrifice
> To him Elijahes fate was given
> He rode on Flames of Fire to Heaven."

As I passed through the churchyard I saw a Cross with a lifebuoy attached, to the memory of Catanese Domenice. The wreck occurred on the 20th December, 1893, during a snowstorm and all the crew were rescued with the exception of the poor boy Catanese. The crew had jumped on to the ledge of rock at Lye, but the boy fell between the vessel and the cliffs and was drowned. The corner of the churchyard was set aside for the burial of bodies washed up by the tide, and here they were carefully interred far away from their homes and friends. I noted that the lifebuoy had been freshly painted and was reminded of the epic as told by Joseph Brown, in his *Musings on Tintagel and its Heroes* (1904), and his concluding lines:

> "We took him to Tintagel Church, there due respect was paid
> And in our quiet churchyard that sailor boy was laid:
> For years and years to come by us he will not be forgot
> As a kind hearted friend has placed a tomb to mark the spot."

I shall always remember Tregatta and its neighbourhood, for it was associated with one of the great disappointments of my boyhood. In August 1914, all plans had been laid for a great Boy Scout camp at Tregatta. The site had been marked, the tents were on their way and I was full of excitement and anticipation, for this was to be my first camp away from home. Uniform had been pressed; even the brim of my scout hat had been ironed and stiffened with some secret preparation. Then came the war and the camp was cancelled.

That is why I shall never forget

> "Trevena, Tremale, Tregatta, Treknow,
> Upton, Trecarne, Trebarwith, Beslow,
> Eight little villages all in a row."

*Paynter in his study with some of the Cornish charms he collected
(Courtesy of Jeremy Tucker)*

Cornish Ghosts & Haunted Houses

A considerable collection of Paynter's research on ghosts survives in manuscript, the most significant part of which is printed for the first time in this chapter. Paynter's work on ghosts contained both eye-witness accounts, traditional Cornish ghost stories and the results of his own ghost hunts and historical research. This selection includes the extant text of the unpublished book on the subject prepared by Muriel Hawkey and Paynter in 1949 (but excludes John C. Trewin's Preface), Paynter's rejected 1953 article, the script of a 1956 radio broadcast, tales concerning John Wesley and strange happenings at Looe, and the story of the Black Cockerel of Lanreath.

CORNISH GHOSTS AND OTHER STRANGE HAPPENINGS IN CORNWALL
[1949][1]

INTRODUCTION

In presenting this collection of strange happenings in Cornwall we have included stories of modern and olden times. So far as the present-day stories of ghosts and haunted houses are concerned, we have included only true accounts, that is to say, true in the sense that the people who experienced them really believed they happened; but we make no claim that the stories in the legendary section of the book are true. We think it probable that some of the tales retold by William Bottrell and Robert Hunt had at least some foundation in fact, particularly in the cases where these writers heard them from the percipients or from people living in their time who remembered some of the incidents. Many of the stories recounted by Bottrell and Hunt have come down from very ancient times, and we feel that a book of Cornish ghost stories would be incomplete without a few, at least, of these legendary stories of Cornwall.

We have included many kinds of ghost stories, among which are phantoms of the living, the dying and the dead; and among the strange happenings in Cornwall we have included some interesting dreams which may be termed telepathic or prophetic, as well as some strange glimpses into the future for which there seems no explanation. Miracles, too, have played their part in Cornwall, but we have included only those which took place at St. Michael's Mount in the 13th century and one story, which has something of the wonder and enchantment of a fairy tale, about the donkey which returned to St. Hilary for Christmas, as we think this should be included as coming within the realm of the miraculous.

We would like to express our gratitude to all those who have been kind enough to send us their experience or to tell us of possible sources of information about ghosts and strange happenings in Cornwall. Without their co-operation and help this book would not have been possible and we ask them to accept our grateful thanks.

M. H.

W. H. P.

CONTENTS

The Ghosts of Stanbury Manor

The Phantom Guest House

Jamaica Inn

The Murder of Charlotte Dymond and Subsequent Appearance of her Ghost

The Ghost in Carpet Slippers

A Midnight Apparition

Strange Happenings in the Wadebridge District:

    The 'Maizey' Lights

    Haunted Cottage at Daymer Bay

    Haunted Inn on the North Coast

    Photograph of a Phantom Smuggler?

The Phantom Brougham

The Murder of Nevell Norway

The Mysterious Visitor

Phantom of a Wounded and Dying Soldier

The Helpful Spirit

The Ghost of a Little Old Lady in a Poke Bonnet

A Haunted House in West Cornwall

The Third Server

Phantom Hound on Trencrom Hill

Phantom at Dead Man's Cove

"A Remarkable Narrative of the Apparition of a Young Gentlewoman to her Sweetheart"

Haunted House near St. Ives

The Donkey which Returned to St. Hilary for Christmas

Miracles at St. Michael's Mount in Cornwall in 1262

Strange Happenings in Helston District:

    The Duel

    The Mysterious Couple

    The Black Dog

    A Mother's Love

The Ghost of Pistol Meadow

The Phantom Hearse

A Haunted House near Looe Pool

Seen in a Dream

The Dream of Mr. Williams of Scorrier House

Phantom House near Truro

Dream of a Lost Brooch

The Ghosts of Pelyn

A Haunted House at Looe

Looe Island Ghost

A Talland Ghost Story

Unknown Places "Seen" in Cornwall:

    A Surrey Laundry

    A Cornish Rectory

A Phantom at Antony House

The Haunted Farmhouse

The Mysterious Bedroom

A Cornishman's Dream

A Ghost by the Wayside

Phantom of the Drowning

The Phantom Hound of Linkinhorne

The Botathen Ghost

Parson Ghost Layers

LEGENDARY GHOST STORIES OF CORNWALL

The Stockadon Spider

The Lost Child of St. Allen

The Ghosts of Kenegie

Laying Wild Harries's Ghost

The Haunted Lawyer

The Haunted Mill-pool of Trove

The Ghosts of Chapel Street and St. Mary's Chapel Yard, Penzance

A Ghostly Ship's Bell

Phantoms of the Dying

The Smuggler's Token

The Death Fetch of William Rufus

The Ghost of Rosewarne

Dorcas, the Spirit of Polbreen Mine

The Pilot's Ghost Story

The Spectral Coach

THE MURDER OF CHARLOTTE DYMOND AND SUBSEQUENT APPEARANCE OF HER GHOST

Rough Tor, situated on the Bodmin Moors, about three miles south-east of Camelford, is crowned with fantastic masses of rough, naked granite rocks, piled up in weird confusion, one above the other, with wind-swept horizontal crevices and scores of water-filed basins. Around, amongst the coarse grasses, rushes and bracken are strewn innumerable slabs and boulders of the same rock, hoary with lichen.

In viewing the rugged summit of Rough Tor the impression first formed is that one is contemplating the dejected ruins of some ancient stronghold, the work of human hands, but a closer acquaintance shows that natural forces are almost entirely responsible for the placing and shaping of this chaotic collection of rocks. The only evidence of human effort here to be found are the remains of some early British bee-hive huts and the traces of a small building reputed to be a chapel to St. Michael on the crest of the hill. It is at the foot of the hill, amid the heather, ling and gorse, and near a rippling, crystal brook, that the traveller comes across a rude monument. On its face, which is well raised from the ground, one discovers lettering, largely illegible because of the tightly clinging lichen which grows upon it. At first the letters are puzzling, but after clearing away the growth one is able to trace a few words which tell of a moorland tragedy—the very last thing one would expect to find in such a quiet, peaceful scene.

"CHAR….. DYMOND"

"Sunday, April 14, 1844."

A man's name is coupled with this woman's, that of "Matthew We..s" and by occasional words recovered here and there from among the lichen, one learns that a murder has been committed.

It is now over one hundred years since this romance of humble life with its terrible ending was enacted.

In 1843 there lived at the small farm of Penhale in the parish of Davidstow a widow named Philippa Peter. Making a living from the moor was indeed a struggle and she had to work hard through she did not live unpleasantly. She knew the soil of the moor and lived by working it. Gazing out over the great waste of moorland the few farmhouses made the loneliness more lonely. When a doctor was required it was necessary to go several miles, and there were no roads most of the way. No wonder that the minister of the parish is said to have erected guide-stones or posts across the Moor so that he might find his way in misty weather. Then there was the fear of the marsh. Winter and summer it was always wet. Cattle wandered into the marsh brimming with water, and to lose a bullock was no small loss.

Charlotte Dymond, a Cornish girl of about 18 years of age, was employed at Penhale and worked in the house, while Matthew Weeks, who had been at Penhale for a number of years, laboured in the fields and on the moors when the peat cutting season was at hand. For some time the pair "kept company," or as Mrs. Peter remarked after the tragedy, "they had courted each other."

On the 14th April 1844, the day on which the murder was committed, Weeks and Charlotte left Penhale together at about 4p.m. On their leaving the house Mrs. Peter asked where they were going as it was "too late for church or chapel in the afternoon, and too early for preaching in the evening." They made no reply, but some minutes later Charlotte returned saying she would not be back for milking, but that Matthew would be back to do it. Charlotte apparently was often in the habit of not returning on Sunday evening until after milking time. "I have milked for four Sundays" remarked Mrs. Peter, "and I can do it again." The couple appeared to be very friendly when they left the house, and Charlotte was wearing a red diamondy shawl, pattens and a whiff.

At about 9.30 the same evening Weeks returned alone to the farm and for a day or two professed that he did not know what had become of Charlotte. On the Tuesday, however, when pressed for further information concerning Charlotte he said she had gone to Mrs. Lanxons at Blisland, who had got an easier place for her. Owing to the distance he said that Charlotte was going to sleep at Caius Spear's at Brown Willy the first night, and go on the next day to Blisland. "I went as far as Higher Down Gate with her," said Weeks, "and after leaving her I went on to All-Drunkard." He further stated that he called to see Sally Westlake who lived there, but she and her husband were not at home. During the remainder of the week he persisted in the same story.

On the following Sunday evening, he had a conversation with Mrs. Peter in which she said that there was very bad talk about him and the maid; that the neighbours said he had certainly destroyed her, and that he was a very bad man if he had done so as they were always so loving together and further, if it was true, that he ought "to be hung in chains." Immediately after this conversation Weeks left, intimating, however, that he would be back to dinner, or directly after. He took no clothes with him except those which he was wearing. In the meantime Mrs. Peter's son and John Stevens, another servant, had left to go to Brown Willy and on to Mr. Lanxons at Blisland to make enquiries.

The body of the unfortunate Charlotte was found in an old river place a little below Rowtor Ford, and the murder had been committed on the brink of this place. Immediately after the discovery of the body Weeks was arrested and taken to Tregeare, near Launceston, the residence of Mr. J. King Lethbridge, the nearest magistrate. Here a cast was taken of Weeks' boots. These were compared with the footprints discovered near the scene of the crime, proved to be identical, and he was charged with the murder of Charlotte Dymond. At first he denied all knowledge but later made a statement in which he confessed his guilt. He was thereupon committed for trial at Bodmin.

It is from the Brief for the Prosecution, a document of some 60 pages, which was in the possession of a lady living at Bodmin and to whom we are indebted for its loan, that we have gleaned the full story of the courtship of Matthew and Charlotte and of its tragic conclusion.

At the trial Weeks was described as a person of a very jealous temperament, and the fact that he was lame (which might constitute a defect in a woman's eye) might have led him to be suspicious of anything in the nature of a slight to himself or a preference for any one else. A man named Thomas Prout of Helset in the adjoining parish was said to be very friendly with Charlotte but, as Mrs. Peter once remarked to Weeks, "It's no use putting Charlotte down to Blisland to keep her from men, as there are men there as well as here." On one occasion when Prout visited Penhale, Weeks remarked that he wondered what he and Charlotte had to talk about. Mrs. Peter's son, John, remembered saying to Weeks that Prout wanted to come and live at Penhale, and that if he did Prout would take Charlotte from Matthew.

Matthew Weeks was found guilty and was hanged at Bodmin Goal on the 12th August 1844, for the murder of Charlotte Dymond at Rough Tor.

Charlotte was buried in Davidstow Churchyard where her grave is marked by a cross. This, however, was not the end of the affair for it was believed by many that her ghost frequented the moor long after the tragedy. There are still living some members of the old Volunteers who recall their great camp in the Rough Tor neighbourhood and the first occasion when ball ammunition was fired. Great difficulty was experienced in keeping sentries posted at night for one of them alleged that he had seen the ghost of the murdered girl making her way across the moor. We have had accounts from several people who say they have seen the apparition but the strangest of them all is the following, which is well authenticated.

A guest—a stranger to Cornwall—staying at Tredethy near Bodmin, went for a day's fishing in the moorland streams. On his return to Tredethy he described his day's sport and remarked on the solitude of the moors, saying that the only living thing he had seen, apart from the wandering troops of ponies and horned sheep which roam in perfect freedom about the wild moorland, was a woman apparently making her way across the moor.

"A woman?" said his host. "What was she like?"

A description was given in which she was described as wearing an old-fashioned dress of a blue colour. "I watched her," continued the visitor "and she kept stopping and shading her eyes from the sun with her hand, as if looking out for someone."

"You have seen the ghost of Charlotte Dymond" said his host, "for your description exactly corresponds with that of the poor girl who was murdered at the foot of Rough Tor by her sweetheart Matthew Weeks."

A MIDNIGHT APPARITION

"About two years ago I had business in a town in North Cornwall which necessitated my staying there for some weeks. Fortunately I was able to obtain comfortable lodgings at an old house quite near a delightful old church.

"For the first couple of nights nothing happened but on the third night I saw such an appalling sight the like of which I had never seen before and hope never to see again. I had spent a busy day and decided that an evening at the cinema would be a complete change. I dined early and then wandered into the cinema where I enjoyed the programme, and on leaving at about 9.40 p.m., I wandered into a nearby pub. I only had a small beer, in fact I could not have any more as the landlord called time and I had to leave. I reached my lodgings soon after 10 p.m., gave a brief description of my evening to my landlady, and then retired to bed.

"My room was on the second storey of the house. It was surrounded by a wainscoting of oak to the height of five feet. It was somewhat lofty, but owing to the narrowness of the windows, it was very gloomy, even on the brightest day. My landlady had given me a fire and as I undressed I counted my blessings. I got into bed, which was quite a modern one—nothing four-posted about it and no drapings. I read for some little time and then, on hearing the town clock strike the midnight hour, I switched off the electric light.

"Soon afterwards I heard footsteps coming up the stairs. They were just ordinary footsteps, although once or twice, as they drew nearer my bedroom door, I fancied they seemed to drag a little. Whose footsteps they were was no business of mine, probably a fellow lodger, or perhaps the landlady, but when they stopped outside my door I became a little more interested. For a while all was quiet, then a faint light began to filter under my bedroom door.

"Up to this time there had been no light and whoever was responsible for the steps was certainly moving in the dark. Anyway, the light began to creep under my door, at first very faintly, then much brighter. Again my thoughts turned to my landlady. Perhaps she was doing a little nocturnal cleaning, although I could hear no sound of brush or cleaning materials.

"By this time the light underneath my door had turned a blueish colour. I sat up in bed and saw a kind of mist entering my room from beneath the door. As I watched it grew in density until the whole of the door was blotted out. But was it mist or was it smoke? I became afraid, horribly afraid.

"I tried to get out of bed but fear had gripped me and I could not move. I was completely paralysed and trembled in every limb. All I could do was to stare at the ever-growing mist or haze. Suddenly the mist began to take shape. First a head was formed, then a body, then arms and legs, until there stood in the doorway a complete human form but without a face. I exerted myself to speak, but in vain; my tongue cleaved to the roof of my mouth and I was obliged to remain a horror-stricken and inactive spectator of the scene before me.

"Then the figure, the horrible shape, slowly, and almost imperceptibly advanced towards the spot where I lay. As it drew nearer I prayed that it would do me no harm. Then a miracle happened. Suddenly I was given the power of speech and addressed the apparition, for apparition it certainly was. I shouted at the top of my voice:

"'In the name of the Lord get out of here and leave me alone.' I had no sooner uttered these words than the shape withdrew, backing slowly to the door. Here it began to dissolve, the head first, then the remainder of the body, and it became once again a cloud of vapour. Then it slowly passed, as it had entered, under the door. The strange light also faded, and I heard the steps retreating along the passage and down the stairs.

"I did not close my eyes again that night and early the next morning I asked my landlady for my bill. She seemed surprised and asked what had caused the sudden dislike of the accommodation. I gave her an evasive answer and left her, but I thought I observed a kind of lurking consciousness in her face of something wrong, and I think that she was probably aware of the mysterious visits of the apparition.

"This, then, is my story and this is the basis on which I build my faith in supernatural appearances. As far as reason and argument may go to ridicule and confute the idea of the existence of such things, I must be allowed to persist in believing that which my own eyes have witnessed."

The name of the percipient is withheld at his request, also the address of the house where he had this strange experience.

THE MYSTERIOUS VISITOR

'Miss Lerryn' was a Cornishwoman and her brother was for many years the Rector of a Cornish parish. At the time of this story, however, he had a living in London and his sister was on a visit to him. She had been very ill for some weeks after her arrival but had reached the stage when she could sit out in her bedroom for an hour or so and do a little reading and writing. Her bedroom was large and comfortable but was in a wing of the house at some distance from the other rooms.

On this particular afternoon she was feeling rather depressed at being held a prisoner so long by her illness. She had been sitting by the fire reading and felt very drowsy so walked about the room for a while and, not liking the idea of getting back to bed again so soon, she settled in a comfortable chair at some distance from the fire hoping that the drowsy feeling would pass. She does not know if she fell asleep or not but she did close her eyes for a little while. When she opened them she saw a woman sitting in the chair beside her bed. She was quite young and rather attractive, and was dressed in somewhat countrified clothes. They looked at each other and then the stranger spoke.

"You'll forgive me, won't you," she said, "but I want to know if you will help me?"

Although Miss Lerryn had never seen the woman in her life she was not in the least startled although she was certainly surprised when she opened her eyes to see a stranger in her bedroom and wondered how she had got there.

"Yes, certainly I'll help you," she replied, "but you must known I'm still a sick woman."

The stranger thanked Miss Lerryn and after a pause asked her if she knew Woking. "Yes," replied Miss Lerryn, "it's about an hour's train run from London."

"Well, I want you to go to the Parish Church and inspect the Register there and find the exact date when 'John Kit' married 'Mary Hill.' When you find it send a copy of the entry to this address."

She gave the address to Miss Lerryn, remarking that when she had obtained the necessary information there was no need to write a letter. All she need do was to write the information on a slip of paper, place it in an envelope, and post it to the address given.

Miss Lerryn willingly agreed to do this as soon as she was well enough but asked "How do I know that all this is genuine?"

The strange woman looked at her for a moment and then replied "By your railway ticket."

"By my railway ticket; whatever do you mean?"

"At the end of your journey you will still have it intact."

"Still have it, but …" Miss Lerryn remembers no more for a drowsy feeling came over her again and she fell asleep. When she awoke the woman had disappeared.

Just then her brother came in to see how she was and to ask if she was not tired and would like to get back to bed.

"Where's my visitor?" asked Miss Lerryn.

"Visitor?" queried her brother. "You've had no visitor."

"Oh, don't be silly dear," said Miss Lerryn, "of course I had—the young woman who has been sitting here talking to me for several minutes."

Her brother smiled and said she'd been dreaming as not a soul had entered her room all the afternoon.

"But surely I know" said Miss Lerryn.

"My dear girl," replied her brother, "I've been in the study all the afternoon and not a soul has entered the house. Besides, they would have to pass the study door and it's been open all the time. You've been dreaming, that's what it is."

"I'm sure I have not," Miss Lerryn answered, and at that moment she noticed the writing pad on the bedside table. She picked it up and read the following words: Woking Church, Register, Date John Kit and Mary Hill. Send to following address (an address in London was given). "There you are," she said, passing the pad to her brother, "what stronger evidence do you want than that?"

Her brother smiled but he looked puzzled. "It's not your writing I agree, but you've been ill. Been scribbling I expect and don't remember it."

His sister assured him she had not written a line and besides, how did I know John Kit and Mary Hill? As for Woking, she had never been there in her life and the address, too, was a part of London quite unknown to her.

The following morning, in spite of numerous enquiries, the mystery was still unsolved, but Miss Lerryn was quite determined to get to the bottom of it and to go to Woking as soon as she was well enough to undertake the journey.

Some weeks later she set out and took a return ticket to Woking. It was a pleasant trip but as she left the station the ticket collector turned his back on her and she passed out of the station with the ticket in her hand.

She found the Church, and after some hours with a friendly and interested Vicar, discovered the entry in the Register. She carefully noted it and then, after having some refreshments, returned to the station. Here again she passed through the barrier without showing her ticket, and this happened again at Waterloo, so that when she arrived home she still had the ticket intact in her handbag.

That evening she wrote on a plain sheet of paper: "John Kit married Mary Hill at Woking Parish Church, on the …" giving the date, and posted it to the address which the mysterious woman had given her.

There, as far as Miss Lerryn could tell, the story ended but it had a very strange sequel. Several months later when she was on a visit to Scotland she was one of the guests at a dinner-party. During dinner a lady sitting near Miss Lerryn congratulated a lady and gentleman opposite on their successful lawsuit.

"You must be relieved," she said, "to have settled it all and to know that the property is really yours at last after such a long delay."

"Yes," replied the man, "we are very glad it is all settled; the missing link was a marriage."

"Indeed?"

"Yes, we simply could not find out when a certain John Kit married a Mary Hill."

"Well, how did you find out?" asked the lady sitting near Miss Lerryn.

"In a most mysterious way; one morning we received an anonymous note stating that John married Mary at Woking Parish Church on a given date."

"How very extraordinary," exclaimed the lady, "but have you ever found out who send it?"

"We haven't the faintest idea" was the reply, "but if we did, well … I don't know how we could reward them."

Miss Lerryn felt that the time had come for her to speak and she told them all the circumstances as far as she knew them. There was natural incredulity, but she was able to prove her story although she could give no explanation.

HAUNTED HOUSE NEAR ST. IVES

Miss H. W. Buchanan of Looe has sent us the following account of a ghostly experience:

"Some years ago I had a position as private secretary to the Manager of a Tin Mine situated a few miles from St. Ives. The mine has long since been dismantled but the house I stayed in is still there and, I understand, is now occupied by an artist.

"I will now explain the happenings which occurred in the house at irregular intervals during the eight months I was engaged at the mine. The first incident happened a few weeks after I arrived; then there would be a lapse of perhaps a month or six weeks, and so on.

"I actually *saw* nothing whatever but I *felt* a presence coming through the door and floating towards my bed, where it stood, apparently looking down at me for two or three minutes, with bent head. It appeared to me to be a tall, gentlemanly sort of man, in black, but how I sensed this I fail to understand because, as stated, I *saw* nothing. Then the thing turned and went the way it came, through the door. And what a relief it was when I felt the air clear again!

"A short time before the Mine was to be closed down the Manager and his family arranged to go to London. A lady visitor called to say goodbye to his wife and I was in the room at the time. Strangely enough the subject of Ghosts happened to come up and then, for the first time, I related my experience in the bedroom. My hostess was very surprised and asked why I had not mentioned the matter before. I replied that I thought they would laugh at me for imagining things, as they were always joking about one thing and another, but she looked quite serious and told me that a room in the house was supposed to be haunted, though they did not know which room it was. As several people had previously slept in the bedroom I had occupied, and nothing had been reported, they decided the best way was not to mention the matter to anyone. According to the story they had been told, a lawyer from St. Ives had hanged himself in one of the bedrooms many years before."

THE PHANTOM HOUND OF LINKINHORNE

A phantom black dog is reputed to appear periodically on a lonely stretch of road between Linkinhorne and Rilla Mill, near Callington. In the early spring of 1937 it was seen by several people on the road known locally as "Bangor's Hill." People who have seen this phantom dog say that it is of huge proportions and that it appears very suddenly. There is no sound of its approach and it vanishes as silently and swiftly as it appears.

Mrs. Hocking of Plusha Bridge gives the following account of meeting the dog: "I had been visiting some friends at Linkinhorne and was returning to my home. It was just after 10 o'clock and a clear, starlit night. I had not gone far before I saw a black dog slinking along at my side. It was a huge dog, about the size of a sheep, and had a long tail. 'Hullo, old chap,' I said, 'Who do you belong to?' I had my finger on the switch of my electric torch and immediately flashed on the light, but there was no dog there. I experienced a nasty, cold feeling, such as I cannot describe. The dog had vanished as if into thin air. It was quite impossible for it to have climbed the hedges, for they are very high, and the interval between speaking to the dog and switching on the light was so short that there was no time for it to get away without being seen. I shall never forget the shock. It was indescribable. A man was coming up the road about 200 yards behind me. I shouted to him and asked if he had seen anything, but he said 'No.' People to whom I have related my experience have laughed at me, but I am positive and most emphatic that I saw the dog distinctly. I am not a nervous woman and am not given to imagining things. I have heard since that the road is haunted by the ghost of a black dog, but on that night I knew nothing whatever of the story. The next time I walk along that road I shall take my own dog with me."

The man to whom Mrs. Hocking called, who was walking some 200 yards behind her, did not see the ghost dog that night, but he had seen the dog on a previous occasion. This man, Mr. Joe Mitchell, a mason of Linkinhorne, told how some time before he was walking along the road at midnight when he saw a black dog. He lifted his foot to kick the dog, but it took no notice of him at all. He said it seemed as if he was just kicking the air, but he saw the dog pass on quite unfrightened.

Mrs. Edwards of Cellars, Linkinhorne, whose house adjoins the haunted road, said that she was returning to her home between 11 and 12 at night when she saw a black dog suddenly coming towards her. "It crossed the road towards me," she said. "Then I felt it rubbing itself against my leg, and presently it just vanished. It made me stiff with fear. It was a large dog, and it was quite impossible for it to climb the hedges as they are very high. Had I not been carrying a lot of parcels I should have run all the way to my home at the foot of the hill. I know of no one in the district who owns a black dog."

Mr. Thomas Harris, a naval pensioner, living at Plusha Hill, also met this ghost dog. "I was returning to my home about midnight," he said. "I saw something sitting in the middle of the road and from its size I judged it to be a calf. On closer inspection it proved to be a great black dog. I went to smooth it, but it vanished immediately."

Old people in the district say that many years ago it was a common experience for villagers returning late from market to encounter the ghost of the dog as they walked along the haunted road. Its appearance, they said, was believed to foretell tragedy of some kind.

This hound was supposed locally to have been a man killed in the Mark Valley Mine, but his name unfortunately has been forgotten. His route is from Mark Valley Mine, through Rilla Mill, up Cellars, and past Two Gates, in Linkinhorne, to Stoke Climsland.

It seems that the story of a ghost dog in this district has come down through many generations. There is a very old legend which may have some bearing on this. On St. Stephen's Down, near Launceston, there was a large tumulus, or ancient burial mound, and there on Midsummer Eve the people lighted a great bonfire and indulged in wrestling and general merrymaking. Long years ago it is recorded they were so enraged when into their midst dashed a huge black dog, which so scared them that they all fled. Ever afterwards when wrestling matches were attempted there the contestants always came to serious hurt and the sport was abandoned. The idea of the miners and rustics was that the spirits of the giants buried in the tumulus resented sports at their burial place and had sent an evil spirit in the shape of a black dog to put a stop to the profanity or sacrilegious sport. It is said that the possible reappearance of the black dog struck such terror in the community that none would wrestle there even in fun lest something awful might happen to them.

GHOSTS

[1953][2]

The Westcountry and especially Cornwall is a haunted land. It is noted for its ghosts and "things that go bump in the night."

There are ghosts in old time costume that walk through walls and up and down stairs and passages; Ghosts with hollow mocking laughs; Ghosts that grope at one's neck with bony fingers and try to strangle and even mischievous spirits who steal the bed clothes; Ghostly footsteps; Ghost birds, one even in the form of a black cockerel; Phantom bells and clocks; Ghostly coaches and headless horses; Nuns and Monks; Ghosts in armour; Phantom dogs

Caricature of Paynter as the 'Ghost Hunter', 1954
(Courtesy of Jeremy Tucker)

that haunt the roads and lanes and even the ghost of a donkey said to return each Christmas to a certain rectory; Screaming skulls; Chests and boxes which mysteriously move from place to place and even pictures which gently slide from walls and fall to the ground without hurt or damage.

It must be remembered that Westcountry people are not fiercely matter-of-fact, blindly cynical. They believe in ghosts, and the stories they tell are true in the sense that they who have experienced them believe they happened.

Well attested facts cannot be swept aside by idiotic ridicule of the "all rubbish school." Even the most sceptical will admit that there is a meagre residuum of evidence for which a matter of fact explanation cannot be easily found.

Most people do not believe in ghosts yet half, in fact a little more than half, are afraid of them. To quote from the famous Dr. Johnson, "All argument is against it, but all belief is for it."

THE GHOST OF THE NEGRO SAID TO HAUNT THE QUEEN'S HOME FARM

Stoke Climsland, near Callington, which Her Majesty the Queen has made the chief scene of her operations as a farmer, enjoys the distinction of having had direct associations with royalty for a long period. There is in fact no evidence that the lordship of its manor was ever held by any but royal hands.

Today Stoke Climsland contains a number of farms that were gentlemen's seats in bygone centuries, and to this category belongs Whiteford, the property of the Queen, which retained its original status longer than any of the others.

Just as it was falling into decay there arrived home from India a highly successful and distinguished engineer Sir John Call, Bart, who brought with him a considerable fortune and a retinue of native servants. He bought Whiteford, rebuilt the house in sumptuous style, and laid out the ground with lakes and artificial fountains. Parochial records tell us that there was a park with thickly wooded grounds surrounding the house, while the house itself contained as many window and doors as there are days in the year.

Some little distance from the house, which has now disappeared and in the remains of which the present Whiteford house is built, stood a Grecian Temple, also built by Sir John in 1799. In this splendidly furnished building Sir John and his son Sir William Pratt Call, entertained their friends, celebrated birthdays and held balls which continued all night. The avenue leading from the mansion to the temple was on these festive occasions lighted each side with flaming torches. Sir John lived here for nearly thirty years, during which time he was High Sheriff of Cornwall, and Member of Parliament for Callington in 1784, 1790 and 1796. He was also a banker, manufacturer of plate glass and a copper smelter. He died in 1801 at his Mansion House, Old Burlington Street, and his memory is perpetuated in Stoke Climsland Parish Church by a marble tablet which bears a long epitaph.

According to the story told by the oldest inhabitants of Stoke Climsland, one of the native servants was a six foot Negro, who met with a mysterious and untimely end. The church register contains an entry that "a man of colour was buried in the churchyard during the period Sir John was at Whiteford."

Following the Negro's death strange and weird happenings were reported both in and about the house, and his apparition is said to have haunted the place ever since. Although the mansion has long since fallen into decay (the beautiful mantelpieces, locks and fittings can be seen today in the Queen's Home Farm at Stoke Climsland, while the ceilings were taken to London), I have met people who have seen the negro apparition and who state with no uncertain voice that he moved backwards and forwards and then gradually disappeared into space.

A few years ago, one of the workmen at the Royal Farm was at dusk returning from work, and while proceeding towards the Temple, which is still standing and used as a cattle-house, he noticed a squatting figure before him. He shouted, and receiving no reply, approached the recumbent figure and asked what his business was. To his amazement, the huddled mass stood upright, revealing a tall, strong and powerful Negro; before the workman could say any more the apparition had disappeared into thin air.

The apparition was later seen by a woman staying in the village. In her own words she told me that while returning from a walk in the late afternoon, she passed what she described as "a big six foot negro." "He looked at me and I noticed his eyes were those of a haunted man, with an expression of extreme fear written on his face, and then he disappeared." On return to her lodgings she reported that she had passed a horrid negro, who after looking at her, seemed to fade into nothing.

"Imagine my surprise" she said, "when I was told I had seen the Whiteford Negro." "Being a stranger to the district and not knowing anything about the circumstances it could not have been my imagination."

Although I have made recent enquiries, the Negro Ghost has not been seen of late but there are many people in the parish who will not venture anywhere near the old Grecian Temple after dark.

The alleged bloodstains which appear on one of the floors of the kitchens at the Queen's Home Farm I have not seen myself but I have been assured that the stain which mysteriously appears from time to time looks like a splash of blood. It only remains for a short while, disappearing as mysteriously as it comes. According to old wives' tales it is the blood of the poor old negro who was killed under very strange circumstances. …

THE MYSTERY OF THE FLOWERS

Within the last few weeks I have been invited to visit a Cornish farmhouse to try and get to the bottom of the disappearing flowers. The story according to the farmer and his wife is that in one particular room it is impossible to keep flowers. No matter how they are arranged or where they are placed, they are mysteriously moved during the night. From table to floor, from piano top to windowsill, from bookcase to fireplace, and they are always removed from their glasses or vases. The windows and doors of the room are always closed at night; in fact the room is searched for stray animals or birds, but in spite of this the flowers continue to be moved.

Is it a poltergeist? What unseen hand removes the flowers? The chief feature of the poltergeist is unaccountable and even malicious mischief. Articles, especially breakable things such as crockery and glass, are thrown about and often smashed by the unseen agency.

Bedclothes are pawed, disarranged and often thrown off the bed. Fires have been known to start and stone, bricks, pieces of wood and even metal have been hurled through the air.

The practical joker was always believed to be the alleged Poltergeist, but it has been established that poltergeists are true psychic phenomena.

It is interesting to recall that the bringing of Hydrangea blooms into the house is considered unlucky by many Cornish folk. The late Sir Arthur Quiller-Couch detested these flowers, considering them flowers of ill-omen. Not a great while before he died he was very annoyed to find that Hydrangea blooms had been included in a floral display by a florist for a special occasion at his house. Sir Arthur seized the offending blooms and opening a window threw them out, with the remark, "I'll not have them in this house."

It will be interesting to learn if the flowers that move about so mysteriously in the farmhouse are Hydrangea blooms!

THE HAUNTED MANSION AT LAUNCESTON

Referring to the night I spent in a haunted house at Launceston [at Madford House, on 15 December 1947]. Alas the mansion is no more!

The carved oak head of the banister post finds a home on my desk as a paperweight, and as I look at it, I wonder what happens to the mysterious footsteps now the mansion is no more. The footsteps which were heard by many started in the cellar, paused at the foot of the stairs, as if to rest for a while with one hand on the oak head of the banister post and then slowly proceed up two flights of stairs to fade into a wall at the end of the corridor.

Was this the hand and footsteps of an old servant, perhaps a butler or footman?

Apart from legend and fiction, the ghost idea cannot be swept quite away. Science as yet leaves much unexplained. We often laugh but we must remember that our grandfathers and grandmothers would be been equally mystified and unbelieving if we could tell them that we listened to music played from an orchestra in Vienna or New York.

The inexplicable of yesterday is the common place of tomorrow.

ST. MARK'S EVE
[1956][3]

The evening of April 24th is St. Mark's Eve and that is when, it was formerly believed in the Westcountry, any person who had the courage to do so, could wait in the church porch, from 11pm to 1am, and see the spirits of all the people who will die in the parish during the next twelve months.

I said courage, for indeed, those who kept the vigil ran two very serious risks. First, it was essential to keep wide awake, for if the watcher fell asleep he would never wake again, and further once you kept the vigil you had to do it every year to the end of your life.

What if the watcher saw himself in the pale procession that walked the gloom? Very awkward eh!

Ghosts it must be remembered are of very respectable antiquity and we find legends of apparitions going back into the very long and distant past.

Do you know that the shortest story in the world is a ghost story. It runs as follows: "Do you believe in ghosts?" I asked. "No," replied my friend. "I do," and with that I vanished.

The Westcountry, and especially Devon and Cornwall, is a haunted land. It is noted for its ghosts and things that go bump in the night …

"Come, come" you say, "You've got to go," as the old Cornish dame said, "to foreign parts abroad to meet with these things." Darkest Africa and such places, that's where you find witchcraft, sorcery and magic. No, no need at all to travel abroad, they can all be found in parts of our own country.

Here in the Westcountry strange and curious things do happen for which there is no accounting. You can still find people who believe in witches and the power of the evil eye, in ghosts, as well as in pixies and fairy folk.

For a great number of years now I have been searching out witchcraft and trailing ghosts in the Westcountry and believe me, they are by no means dead.

It must be remembered of course that Westcountry people are not fiercely matter-of-fact or blindly cynical. They believe in ghosts, and the stories they tell are true in the sense that they who have experienced them believe they really happened.

After all, well-attested facts cannot be swept aside as idiotic ridicule of the "All rubbish school." Even the most sceptical of us must admit that there is a meagre residuum of evidence for which a matter of fact explanation cannot be easily found.

Most of us do not believe in ghosts yet half, in fact a little more than half of us, are afraid of them. Remember what the great Dr. Johnson said, "All argument is against it, but all belief is for it."

Whether advancing science will ever enlighten us as to the reason for these phenomena we know not. It may be so.

But to return to St. Mark's Eve. Will ghosts, outside those who march in procession to the church, be extra active on this evening? According to Westcountry beliefs they will, and in all probability I shall glean a few more stories from those who have been fortunate enough to see them.

Let me tell you of two Ghost stories I have quite recently added to my ever growing collection.

"Some years ago," said my informant, "I had a position as a private secretary to the Manager of a mine in the Westcountry. The mine, by the way, has been closed down now but the house I stayed in is still there and is now occupied by an artist. Now the strange happenings in the house occurred at irregular intervals and the first happened a few weeks after I arrived.

What did I see? Well actually I saw nothing whatever but I felt a presence coming through the door and floating towards my bed, where it stood, apparently looking down at me for two or three minutes, with bent head. It appeared to me to be a tall, gentlemanly sort of man, in black, but how I sensed this I fail to understand because, as I said, I saw nothing. Then the thing turned and went the way it came, through the door. And what a relief it was when I felt the air clear again.

A short time before the mine closed down my employer and his family arranged to go to London. A lady called to say goodbye to the wife and I was actually present at the time. Strangely enough the subject of ghosts happened to come up and then, for the first time, I related by experience in the bedroom.

'But why did you not mention this before,' I was asked, and replied that I thought they would laugh at me for imagining things. It is quite true, they said, there is a room in the house supposed to be haunted but we do not know which room it is.

'But who is it supposed to be haunted by?' I asked. 'By a lawyer who hanged himself in one of the bedrooms many years ago.'"

Now for a yet stranger story.

A Westcountry vicar's children were always eager to go to bed and the parents were puzzled as any parents would be. They took to listening outside the children's room, and one night heard one of them say "I wonder if she will come tonight." To which the other replied "Of course she will, if we're quiet." The following evening after hearing further snatches of conversation and one "She's come," they burst open the door. Imagine their surprise on being told "Oh Mammy and Daddy you've spoilt it." "Spoilt what?" asked the parents. "Why," said the children in unison, "When you came in the old lady went away." "What old lady?" "Why the nice lady that sits in the chair by our bedside. She is a dear, she nods and laughs to us, but when we get out of bed to speak to her or touch her, she goes away." "And does she come back?" asked the vicar. "Yes Daddy," was the reply.

Some time later the vicar, attending a gathering of clergy, met a friend he hadn't seen for years. He was asked where he was living and when he mentioned the village and the vicarage the other said "What a coincidence! I was vicar there many years ago. It was in one of the bedrooms that my children saw the old lady."

Strange isn't it.

JOHN WESLEY AND THE GHOST
[c.1969][4]

John Wesley, when in Cornwall, once could find no house to pass the night save one that had the reputation of being haunted. This, however, so far from deterring him, caused him to enter the house and go to bed. He was unable to rest for there arose a terrible tumult below—the sound of carriages, the rustle of silk dresses, the noise of oaths, and the tramp of feet prevented him from sleeping. He arose and went into the hall where he found a large assembly of guests. They greeted him with loud welcome and begged him to join the feast. He consented, saying however that he must first say grace. This remark was hailed with noisy derision, but nothing daunted he began "Jesu, the name high over all…" He did not finish, for in a moment the lights and the guests vanished and he was alone. He returned to his bed and passed the rest of the night undisturbed.

A STRANGE STORY FROM LOOE ISLAND
[1969][5]

And now for a strange story told to me by the late Beatrice Chase, the Devonshire authoress, who once lived in a house where they could never keep doors locked or bolted. Time and time again the doors were duly locked and bolted at bed time, but next morning they were always found open.

Unfortunately she would not tell me where the house was situated. It was one of her secrets. But back to the story she told me and from what I can gather [it] has never been told before.

Many years ago [there was] a sewing-woman of Looe. Sewing-women, by the bye, were usually widows or middle-aged spinsters who augmented their living by taking in sewing and visiting people's houses to do the family sewing and mending. Well this good woman went over to Looe Island to do the sewing and mending for the farmer and his family who lived there.

Now on the second day of her visit, the weather was so lovely that she decided to take her mending and sit on a seat on one of the points of the Island. She also took the farmer's two children with her, but soon after arrival the two children began to whimper and cry. Asked what was the matter with them, they said someone was pinching them and pulling their hair. The woman said this was nonsense as apart from themselves, there was no other person present.

The children continued with their complaint and them to the woman's amazement she could not keep her needle threaded. Every time she threaded the needle, the cotton was mysteriously pulled out. She became annoyed and collecting the children she returned to the farmhouse not saying a word of her adventure to the farmer or his wife.

That night she retired to bed and had not been in bed long before she heard footsteps, just ordinary footsteps, though once or twice, as they drew nearer her bedroom door she fancied they seemed to drag a little.

Whose footsteps were they? When, however, they stopped outside her door she became a little more interested.

For a while all was quiet, then a faint light began to filter under the bedroom door. Up to that time, there had been no light, and whoever was responsible for the steps was certainly moving in the dark.

Well, as I say, the light began to creep under the door, at first very faintly, then much brighter. Again the woman's thoughts turned to the farmer's family, and she wondered if the wife was doing a little nocturnal cleaning, though she could hear no sound of brush or cleaning materials.

By this time the light underneath the bedroom door had turned a blueish colour and the woman, sitting up in bed, saw a kind of mist entering the room from above and below the door. As she watched it grew in density, until the whole of the door was blotted out. But was it mist or was it smoke?

She became afraid, horribly afraid. She tried to get out of bed. Fear had now gripped her, and she could not move. All the poor soul could do was to stare at the ever growing mist or haze. Suddenly the mist began to take shape. First a head formed, then a body, then arms and legs, until there stood in the doorway a complete human form, but without a face.

Again the woman exerted herself to speak but in vain, her tongue cleaved to the roof of her mouth, and she was obliged to remain a horror-struck and inactive spectator of the scene before her.

Then the figure, the horrible shape, slowly and almost imperceptibly, advanced to the foot of the bed. As it drew near, she saw it was a very tall figure, with very long arms and hands that reached well below the knees. The woman prayed that it would not harm her, and then a miracle happened.

Suddenly she was given the power of speech, and addressing the apparition, for an apparition it certainly was, she shouted at the top of her voice, "In the name of the Lord, get out of here and leave me alone."

She had no sooner uttered these words, than the shape withdrew, backing slowly to the door. Here it began to dissolve, the head first, then the remainder of the body, and it became again a cloud of mist or vapour.

Then to the woman's amazement, it slowly passed, as it had entered, over the top and under the door. The sickly light also faded, and she heard steps retreating along the passage, and into the distance. She then roused the farmer and his family and related to them the terrifying experience. To this she added the story of the children and their pinching and hair pulling, and of her strange experience with her needle and cotton.

The farmer was so interested that the following day they began digging near the seat and at no great depth unearthed a skeleton of an exceptionally tall man with very long arms and long fingers BUT WITHOUT A SKULL.

According to Miss Chase, it was believed to be the skeleton of a man who had been murdered on the Island, while others contended it was the remains of a man who had been drowned at sea and his body washed up on the beach of the Island.

But during the past few weeks a sequel to my story has come to light.

While discussing the Island with a well-known Looe inhabitant, now well over eighty years of age, he said "do you know Mr. Paynter my father was the official boat-man to the Island, and I remember as a boy being on the Island when they dug up a skull. There were no other bones, just a skull. Nothing was said about [it] and for a long time it was kept in a cardboard box in the cottage on the Island. Whose skull it was we don't know." I then told him Miss Chase's story of the finding of the previous skeleton WITHOUT A SKULL.

THE BLACK COCKEREL
[1969][6]

In one of our Cornish villages there is an old inn, and in this inn there is a great big open hearth, and in the hearth there is an old cloam oven. An extraordinary thing about this old cloam oven is that the lid or cover to it is cemented on. You can't take it off and when you see it the first thing you will say is "Well, how can you do any baking if you can't take the cover or lid off?" And if you keep enquiring someone will quietly sidle up to you and say "There's a ghost inside."

What is the story?

Let us go down the village. Down the village they tell us that many, many years ago the old vicar there was a doddery old bachelor, and one day he surprised everybody by bringing to the parish a very charming, good looking young lady of about 22. And still more surprising, not a great while after, they were married. But the marriage didn't seem to do the poor old boy any good at all. He got more doddery than ever and he got so doddery, in fact, that he couldn't do his Sunday services, and so he advertised for a curate, and the Curate duly arrived—a tall, good looking chap of about 24.

[Some while later] it was Christmas Eve. The old vicar said to his wife, "Look, our curate is down in lodgings in the village, very comfortable, but don't you think it would be nice if we invited him to come and spend the evening with us and have an evening meal?" An invitation was sent and the Curate duly arrived. As the dear old vicar was helping him to take off his hat and coat he said, "My son, this is a very important occasion and I want you to come down with me into the cellar and find the oldest bottle of wine I have, and that we are going to drink with our evening meal."

Imagine the scene—A doddery old vicar carrying a guttering candle followed by the curate, opening the great cellar door and preparing to descend the steps. Suddenly there was a scream and the poor old vicar toppled from the top of the steps to the bottom, landed on the cellar floor and broke his neck. Well, you know what they said up village: "Wadn't no accident, 'ee was shoved."

Not a great while after the good looking curate married the poor old vicar's widow, and thought they were going to live happily in the parish. But it was not to be. For the old vicar knew all the while they were, as we sometimes say in Cornwall, "they was carrying-on." And so he decided to come back and haunt them, and he came back to haunt them in the form or shape of a villainous black cockerel: a bird that attacked everybody on sight—pecked people's faces, arms and legs; children were pulled in after school; everyone was terrified of this villainous black bird.

Several attempts were made to shoot it but it always got away. Then came the day when it was reported that the great big black cockerel was up in the village feeding in a corner surrounded by 3 high walls. Word was quickly sent to all the farmers to come and bring their scatter guns, "'cause" they said, "now's got 'un for sure."

Again, imagine the scene—A whole line of farmers marching solemnly through the village with their guns at the ready to shoot the villainous bird. And there he was in the corner. He saw them coming and he went that way, and he knocked into that wall; and then he flew that way, and he knocked into that wall; then he flew this way, and he knocked into that wall; his only hope of escape was to fly over the heads of the farmers and their guns. And that's what he did.

It so happened that the window of the inn was open and the great big black cockerel came in through the open window. Strange though it may sound, the landlord's wife had just cleaned up the old oven prior to baking and she'd actually got the lid or cover in her hand. When the great big black cockerel coming in through the open window was travelling at such speed, he couldn't pull up, and he went right into the oven and she jammed the cover on, and he's been there ever since.

Cornish Hugger Mugger

Various draft scripts on folkloric themes prepared for B.B.C. regional radio programmes during the 1930s and 1950s are presented in this chapter. In them Paynter focused on contemporary beliefs and examples of superstitious practices in Cornwall, and he also cited cases of snake charming within his own experience. The full text that accompanied Paynter's own "Hap Da" talisman, sold at The Cornish Museum, Looe, is also included, along with the script of the presentation Paynter gave to the Liskeard Old Cornwall Society on Midsummer Eve 1948, in which he detailed the various customs associated with the night over the years, drawn from both Cornish and British examples.

"MORE LOVE CHARMS"
[1939][1]

(FADE UP SIGNATURE TUNE "THE GHOST WALK" BY BORRAH MINEVITCH.)

(CROSS TO FADE UP NOISE PRODUCED BY BLOWING INTO A BOTTLE.)

Compère: No that is not the sound made by one of Cornwall's famous 'blow-holes,' but Whyler Pystry, Mr. W. H. Paynter of Callington, the well-known authority on Westcountry Witchcraft and the Supernatural, blowing into an old Spanish scent bottle, used by a Cornish witch for mixing her love potions. Cornwall's witch-finder has brought this "love potion bottle" to the Studio with an ABRACADABRA charm, and a black bag containing another potent charm, and is going to tell you more about the many love charms he has discovered while hunting witches in various parts of the Westcountry.   Mr. Paynter.

Paynter: Love charms are almost as popular with girls and women today as they were in the Middle Ages, especially as their users now run no risk of being burnt or drowned as witches. Dragon's blood used just before midnight on a Friday, and remember this is a Friday night, will it is claimed bring any man to his knees, while tormentilla root serves to reinspire the lover whose passion is cooling.

Compère: But did people in Cornwall really go to the owner of his magic bottle for charms and for advice how to lift and even cast spells?

Paynter: Yes they certainly did AND still do visit witches not only in Cornwall but other parts of the country as well. Here's a charm to cure a wayward lover which actually came out of the bottle: Over a resin-wood fire—lit in the open on a Friday night when the moon is full, place a copper pot. In the pot throw equal handfuls of borage, oleander, or as some call it, rosebay, and a good sprinkling of saffron. Add a third of a tumblerful of dragon's blood and brew for one hour. Strain through a piece of silk and bottle. To cure your wayward lover of his waywardness pour a teaspoonful of this magic brew into his drink, BUT be careful not to show the spell to anyone or it will be broken.

Compère: Isn't there another charm in which dragon's blood is used? I've heard of it being used in the Westcountry, but from what I can gather a great deal of mystery surrounds its employment for this purpose and it is only with difficulty details are obtained.

Paynter: Yes there is, but I hesitate to give the formula for as you know I am not a wizard. Besides, some love-sick maiden might try it later in the evening.

Compère: But this is Friday night, couldn't you…..!!!

Paynter: Well, here goes. Buy three pennyworth of dragon's blood at the chemist's. Don't eat or even touch any food or drink between eleven and twelve at night; and as the clock strikes twelve place the dragon's blood on a piece of white paper in the grate and set it alight. While burning keep the name of your lover in mind and repeat the following:

> "Dragon's blood, dragon's blood,
> 'Tis not your blood I wish to burn,
> But my true love's heart I wish to turn.
> May be never sleep, rest, nor happy be,
> Until he comes or send to me."

And within three days you will see or hear from him.

Compère: Then what about the ABRACADABRA charm Mr. Paynter. I see it is heart shaped and written on parchment. Will you tell us something about that and how it works?

Paynter: This actual charm was given to a Westcountry lass by a noted White Witch in consideration of a small fee, and it worked wonders although the girl only wore it for three days. It proved so potent in fact that the indifferent lover returned within the three days and a few weeks after they were married. To prepare this charm take a piece of virgin parchment, or fine linen and write the word ABRACADABRA in the form of a triangle. That is, omitting the last letter in each line and ending with the letter A. Then carefully fold it and place it in a white bag and wear it next to your heart and you will always have a lover.

Compère: Oh, before you resume your witch hunt Mr. Paynter, you've not told us about the little black bag. What can you produce from that in the way of charms?

Paynter: Secure three hairs from the head of the woman whose love you require and keep them until Friday night following and on that day before sunrise, with your own blood write your own name and her name on a piece of parchment or fair linen and then burn the hair and the letters together to dust in a red hot fire. Carefully gather up the ashes and place them in her meat or drink and she will always love you.

(FADE UP "THE GHOST WALK.")

ST. JOHN'S EVE—SOME ANCIENT CUSTOMS AND SUPERSTITIONS
[1948][2]

Today we've reached the noon of summer. The sun has got as far north of the equator as it's possible for it to reach. Tomorrow it will have resumed its journey southwards. It's interesting to recall that the custom of lighting bonfires, as we are doing in Cornwall this evening, was once celebrated over the whole of Europe, Midsummer Eve and Midsummer Day. In our own country they were indeed common but the custom died out many years ago. In our own delightful County, however, it was retained until quite recently. With bygone generations Midsummer was the counterpart of Yuletide. It was kept as one of the chief holidays of the year.

The festivities began on Midsummer-eve with dancing, singing, feasting and drinking, sports and pastimes, and the lighting of bonfires. Mingled with all that was the observance of various old rites and customs which had come down from pre-Christian times and which the Church had allowed, nay, even sanctified, by directing them to their right source—the maypole dances, for example, and the midsummer fires which instead of being dedicated to Bel or Belinus, now honour St. John the Baptist.

The past goes further back in Cornwall than in any other part of England. It's well to remember that it is to the Celtic blood and age that we owe so much of our mystic temperament, which is especially noticeable to-day in persons dwelling in isolated villages and on the moorlands. The beacons that heralded the Spanish

Armada off the coasts of Devon and Cornwall have, I'm afraid, rather led to the popular supposition that our ancestors only lit bonfires and made the gleaming blaze from beacon to beacon on very great occasions. But this is not so—at least once a year in former times—on St. John's Eve—the land sparkled with ten thousand bonfires. "At these fires the Cornish attend with lighted torches, tarred and pitched at the end, and make their perambulations round their fires and go from village to village carrying their torches before them."

Our miners likewise celebrated. To them it was a high holiday—the day was saluted by much noise. Holes were bored in the rocks which, being loaded with gunpowder, were discharged in rapid succession. Flags marked the mine boundaries, holly or holm bushes, surmounted the main shaft head, large poles crowned with flowers, herbs and laurel branches were set up and around them the miners danced and sang. Sums of money were also awarded for the best samples of tin, etc. placed on the tin hutch during the day, to be won by those who were unfortunate enough to be at the "bal" during the day.

In Devonshire the custom was also common, but our Cornish records are the more numerous. Let me remind you, however, that the kindling of the midsummer fires was not a frivolous undertaking. In every homestead, as night drew in, the old fires upon the hearth were extinguished to be rekindled with the glowing embers taken from the midsummer fire. It was supposed that the old fire in a twelvemonth had got exhausted. But these live coals were not only used to ignite the new fire on the family hearth, they also brought good luck to the house. The ash and charcoal were carefully preserved until it could be renewed upon the next occasion, being employed meanwhile as charms, etc. It was sewn up in little bags and in the clothes of women to preserve them from the fairy folk, the piskies in particular, as charms against witchcraft, medicine for sick animals and scattered over small fields and herb gardens to ensure good crops.

In other parts of the county cattle were forced to pass over the expiring embers with religious solemnity in the belief it would preserve them from disease and the evil eye, while in the case of cows to cause a plentiful supply of milk. Others again temporarily folded their cattle some distance from the fire and during the night, with their friends, carried bunches of blazing grass and furze so that the smoke was wafted about the cattle. Those so engaged took the great precaution of going around the fold in the direction of the sun. That was a precaution against the influence of witches.

Sprigs of St. John's wort, green branches, and bunches of flowers and herbs were also hung over the cottage doors and the cattle houses.

People danced around the fires, and at the end went through them with members of their family. New born children were passed through the fire. Those about to undertake long journeys leaped backwards and forwards three times through the fire to give them success in their undertakings, others who were about to marry leaped o'er the fire to purify themselves for the marriage state. Others again seized flaming torches, which they swung round their heads to be preserved from evil throughout the ensuing year.

Since those days the human outlook on life has changed considerably. No longer do we believe the fire has the power to driving away evil influences from the crops and preventing diseases among cattle.

With the disappearance of the human sacrifices from the sacrificial fires it was customary to throw some live animal into the flames—a cock, a cat, a rabbit or pig, in the belief that the death of some living creature was necessary for the beneficent effect that the ashes of such bonfires were supposed to possess. In their place we now throw a garland of emblematic plants and weeds. It is scythe-shaped and contains all the plants to be gathered on this evening as possessing peculiar properties. The whole is secured by ribbons, saffron coloured, symbolical of Justice, red of sacrifice, white of purity, and blue of truth.

Surely this reflects to us some little of the beliefs, superstitions and customs of our forefathers. The evening was also considered a most suitable time for love divinations. Personally I cannot imagine the youth of both sexes, especially the girls of today, who have sweethearts meeting to determine whether they are constant and those whose choice it is yet unfixed to enquire whom they are fated to marry. And yet, I don't know, young people are as superstitious as ever, with their lucky pigs, horse-shoes, white heather, four-leaved clover, etc.

It is really extraordinary, that in spite of the march of intellect and the spread of education what a large number of superstitions still prevail. Still prominent in Cornwall are those regarding mermaids, dreams, good and bad luck, witchcraft and the evil eye. Witchcraft is not dead. We still have our witches and our charmers.

Aubrey tells us that in the seventeenth century Midsummer-Eve was called 'Witches Night,' and according to our folk-lore, the witches of West Penwith meet on Midsummer-Eve at Zennor to renew their vows to their Satanic master; and anyone touching the Witch's Rock there nine times at midnight is proof against being "ill-wished" during the coming year.

A wreath of elder-blossom hung up in the stable will prevent the cattle from being harmed by witches, while a wreath of St. John's wort or Camomile if hung up will scare away any witch.

If any baptized person here is courageous enough to deck himself or herself with a wreath of St. John's wort or Camomile and stand upon an elevation near the fire he will see the witches rushing through the air as they are being driven out from the villages.

Or still, if you have time to gather and make a girdle of common wormwood or mugwort, and throw it into the midsummer fire it will bring you the very best of good luck for the rest of the year.

It is easy to laugh at such superstitions and despise the credulous people who hold them, yet strange and curious things do happen in the country, and it is not very wonderful that people who live in remote places should seek to account for them in the same manner as their fathers and mothers were accustomed to do. Even in the town and among educated people practices are still followed which have their base in the customs and belief of primitive people.

We may leave it at that.

WESTCOUNTRY MOON-LORE
[1956][3]

Observing a countryman bow three times to the new moon and then hold up a silver coin against it, reminded me of the many superstitions and customs associated with the Moon which still exist in the Westcountry.

To bow to the moon is unconsciously to preserve alive one of the oldest forms of idolatry in the world. All mankind, in its primitive stages of religious and intellectual development has embraced Moon-worship.

In the Westcountry to point to the stars or do anything that might be considered an indignity in the face of the sun or moon is till to be dreaded and avoided.

The Moon was also said to influence childbirth and there are still people who believe that when a child is born in the interval between and old Moon and the first appearance of a new one, the child will never reach the age of puberty—hence the saying "No Moon-No Man."

The notion that the weather changes with the Moon's quarterings is also believed in with great vigour, while the influence of the Moon upon vegetation is an opinion hoary with age. Sow peas and beans on the wane of the Moon. Turnips, leeks, cucumbers and a number of other plants are said to increase during the fullness of the Moon, but onions are much better nourished during the decline. Cabbages, says an old gardener friend, grow more swiftly in the full moon.

It is still the custom in Cornwall for people to gather medicinal herbs when the Moon is at a certain age. Herbs, a gipsy once told me, should always be gathered at night because their properties are more potent after dark than in the day time.

Mushroom gatherers also believe that their harvest is influenced by the Moon. Gather them when the Moon is full but never on the wane.

Quite recently an old dame living near the Cornish Moors told me she was a great believer in the phases of the moon, and in addition to cutting her hair, finger and toe-nails, sewing beans and cutting down trees and gathering certain herbs on the wane of the moon, the stumps of her teeth stuck up during the grow'n and were very painful but went back when the Moon waned.

Many people believe that the Moon influences physical health and disease and there appears to be no malady within the whole realm of pathology which the Moon's destroying angel cannot inflict; from the crown of the head to the sole of the foot, man is apparently at the mercy of her beams.

Oh! and then there is that very general belief that the effect of moonlight on the eye is injurious. Do not sleep exposed to the rays of the moon, or your sight will be impaired or destroyed.

Some medical men have admitted that the full Moon can have a curious effect on certain people. This was illustrated some years ago in a Westcountry Coroners Court when a juror asked whether the death of a woman from injuries received from a fall from her horse might not have been caused by the full moon, which sometimes made certain people giddy.

During a recent visit to Gloucester I was reminded of the idea connected with moon, namely that if corns are cut after the full moon they will gradually disappear … Then again there is the very general belief that the condition of the weather depends a great deal upon the day of the week upon which the new moon happens to fall. New Moon on Monday is universally held as a sign of good weather and good luck.

A Sunday new Moon is believed to bring fine weather but if the horns point upward, then look out for a breezy spell. According to a Cornish proverb, "So many days old the Moon is on Michaelday so many floods."

In my Luna collection, as I call it, I have many interesting and indeed amusing superstitions and customs. Do you know that apples are said to "Shrump up" if they are gathered when the moon is waning. Always set eggs under a hen at the new Moon. If mistletoe is gathered on the first day of the new Moon, without being touched by iron or allowed to fall on the ground, it is said to be a certain cure for falling sickness or epilepsy.

During a recent visit to Somerset I gleaned that the new Moon, aided by certain charms has the power of curing Kings Evil.

Westcountry moormen tell us that turf intended for fences should always be cut when the moon is on the increase, and that intended for fuel when the moon is on the wane, for it dries much more quickly.

An Old farmer friend told me the proper time to scythe grass is during the full moon.

A halo around the moon foretells a storm while in Cornwall we say a misty moon always brings misfortune in its train.

And finally we don't like seeing the new moon for the first time through a pane of glass, it is said to bring bad luck. On the other hand to observe the new Moon for the first time after her change on the right hand, or directly before you, is as we say a proper job, for it betokens good fortune to come.

All Moonshine did you say. I wonder!

WESTCOUNTRY SNAKE-LORE
[1957][4]

Observing a very fine grass snake basking in the sun, on a recent walk across the Cornish Moors, I was reminded of the opinion once held, that about Midsummer, the snakes met together in companies, and joining their heads, began a general hiss, which they continued until a kind of bubble was formed, which immediately hardened and gave the finder prosperity in all his undertakings.

Carew the Cornish Historian, in his "History of Cornwall," written in 1602, mentions the making of the stone ring of blue colour, and of his being presented with one of these magic stones, which he says if soaked in water and the water given to beasts which have been stung will there-through recover.

The old Westcountry belief that if a circle is traced with an ash stick around an adder, and the sign of the cross made within whilst the first two verses of the 68th Psalm are repeated, the reptile will be unable to pass its bounds.

In a report recently made to the members of the Devonshire Association reference was made to the rare but interesting gift of adder charming, and of known practitioners living to this day on Bodmin Moor and on Dartmoor.

I have seen this charming done on several occasions, and quite recently by a Cornish Charmer. I was climbing down the rugged pathway which leads to the romantic and legendary castle of Tintagel when an adder, disturbed from its mid-day slumber by a party of picnic-makers nearby, joined us in the [descent]. I raise[d] my stick, a sturdy ash rod, to kill it, but a charmer stopped me and taking the stick, made three distinct circles around the snake, and the sign of the cross within. A short incantation was muttered, and then he took the adder up by the tail. "Where shall I place it?" he asked. I pointed to a ledge partly hidden by a clump of dried grass. He did as commanded and as we struck the trail again, he remarked that it would be in the same place at sun-down. Rather doubting the statement I returned in the evening and had a cautious peep, and there, sure enough, was the adder still in the trance. Later, in company with the charmer, I again visited the motionless adder, and after he had removed the spell it hurriedly crawled into a hole not many inches from where it had laid for so many hours.

By the bye, do you know that snakes are said to dread the ash, and according to Westcountry folk, snakes are never found near an ash tree. If a snake is placed near a fire, and both are surrounded by ashen twigs, the reptile will choose rather to run into the fire than cross the ash branches. Ash trees certainly possess strange properties, for it is said that if a boy is beaten with an ash stick he would never grow afterwards.

Charms against snakes and snake bites are still used in the West, in fact, on many of our Westcountry moors when anything happens, the "white witch" or charmer is sent for and is often preferred to the doctor or the veterinary surgeon.

A farmer told me quite recently that his dog had been bitten by a viper and its head was swollen to the size of a football. He took it to a charmer who repeated a charm over it and immediately the swelling diminished, and the dog recovered. I later spoke to the charmer and he told me that in the case of a person belief in the efficacy of the charm was necessary, but it did not matter in the case of animals.

Another popular remedy against the bite of an adder is to fashion a piece of ash or hazelwood into the shape of the Cross, place it softly on the wound, and repeat a certain charm three times in a loud and clear voice, while another Westcountry cure for the sting of an adder or a wasp was to count thirteen backwards, three times each day over three days, say the Lord's Prayer after each counting.

The body of a dead snake, or "long-cripple" as it is known in some parts of Cornwall, bruised on the wound it has occasioned, is an infallible remedy for its bite.

One of the oldest snake superstitions is that if you eat snake you will keep young, while an adder's skin hung to the rafters of a house will prevent it from catching fire.

In parts of Somerset, the skin of a snake is said to draw out thorns or splinters from a body, while from the same county I have gleaned that the bite of a snake can be successfully cured by tying a circlet of ashtwigs round the neck of the patient.

An East Cornwall man had a prickle in the knuckle of a finger that began to fester. His mother had once picked up an adder's udd or slough by a hedge, and she tied a piece of this the opposite side of the festered finger for a night, and the thorn gave no more trouble.

Do you suffer from headaches? If you do you can try wearing a piece of snake skin around your head. In fact, I have come across moor men in Devon and Cornwall, who always wore a piece of snake skin inside the linings of their hats; they assured me they never had headaches. Snake skin will also keep snakes from entering a house, and I have records of Westcountry lads who were born and bred on the moors, carrying in their pocket a piece of snake skin to keep away malaria, if ever their National Service took them overseas.

Some years ago while spending a holiday on the North Coast of Cornwall, I saw an old lady leading her donkey towards the village. On my asking where she was going with her animal she replied "Up to Delabole me dear, to have 'en charmed. 'Es been stung by an adder." Goats and snakes do not appear to like each other, for where goats are kept snakes never appear.

One of the most extraordinary snake stories I came across was in Devonshire, where an old sexton told me that he always beat the grass, bordering the path leading to the church on the morning of a wedding for he maintained should a snake slither out of the grass and cross the path of a bridal party on the way to the church their married life would be very unhappy.

And finally the story of the Cornish child who used to share its bread and milk with an adder. The snake came each morning to the cottage doorway and the child was able to handle it without harm. Eventually the mother discovered the child's unusual playmate, but in spite of her attempts to drive the reptile away it always returned. As a last resort the mother bound an ash twig around the child's waist and the adder never came again. There is a sequel to the story, however, the child so pined for its strange companion that it pined and died of grief.

AMULETS AND TALISMANS
[1959][5]

From the earliest times, humanity has had faith in inanimate objects which they believed were endowed with some occult influence. In ancient records, and the tombs of the dead, we find talismans and amulets which played their part in the early religions of the world and were believed to bring good fortune and to avert danger. Many of them were considered solely protective, diverting evil influences from the wearer, whilst others were thought to bring good health and fortune.

Charms were once regarded as essentials in every cottage throughout the country, and people used herbs and charms to cure various diseases, often accompanying their application with sundry mystical incantations. (See *PRIMITIVE PHYSIC—A Hundred and One Old Fashioned Cures and Remedies*, obtainable from the Museum at East Looe).

Nowadays we do not generally believe in, or fear the Evil Eye, and the charms which were once used to avert it, have been passed down to us as talismans. However the belief in the power of an authentic charm is so old and world wide that it cannot be swept aside as a stupid and ignorant superstition. Further, the source of the particular power that is exerted by a talisman still remains a mystery, and we only know that some mysterious, perhaps occult force often influences the life and fortune of the wearer.

In Cornwall genuine charms are held in high esteem, and the legends concerning them have been handed down from one generation to another thereby preserving them in the full efficacy.

The "Hap-Da" Talisman

At the request of a number of people, I have designed a talisman based upon genuine Cornish Talismans and Charms.

In itself, it is a fascinating souvenir, and depicts various phases of Cornish Lore, such as the Dolmens, the Cromlechs, The Celtic Crosses and the Cornish Chough; which is thought to be the Spirit of the Great King Arthur.

The centre of the Talisman displays the Five Pointed Star and the Celtic Mystical Sign, which has always been credited with the power to influence our lives and fortunes. It is considered to be the symbol of achievement and the Protector of Bodily Health.

I therefore offer this Talisman with every confidence in the authenticity of the symbols depicted and their alleged power to influence the Health and Fortunes of the Wearer.

*Advertisement for the "Hap Da" Talisman, 1967.
(Author's Photograph)*

Tales of Mystery and Imagination

This concluding chapter includes six of Paynter's stories, written during the 1930s to 1950s. They illustrate how he drew upon his extensive knowledge of Cornish folklore for their content, at times barely disguising the source material he drew upon. The tales were often published as Christmas ghost stories and those included below feature uncanny coincidences, fantastical devilish conventicles, doppelgangers, communication from beyond the grave, and a prophetic dream. Some of the stories were also read aloud as part of Paynter's 'Cornish Ghosts and Haunted Houses' lectures.

THE PICTURE OF "THE LADY"
[1937][1]

A Weird but True Story

We came across the picture a week or two before Christmas, while turning out a lumber-room in the office.

The principal said he knew it had been in the office for at least 40 years, and as far as he could remember, was taken by his predecessor in part payment of costs from a client who had fallen on evil days.

Now the picture, which measured some 26 inches by 18 inches, was a portrait in oils of a lady; in fact, a small name plate on the very elaborate frame read: "The Lady." Apart from this there was no other name or initial on the portrait or frame to give any clue as to who was the sitter, or the artist, whose work it represented.

By-the-bye the lady had an Eastern looking face, almost Egyptian, very curious eyes, and was attired, or at least draped, in an early period costume.

To the principal and members of the staff the find presented little interest, even the office boy sniggered, and was heard to remark, "She's no angel!" To me, however, it was fascinating. There was something about "The Lady"; well, I don't know what it was, but it appealed to me.

Now some days later, when the suggestion was made that the picture could be thrown away with the other rubbish, I asked if I might have it.

"Yes, certainly," said the principal, "Glad to get rid of it. It's a pity to destroy it, and after all it may be worth something, but I rather doubt it."

And so I became the proud possessor of "The Lady."

My pleasure was short-lived, however, for on reaching home my wife was not a bit thrilled with the gift. As soon as she saw it, she said it was horrid, and not fit to hang on any wall; no, not even in the kitchen.

I tried to reason with the wench, but it was all to no purpose; she would not have the picture at any price.

"It's uncanny," she said, "and will bring us nothing but bad luck, I know it."

I laughed and remarked that it might, on the other hand, be worth a little fortune; that would indeed be good luck.

"But I don't like the woman's eyes," said my wife, as I packed it up again, "they seem to stare right through one. It's uncanny, take it away for goodness sake."

That evening I carried "The Lady" to a spare room, where she reclined, and was eventually forgotten until the day we decided to turn the spare room into a nursery.

Again it was a few weeks to Christmas, and in the grand clear out "The Lady" was re-discovered and I was just in time again to rescue her from being carried away with the rubbish.

The following morning I found a place for the picture over my writing-desk in the study, but imagine my surprise, on my return from the office in the evening, to find it missing.

"What's happened to the 'The Lady'?" I asked.

"Well," said my wife, "I went into the study after lunch to fetch a newspaper, and as I opened the door, the horrid picture swayed from side to side."

"Must have been your imagination or the wind," I remarked.

"Oh no, as I say, the picture swayed, then the eyes of the horrid creature moved, and her lips seemed to part."

"What nonsense," I said.

"Well, believe it or no," rejoined my wife, "it's uncanny and I've got rid of it."

"You've not burnt it I hope?"

"No, I've just given it away, that's all."

"But who've you given it to," I asked.

"If you must know, just after lunch a man called buying rags and bottles. I told him I had none, but wondered if he bought old pictures. 'No,' he said, 'they're not in my line, but if you want to get rid of any, perhaps I can give you a trifle for them, the glass might be useful. I occasionally get enquiries for odd sheets of glass.

"I got the dreadful picture, closing my eyes as I took it from its nail, and showed it to him. At first he said he could do nothing with it, and remarked that it was rather weird. 'The old bird's got queer eyes, ain't she,' he remarked. However, he offered me a shilling, I pushed the picture into his hands, and as I closed the door, heard him muttering 'Don't like them eyes.'"

Now I cannot tell you how annoyed I was, and how I censored my wife for parting with the picture, but it was no good, "The Lady" was gone, and my wife seemed greatly relieved.

The following day I decided to try and trace the picture, and after numerous enquiries found that it had already changed hands several times, the last purchaser paying £5 for it. Then it got into the hands of a dealer, and from that moment I lost all trace of it, and so gave up on the quest.

Now two or three days before a subsequent Christmas I happened to be in London with my wife and chanced to see a newspaper report that a famous picture had been discovered and was on view in a certain art shop in Regent Street.

"That's interesting," I observed, "if we happened to be anywhere near the exhibition we'll have a look at it."

"Still thinking about your poor old missing 'Lady'?" asked my wife. I did not reply, but just bit my lip.

The following afternoon, while returning from a shopping expedition, I noticed a large poster and found that we were within a few doors of the very art shop where the picture was being shown.

"Let's have a look at the masterpiece which has been discovered," I remarked, and we casually strolled to the window.

One look was sufficient; there was my "Lady." I stood dumbfounded. A notice read that it was the work of one of the early artists, I forget which now, it had been missing for I don't know how long and had recently been discovered, but no one knew exactly where.

It was priced at Twenty Thousand Pounds!

I turned to my wife; she gave one scream, muttered something about eyes and lips, and fell in a heap on the pavement.

Strange, wasn't it; but true.

A WEIRD CHRISTMAS EVE
[1942][2]
Wine and Cards at a Cornish Inn

It is strange, but most weird and uncanny things happen on a Friday night. Ghosts, for instance, are said to make their appearance, and witches and wizards are unusually active. Here is an example.

It was a Friday night that I set out to spend a long weekend with an old school pal, who lived in an isolated part of Cornwall. All the day it had snowed heavily, and before leaving home, I was reminded by the B.B.C. weather forecast that more snow was expected, and those undertaking long journeys were advised to carry chains for the roads were in a hopeless mess for motorists. My journey, however, was by train to Truro, and from there I had to catch a 'bus to a small village, where my friend would be awaiting me with his pony cart, for the remaining seven or eight miles of the journey.

After some trouble with frozen roads and drifts of snow, I managed to reach the village, but found that it was quite impossible to travel further owing to the condition of the countryside. In places the roads were under water, in others they were completely blocked by snow, while to add further to my trouble, it began to snow pretty heavily again.

My only alternative was to stay the night at the village inn, and try and get on to my friend in the morning. Happily, the inn proved very comfortable, and the landlord, a real Cornish character, promised that my Christmas Eve should not be ruined if he could help it. He showed me to a well-appointed bedroom; a fire burned merrily in the quaint old fireplace, although the lighting arrangement was not quite up to that I was used to. Electricity was quite unknown, so an odd-looking oil lamp took its place. And what a lamp! The innkeeper's wife described it as a "double-burner," a bit smoky at first, but when it got warmed-up she promised it gave a lovely light! It took some time, however, to warm up, and needed quite a lot of attention, for when one wick was turned up, the other automatically went down; however, it eventually did warm up, and I settled down to make the best of the evening.

About eight o'clock I had a hot meal, and then began to hunt the room for a book. What a business that hunting was, for of all the cupboards and drawers I opened, none revealed anything in the reading line. Just as I was giving up all hope, I discovered yet another cupboard, and in it three or four children's Sunday school rewards, and among them a very tattered and torn copy of the "Adventures of Dick Turpin." Now it was years ago that I read the adventures of this famous highwayman, so putting my horse-hair chair a little nearer the fire, I lit my pipe, and settled down once again to enjoy the adventures of Highwayman Turpin.

I had not been reading long before there was a knock at the door. "Come in," I shouted, but no one entered. There was a slight pause, and then came three louder knocks. "Oh, do come in," I called but still the door remained closed. Another pause; and then three heavy bangs.

By this time I was out of patience, and bawled at the top of my voice "For goodness sake come in." The door quietly opened, and revealed a tall, good-looking young man in evening dress, or at least the half of him that I saw, as he peeped round the door was so attired. He looked at me and I at him. Then he spoke, "Excuse me, old boy, but the landlord tells me you are stranded, jolly bad luck. But I'm throwing a party to some friends, and I thought you'd like to join us."

"Won't you come in," I said.

"No, thanks, old chap, I mustn't stay, or my friends will miss me."

"But— —," I said.

"That's okay," was his reply, "don't worry about your togs; come as you are. It's holiday time. We'll understand."

"But where must I come?" I stammered.

"Out of your room, down the passage and the door facing you, come right in."

"Fine," I replied, "I'll be with you in ten minutes."

He withdrew his head and shoulders, and the door closed as mysteriously as it opened.

Strange, I mused, and yet why shouldn't I? After all it's pretty dismal to be alone on Christmas Eve.

I got up from my chair, dropped the book I was reading, turned out my lamp, opened my bedroom door, and peeping out saw the passage, and the door at the far end.

I approached it, and as I drew nearer, heard voices from within. I knocked and waited, but there was no reply. I knocked a little louder, but still there was no reply; and then I remembered my visitor telling me to "open the door and come in." I gently opened the door, which revealed a fairly large room and running down the whole length of it, a table simply laden with good things to eat and drink. About the table sat four ladies in party frocks and three men in dinner jackets, while at the head sat the young man who had invited me.

And so I stood in the doorway "glazing," as they say in Cornwall, but strange to relate no one took the slightest notice of me. In fact, I stood there for several minutes and was about to return to my room thinking I was, indeed, and unwelcome guest, when the young man who had invited me to the party, suddenly looked my way, beckoned to me, and drew out a chair by his side for me to sit on.

Cautiously I passed down the room, sat down, and began to eat. Now the curious thing was, my plate was never empty, nor for that part was my glass; dainty dishes appeared and reappeared before me, and I ate with relish, but who the dickens had brought them or collected the empties, I didn't for the life of me know, for I saw no servants. Then there was another thing which puzzled me, no one present took the slightest notice of me; I ate and drank in silence.

At length the meal came to an end, and then my host spoke for the first time.

"I say, you fellows, while the ladies are retiring, would you like a game of cards?"

A couple of the men nodded; the ladies retired, and I was about to ask if I could be excused, when my host turning to me said, "You'll make one, won't you?"

"Well," I replied, "I don't mind, but I'm not very brilliant at cards."

"Splendid," he replied, and drew from a corner of the room a small card table. From his pocket he produced a pack of cards, and we played for some time and then my mysterious host asked if I had ever played for money.

"Once," I replied, "and lost several shillings."

"You don't mind playing again then?" and I felt forced to agree.

And so we played, first for a shilling and then higher stakes, until eventually I realised I had only ten shillings left. Things looked hopeless; however, I thought it was neck or nothing, so I threw in my ten shillings, the other players did the same, and four ten shilling notes lay on the table.

Now, not being very well-versed in card playing, I don't know the name of the game we played, but as far as I can remember it was like this. We were each dealt five cards, and the remainder of the pack was placed face down in the centre of the table. The idea was, as usual, to make as many tricks as possible, but before attempting it, you had to state how many you intended to make. The one who bid highest led off, and if he failed, there he had to pay out. If you said you were going to make all five tricks, you could discard any one of your cards, and take another from the pack in the centre of the table.

For this final hand, the cards were well shuffled, cut, and dealt, and I picked up my five with very trembling hands. Ace, King, Queen, eight of Diamonds, two of Clubs. "Three certs," I muttered, but what about the other two! Each of the other players scanned their cards, and shouted "pass," and I shouted "Five."

"Good," said my host, "Make 'em."

I played my ace, my king, my queen; three tricks. I was worried to death, three tricks to date; two more to make. What shall I play next?

By this time the perspiration was streaming from my face, I took out my handkerchief to mop my brow, and in doing so dropped it on the floor. I stooped to pick it up, and as I did so, saw protruding from the trousers of my host the two front feet of a bullock. Cloven hooves! I screamed, he sprang at my throat, and I felt his fingers closing tighter and tighter, then I knew no more.

How cold I was, I was shivering. I slowly opened my eyes to find myself lying on my back in the snow. My collar and necktie had gone, my shirt front was ripped, and my throat was so sore and painful that I could hardly swallow.

I got up like a man in a dream, and after wandering about in the snow for how long I don't remember, I suddenly saw a light. I made for it and discovered it was the village inn. I banged at the door, and presently a bedroom window opened.

"Who is it?" shouted the frightened landlord. I told him, and in his nightshirt, carrying a guttering candle, he opened the door and let me in. With horror in his face he asked me what I was doing out at one in the morning, and in such weather. I told him exactly what had happened.

"My dear sir you are dreaming; must have been sleep walking, there's been no party here to-night. Not a soul in the house besides the wife and four kids, and we've been abed these last two hours."

I persisted in my story, and took him to my bedroom. "There," I said, pointing to the chair by the now-expired fire, "that's where I was sitting when the unknown man knocked and opened my door. There's the book I was reading, exactly where I left it with even the very page turned in where I had left off."

"But I tell you, sir, we have had no party," said the landlord.

"But I did go to a party," I shouted, "Come and I'll show you the room."

Together we passed through the door, down the passage, and I pushed open the door in front of us. "Here's the room." Yes, there it was all right, but instead of presenting the appearance of a feast, or at least the aftermath of a feast, it was all straight and tidy. The table I had seen, and sat at, only a short time previously, was now covered with a red tablecloth with a pitcher of flowers in the centre.

"There you are," said the by now, very frightened landlord, "No party here."

"But," I stammered, "I sat here," and I pointed to the chair at the side of the table. "Yes, and there's the table on which we played cards, and here's the spot where the villain tried, and indeed, very successfully, to throttle me."

"All a mistake, sir, had no party here," persisted the innkeeper, "you must have ——." He did not finish the sentence, for suddenly the candle he was holding was violently knocked from his hand, and there was a terrible groan.

The old landlord shouted.

"Keep quiet, you fool," I whispered, "where are you?" He shuffled nearer to me in the darkness, and I touched the heavy curtain by the side of the fireplace. I pulled him toward it.

"For God's sake keep quiet; we'll be all right in a minute."

Then came the groan again, and a terrible gurgling, and from behind the curtain we felt something heavy pressing against us. It remained pushing for a moment or two, and I put my hand out to discover if it was palpable to touch. I encountered an hairiness.

"It's the very devil himself," I muttered, and in drawing back into the fireplace, my foot touched something—the fire irons. I stooped, picked up an iron poker and handed it in the inky darkness to the landlord, and then seizing the fire-tongues, whispered, as bravely as I could, "The next time the terror, or whatever it is, comes near us, hit."

Quietness reigned for a second or two, then came a piercing shriek, and something struck the curtains. "Hit," I shouted, "Hit."

We both did, and in the mighty stroke that I delivered, I fell headlong into space and then: I WOKE UP.

CALL FROM THE DEAD
[1950][3]

A True Telephone Story

The general conversation in the comfortable lounge of a Liskeard hotel suddenly turned to ghosts and haunted houses, and after three or four stories had been related concerning weird happenings in and around the immediate neighbourhood, I chanced to remark: "I wonder whether all the phenomena that occur in reputed houses and places are really due to entities from another world. In my opinion it is very debatable."

"Agreed," said the man in the corner. "Even granting they are not due to trickery, illusion, hallucination, or hysteria, there is still the possibility that, at least, a percentage of them may be due to some quite natural cause."

"As for example," I interjected, "a deeply emotional thought may have capabilities little dreamed of by its conceiver, with effects not merely transient or confined to a lifetime, limited to any definite number of years, or to any limited space."

At this point our little party was joined by a visitor, who, after telling us that he was no stranger to our delightful county, said: "I was always a very strong-minded man, and until the time of which I am about to speak, I always ridiculed the idea of ghosts and things that go bump in the night."

In an instant we were all ears, and our guest, noting our very keen interest, continued: "Let everyone speak as they find, for my part, I am now convinced of my error, though I'm far from wishing anyone to adopt my opinion unless from conviction.

"Not many years ago, I happened to be staying with a friend of mine and his wife not many miles from this very hotel. They were a very affectionate couple; not been married very long, you know!

"Four or five days after my arrival, they had a telephone message to say that the wife's mother was ill, having been slightly hurt in an accident. Vera, that is the name of my friend's wife, was naturally upset, and being a bit under the weather, suggested that her husband, Jack, should hop into his M.G., pay mother a visit, and bring back a full account. Jack agreed, and as we saw him off at the front door, Vera asked him to be sure and give us a ring on the telephone with all the news. 'Okay,' shouted Jack over the roar of the engine, 'Expect a call from me round about ten o'clock,' and away he went.

"Now, I could see that Vera was upset about her mother, and although I tried to distract her attention, I had a feeling all the time that her one thought was for Jack and his telephone message.

"As the hands of the old grandfather clock neared ten, she moved a little nearer to the telephone, but nothing happened. The clock struck, and we both looked at the telephone. The minutes passed—10, 15, 20, and then half-past. 'I can't understand why Jack hasn't 'phoned.'

"Perhaps he's had a breakdown," I suggested. "Come, let's have a drink, Jack won't let us down." I reached for the whiskey and soda, and as I did so, Vera shouted: "Here he is."

"The telephone bell gave a slight tinkle. I did not take any notice, for it was not loud enough for a call. In fact, I thought I was responsible, for in reaching for the whiskey, I moved the table on which the phone stood.

"'Hello! Dear,' said Vera, picking up the phone. 'Is that you Jack? Oh, speak up, I can't hear you, you seem to be thousands of miles away. What, you couldn't get through?' At this point she turned to me and exclaimed: 'I can only just hear him.' 'What Jack? Oh, that's lovely, give her my love. I'm glad it's no worse.' She then rang off.

"A moment of two later the bell rang again. 'It's a call for you,' said Vera. It was a doctor. Could I come as quickly as possible to so-and-so, and for heaven's name, don't tell Vera. Jack has had a smash. I asked Vera to excuse me, telling her that I was wanted on rather important business. As I hurried from the house, I remembered that Jack had said nothing about any smash to Vera. In fact he could not have been badly hurt to be able to speak on the telephone. Some time later I was at the scene of the accident, and could see at once by the doctor's face that something serious has happened.

"Poor old Jack, in his hurry, had met with a tragedy. His car had gone over a bank, he had been thrown out, and his neck was broken. 'Fortunately he was alive when I arrived on the scene,' said the doctor, 'but he died a short while after.'

"'What time did the accident happen?' I asked the doctor, for at exactly 10.30 p.m. he had spoken on the telephone to his wife.'

"'Impossible,' replied the doctor, 'the accident happened round about 10 o'clock, and he was dead before 10.30. But come to think of it, he told me he had to speak to his wife, and was very upset because he could not do so. In fact, his worrying about telephoning hastened his end. Two or three time he tried to sit up, but...'"

Our visitor took a sip of his beer, cleared his throat, and exclaimed: "That is the story."

"But who was it that phoned," we all asked.

"Why Jack, of course," he replied. "That's very clear."

"But how could he? He was dead."

"I don't know; all I can say is that he did telephone. Poor old Jack had made up his mind to do it, and he did, that's all."

TWO STRANGE STORIES
[1950][4]

"Various opinions have been held respecting the reality of the existence of apparitions," said my storyteller, "and here are a couple of happenings which occurred at different times and places."

"They are, as you will observe, totally unconnected with each other, yet they may be said to elucidate the subject. My first story will, no doubt, stagger the cynicism of some, while the latter will have a tendency to moderate the extreme credulity of others."

Old Mr. ____ was a Commoner of one of the Colleges at ____. He was a remarkable old chap, and will be remembered by his curious walk, and the particular habit he had of holding up his gown behind. He was in fact, equally known by his back, as by his face. Now it happened one day, I was talking with a friend, waiting for the dinner call. Suddenly my friend said: "Good heavens, who is that coming out of your college?" I looked and saw as I supposed old Mr. ____. "Look at his face," said my friend. "I've never seen such a face in all my life." "What's wrong with his face?" I asked, "It is the same as always." "What" exclaimed my friend, "it's terrible, so haunting. I shall never forget it." I watched old Mr. ____ without any emotion or suspicion as he came down the quadrangle, through the gate, and then proceed up the street, where we lost him.

The dinner call sounded and I went into the hall thinking no more of old Mr. ____. In the evening prayers were desired for one very sick and in a dangerous condition. When I came out I asked, in the hearing of several others, who it was we prayed for. "Why, poor old Mr. ____" was the reply.

In astonishment, I asked what was the matter with him, for I had seen him go out to dinner that day. "You are mistaken," was the answer, he has been in bed for days." "What nonsense." I replied, "not only did I see him, but my friend saw him as well." Some time later my tutor sent for me, and questioned me rather fully. He regretted that I had mentioned the matter so publicly, for poor old Mr. ____ was really dangerously ill. I expressed my regret, and explained that I had done it innocently. The next day the old chap died. It so frightened me that I contacted my friend, and in the presence of my tutor and several others, and without any prompting from me, he confirmed the story in every detail. Proof of existence of apparitions!

So much for story number one; now for experience number two.

Mr. ____, a tradesman living in a small market town in the west of England, was a member of a club which used to meet every month at a public house in the street he lived in to discuss current events. He was greatly respected by his friends, who elected him as their President. Now Mr. ____ was taken ill and was confined to his room a short time before the monthly meeting of his club. He was duly visited by several of the members, who expressed the hope he would be well enough to attend their next meeting. Their sympathy and good wishes were, however, unavailing, for as time drew on he became worse, and little or no hope was entertained for his life.

The evening of the meeting arrived, and as the members took their seats they agreed that the President's chair should not be filled on that night, as a mark of respect to the absent member.

The evening passed with its accustomed good humour, and they were just about to retire, when their attention was drawn by the entrance of a figure, which everyone knew to be an exact resemblance of their absent President. His face was pale and emaciated. He was dressed in an old dressing gown, with an odd looking nightcap on his head, and walking deliberately towards the head of the table, took his seat in the vacant chair. He looked kindly around on his companions for a few moments, then rose up without speaking, and disappeared.

There was much excitement, but imagine the feelings of all present next morning when they heard that their President had died about the time they had witnessed his extraordinary appearance.

The story was told and re-told, and each member of the club confirmed what he had seen. Now it happened that some years later, while the circumstances were still fresh, than an old woman, who had been employed as a nurse, being at the point of death, sent for a clergyman of the parish, and gave him the following reason.

"I cannot die contentedly without telling you of the particulars respecting the death of Mr. _____. I have hitherto not told a soul, but it was my negligence which caused the appearance of Mr. _____ at the meeting. I was left with him the night on which he died; and finding him very faint, I went out to the neighbours for some brandy. When I returned, I found he was gone, and I became alarmed. Presently I heard the street door open, he came up the stairs in a very exhausted condition, threw himself on the bed, and died. I was afraid to give this account before, as I should have been held responsible for his death, and should have lost my employment.

"It was, then, Mr. _____ who took his place at the head of the table, and not his ghost. He knew it was club night, and in the delirium occasioned by his illness, set off, regardless of his situation, to fill a post which he had so often filled before," concluded the story-teller.

MURDER WILL OUT
[1952][5]

Strange West Country Story

"Strange things do happen," said the man in the corner seat, "and here's one which happened many years ago."

I had occasion to be at _____, a small town in the Westcountry, and the following strange adventure happened to me. I arrived late in the evening on my journey from _____, and after having inquired for the best inn, was recommended to _____ at the other end of the town, facing the market, and adjoining the churchyard.

The following morning I decided to see the sights of the town, and began with the church. After I had surveyed the building I walked through the churchyard, and came across the sexton digging a grave. I stood for a while watching the man, who, without the least compunction or reflection, cast out from the earth the remains of a fellow mortal.

Among the variety of bones taken out of the pit was a skull which appeared whiter than ordinary. This induced me to take it up, and turning it about I heard something rattle within it. Upon closer examination, I found a large nail covered with rust, about four inches long. It puzzled me greatly, for you can imagine my surprise to find a nail in such a place.

Turning the skull about, I found on the forehead a perforation encrusted with the rust of iron, and in which a part of the nail yet remained.

I at once suspected murder, but without mentioning this to the sexton, I enquired if he knew whom the bones he was now removing from the earth belonged.

"Why, yes sir," was the ready reply, "he was the master of the _____ inn 22 or more years ago."

"But how came he by his death?" I asked. "Oh, very sudden; would you believe it, I drank with him the night before, and he seemed hale and hearty, but in the morning he was dead, and I buried him with my own hands in this grave."

"He died suddenly, you say," was my next remark. "Yes, in a fit."

"Strange," I replied, "are you sure? Take a look at this," and I showed him the nail rusted in the skull and the remainder corroded and loose in the cavity. He was astonished.

"Did he leave any family?" was my next question, to which the sexton replied: "He left a widow who at the present keeps the _____ inn," the very inn in which I was staying. Continuing, the grave-digger volunteered the information that within two months of the death of the innkeeper, his widow had married the hostler, and he was at present the landlord.

Without further questioning of the sexton, I enquired for the nearest magistrate, and taking the skull with me, I went to his residence. I explained the reason for my call, and showing him the skull, he agreed that the owner had been murdered. A message was sent to the woman at the inn, and within a short time she arrived at the house of the magistrate.

Questioning began concerning her first husband, and amid sobs she praised him for his kindness and virtue. "But what of your present husband?" asked the Magistrate. "I hope you have no reason to complain of him." "Certainly not your worship," was the ready reply. "But you married him, I understand, very soon after your first husband's death."

"Yes, indeed, your worship. What could a poor woman do, left all alone, as you may say, in a large inn?"

"Your first husband died suddenly," said the magistrate. "Oh yes, he was taken in a fit of apoplexy, fell back in his chair, and spoke no more. We put him to bed and did everything, but it was no good."

"Did you call a doctor?" was the next question, and the reply, followed by much sobbing, was: "I was too frightened to call a doctor."

"You say that you put him to bed. Who assisted you?" continued the magistrate. "Why Robert, the hostler, sir, for I could not lift him myself. We called in the gossips, they saw my dear husband's corpse and helped to lay it out too. Therefore there was no need of the Coroner's inquest and he was buried as you know.

"It was at this point that I joined the cross examination, and remarked, "But immediately before his death, did he not complain of a headache?"—"Not in the least sir."

"Well," I added, "I think a nail half the length would make me complain."—"Nail, your honour? Whatever do you mean by nail?"

"I will tell you," said the magistrate, producing the skull and the part of the nail found in it. The moment she saw the skull and the nail, the woman screamed: "Murder will out," and fainted.

The magistrate caused her to be removed to an inner room, and sent for the husband. He made sundry excuses, and said he could not come, as his wife was out shopping, and there was no one to look after the inn. Eventually, however, he arrived.

At the sudden exposure of the skull, and being told it was the master's, he broke down and confessed.

Later he and his wife were committed to prison. At the Assize, which unfortunately I had to attend to testify as to my part in the strange story, both were found guilty of the murder, and both were hanged at a West Country gaol.

A STRANGE DREAM
[1952][6]

"Belief in the agency of dreams in conveying warnings and news of things to come is still widespread," said the man in the corner seat.

"Even those of us who openly state that the interpretation of our dreams is mere amusement, often secretly fear that there is something behind our dreams and visions which have a powerful influence over our fate.

"Again, how is it that we see in our dreams the very faces and dress of the persons we dream of, we even hear their voices, and receive impressions of what they say, and, very often, we speak to them with our own voices articulately and audibly, though we are fast asleep?"

"Very strange," I replied.

"And yet again," said my companion, "there are numerous accounts in which persons have had the period of their own death pointed out to them in their dreams. The following West Country story supports this, and is worth the telling, not only on account of any supernatural character belonging to it, but simply from the extraordinary coincidence between the dream and the subsequent event. Now for the story.

"An old friend of mine dreamed one night that he was out riding, and came across an old mansion, now a gloomy ruin. It was surrounded by an old-fashioned garden, overgrown with weeds. The paths leading to the house were covered with grass and moss, and the many fruit trees trained against the walls shot out a plenteous overgrowth which hung over the borders. Thistles, docks, and weeds of every description choked the flower beds.

"The only objects which did not bear the evidence of neglect were the fine elms which fringed the lawn. In the old mansion itself all the window planes were broken, the roof was practically gone, while the once fine oak entrance door had dropped from its sockets and was held in place by a rusty chain. All was silent, deserted, and desolate.

"Now my friend sat on his horse in silence, contemplating the desolate scene. Suddenly the sound of voices came from within the building, then laughter, and then, to his amazement, the old front door began to tremble and shake, and fell with a crash to the bottom of the granite steps which led to the entrance. He dismounted, and led his horse to a nearby wall, and tied it to a stake. Then he walked slowly across the once gravel path, mounted the three granite steps which once led to the front door (stepping, by the way, over the fallen door), and entered the building.

"Once inside the house, the rooms became alive, and glowed with warmth and friendliness. People moved from room to room amid much talking and merriment, and the whole place appeared to be a blaze of light and colour.

"But to my friend's astonishment, all the people he saw moving about he had known years previously, and were all dead. In spite of this, however, he was very kindly received by them, and after being given a comfortable seat, he was handed food and drink.

"How long this continued, he could not remember, but eventually he asked to be excused, and was just about to leave, when one of the strange company made him promise he would visit them again in a month's time.

"He promised faithfully to do so, and bidding them all farewell, left the house, collected his horse, and rode home.

"Such was the outline of the dream, and he related it to me in a humorous sort of way, for he thought little about the adventure, not being a superstitious man.

"But, alas, this was not the end of the weird adventure. There was a tragic ending, on the very day, one month later, he was killed while attempting to jump his horse over a high bank. Strange, eh?"

APPENDIX A:

THOMAS-PAYNTER CORRESPONDENCE (1928)

Letter 1: 14, Union Street, Camborne. 8 March 1928

Dear Sir

My sight being bad I am not able to write much, but I don't know that I can tell you anything that would be of any use to you, but if you come to Camborne & you have time to call I shall be pleased to meet you The man who you call Jimmey the Wizard was much oftener called Jimmey the Witch, but his proper name was, James Thomas, but no relation whatever, I never saw him but once, that was not long before he died, he was very fond of a pinch of snuff & a glass of ginn but he done many strainge things which [were] called Witchcraft, but if I have been rightly informed he was not as you say a native of Illogan, but he lived there for many years, but if I have been told the truth he was a native of St. Wendron, & long before my time he married a widdow who lived at Helston who went by the name of Tammey Blee, but often called the Witch of the West & don't think that she took his name, but on the other hand he lernt her box of tricks, & although he was an Engine driver by proficion he never worked at it after he got married, She was many years older then he she died about 68 years ago & the day on which she was buried the[re] was a very severe Thunder Storm the talk was that the Devil was responsible for the Thunder & lightening but not for the rain & it look to me that Jimmey had to seek new fields in which to carry on his buisness so he came to Illogan much of his cures was done by charms & some wonderful stories was being told too many for me to write here, but I remember children who told an untruth to their parents being told if it happen again they would be taken into Helston to Tammey Blee & have their head turned forth & back & that often proved a cure for them, She died about 68 years ago, I don't think her husband is dead no more then about 35 years, I knew a man about 55 years ago who had a misterious sickness & he beleived that he was ilwished by a woman who was accused of being a witch, because he would not keep company with her daughter, so he went over to broad lanes, Illogan to Jimmey who kept him there a day &

night, after he went through lots of straing antics he told him that he was ilwished but did not say the name of the person who did it but said [that] when you enter Camborne you will meet the one that done it walking on two sticks, & he told me at the time that he came to Town through Stray Park lane & as he turned the corner he met the woman who he accused as he was told walking on two sticks & he never saw her walking on sticks before, By trade I am a boot & shoe maker, & that same woman had her Boots at the shop where I was working but she was not a good pay[er], so my Boss told her in my presents that he would make nor mend no more Boots for her nor her family, She said you will be sorry for that & wish that you had done my work for said she I will see that you shall have no work to do in a short time, at that time we was four men working in the shop, he said I dont care about your ilwishing & go out of my shop so she said but you will care, after that I went to America, & returned in about 4 years & went to the old shop to see the Boss, but he was packing up his Kit leaveing for New Zeland he told me that his work began to fail after the old woman had ilwished him, although he did not beleive in witchcraft neither do I but it just turned so, A woman told me that she had child that was very sick, she lived about twelve miles from Helston, She put the child into a donkey cart & drove it into helston to see Tammey Blee to see if she could cure it, but when she got there she looked at the child & discovered it was dead & Tammey did not attempt to bring it to life, so she put it back into the cart & took it back home, my notes I shall want for Hayle, but those little yarns are not in with my notes, & possible these are not the kind of thing that you want if they are let me know

Yours truly
Jim Thomas

Letter 2: Undated

Dear Mr Paynter

I received your Letter alright, much thanks & I took the bottel up to Mr Bennets & he photographed it & brought it back to me again, I have not seen the result but I hope you have before now I trust it was a good one, he told me that was going to give me a copy & I without doubt shall have it, he told me that he thought to send a copy to the newspaper & asked me to write a bit of a note to explain it but I have not done it, thinking I had better to ask your opinion about it, & now I will also ask of you a little favour that is if it is alright, will you write the foot note for me & send it down to me, I am not much now for writeing for newspapers, my day is gone for Jobs of that kind I use to do it but I am not as young as I use to be, I saw a Lady this week whos Husband knew Tammey Blee well in fact he used to be put in the bed with Tammey for her to take care of him, when his Mother wanted to go out on buisness, the woman told me that Tammey was confined to her bed for some considerable time before she died she also told me that there [were] People sometimes brought on stretchers & laid by her bedside entirely helpless, & they have known them of their own strength to rise up from the stretcher & go down over stairs perfectly well, she said that her own mother had a neighbour who was very bad & they could not say what [t]he complaint was, so she & another neighbour went in to Tammey Blee to see if she could tell them what was the matter with the woman when they got in there & asked her what was the matter with her & if she would git well again for when they left the woman was bad in bed, Tammey said give me sixpence & I will tell you all about it They said we have got no money at all yes you have said Tammey Put your hand in your pocket you have a sixpence there & the woman who told me said her mother put her hand in her pocket & found a sixpence which she put there & forgot all about it, it was given her for to go to Copperhouse Fair & she gave it to Tammey & she said go home your neighbour is alright & against you git home she will have Tea ready for you & she is bakeing a heavy cake for your Tea, & against they got home which was about ten miles away, they found the woman down stairs & well, with the heavy cake made & baked for their tea & they sat down & had their tea off it, now I don't know if that little adventure is any good to you or not if so I think it is possible for me to git some more, but do you want them from any other part of the world but Cornwall or must the[y] be all Cornish,

With all good wishes
Yours very Truly
J. Thomas

[PS] I have also got a model of a black heart but it was not Cornish so I thought possible it is no good for you to see thinking your intrest was with Cornish witchcraft alone
    J.T

Letter 3: Undated

Dear Mr. Paynter

You will excuse me I know for being a little slow in returning thanks for your kindness in sending me the cutting from the Independent & your kind Letter with the copy of your letter to the Morning News & also the Morning with the picture of the Bottle, all of which interested me very much, & I thank you very much for them, I have had a very bad cold, but I have ben hopeing to have more yarns for you but I what I have got is nothing very strikeing but I am still on the search with my ears open, the Bottle in the Morning News was very good there was lots of chat about it so much so that the Camborne Branch of the Old Cornwall Society had me to give my paper here at Camborne last Monday evening & everything went of[f] alright, & so it did at Hayle, although I think I did a better job here then what I did at Hayle or Redruth, you know the old saying, every cock can crow loudest on his own dung pile, but they seem to be pleased all around, I trust that you are gitting on with your book alright & gitting more material for it from others who are a bit younger than myself, now I want to ask another question, Tamey Blee called herself the true Pellar Stock or Blood what did she mean by Pellar, because I have heard Fortune tellers say that they was the real old Egyptian stock therefore they were able to looking into the future of any on[e]s life, I forgot to say I have had the photo of the Bottle from Mr. Bennetts & I passed it around at the meeting & also the black heart, it appear[e]d to interest them very much,

Yours truly

J. Thomas

Letter 4: Undated

Dear Mr Paynter

Many thanks for the letter which I received from you this morning, in reference to the meaning of Pellar, I dont know if I told you when you was here, that when I was young that I was very fond of having my fortune told, & on[e] time I went to a Mrs Turner who went over the lines of my hand with a bit of wood with a heart carved on one end of it I asked her what it was & she told me it was a black heart, & that with it she had the power to do good or evil, I said to her you cant do me evil, she said that she could because she was the seventh daughter of the seventh son, well said I, I am the seventh of the seventh, then she said I can do you no harm, she asked me to write the names of girls that I knew, which I did & folded them up in separate bits of paper & laid them on the table in front of her, & she took the piece of wood that she called the black heart & knocked one of the pieces of paper in on the middle of the Table there she said thats your Wife, & nine years after that I was married to that same girl, of course I look at it as nonesence, but they happen to be right sometimes, I think much of it was done like I know it was done here at Camborne many years ago, at that time a woman came here telling fortunes & she told people as true as the day & she done a good buisness & got lots of money, the reason was she made friends with a family who knew Camborne & the people of Camborne well, so that the woman who was a great strainger to the place went to the house of her friend in the evening & got all the news she required for the next day, but their craft was discovered & the woman made herself scarce to save herself from a rough handling,

Uncle Jackey Hooper lived at Blowinghouse near Redruth, how long ago he lived there I dont know, but he was living there eighty years ago & I think he was an old standard there at that that time, because I have reason to believe that he was there twenty years before that time, he told people their troubles & also their fortunes by a bit of smoked glass, if you have forgoten the stories that I told you I will tell you again,

A Mr. Eva from Barripper lost a cow, but the cause of death he did not know, although most people said it was ilwished but he declared that he did not beleive in witchcraft, at last the evidence was too strong against him & he made up his mind & went in to see uncle Jackey Hooper for his neighbours was sure he would tell him all about [it.] Mr Eva met uncle Jackey at the door, well said he thee art come at last, yes said he but what am I come for why said uncle Jackey because theest had a loss, yes said the man but what have I lost, come thee in said uncle Jackey & Il soon tell thee what theest lost so they went inside & uncle Jackey took down from the mantleshelf an old hand lamp, & with flint & steel he soon lit it, then he took a piece of glass & smoked it over the lamp, then he held it up against the light, look here said uncle Jackey thats what theest lost, what is it said the man I cant see anything, upon that uncle Jackey got into a rage, why there it is he said as plain as pikestaff a underground shirt he said, thats what theest lost, oh said the man, you know as much about it as what I thought you would, & I wish good morning, & he came away leaving uncle Jackey in a very bad temper, that happned nearly a hundred years ago, But about seventy nine years ago a woman whos husband was an engineer & over to Spain puting up some machinery but he was taken with feaver, & letter carrying at that time was very slow being taken down through the country on mules backs, & the woman was very ancious to know about her husband, & her neighbours was cirtain if she was to go in & see uncle Jackey he would be able to tell her all about him, so the woman went in & one of her neighbours went with her for company, when they got to the house & knocked at the door, oh come in my dears said uncle Jackey you have got husband trouble he said I can see you have yes said the woman, Where is my husband, & what is he, & how is he, sit down said he & in a few minutes Il tell ey all about en, & as in the other case he lit his old lamp & smoked his bit of glass & held it up to the light, oh he said my dears theres your husband life & well, & by trade he is a sailor & he is at this time out upon the high seas climbing the riggins, here he said you can see for yourself no she said you old Fool I dont want to see you nor your old glass, & she told me that she had a good mind to give him a slap in his old face, to think she said that I walked nine miles to hear a yarn like that, so they came away leaving uncle Jackey in a very bad temper,

I was much interested in the newspaper cutting, I remember many of the old customs sutch as makeing whistles & also about the Farrow & the fires, but you said nothing about maying the Farmers door & demanding the glass of cream, because that was a part of the may morning Festival, Baal worship is much older than the Phoenicians it is my opinion that the first prayer that man ever made was to the sun & that's a long time ago, I thank you I am a little better, with kind regards yours Truly J. Thomas

[PS] I am much interested in Tamey Blees Picture & am hopeing that I shall see it in the paper, I hope it will not pass on without me seeing it

I trust if you ever come this way again that I shall have the pleasure of seeing you because I did not know you when you was here as well as what I do now

Letter 5: Undated

Dear Mr. Paynter

At last very many thanks for the newspaper cutting on Mayday & for the one that I received this week with Tamey Blees Picture. You will forgive me for not writeing before, because I have been very buisy. I have been writeing a paper for to read to the old Cornwall society on the ancient British village here at Caerwynen I took them up there last evening so that job is over. You asked me if I knew anything about Thomas, the cunning man, I know nothing whatever of Bodmin or the people there, but I thought possible it was Jimmey the Wizzard of Illogan, for it about years ago [sic] that he was sent to Bodmin Prison & was away some time from here. Possible he was up there doing a little buisiness, of course I dont know. About Madge Figgey, Jone of Alsia Mill, & The Witch of Treve, I have asked all the people that I know from the west & the[y] appears to know nothing about them but I was told of a White Witch by the name of Eliza Dunn, who lived at Troon Camborne, many 40 years ago, who believed herself that she could remove spells of witchcraft from people or cattle, & most people went to her, she also made salve & medison for Childrens & grown up, in cases of witchcraft she would read a prayer over the sufferor sometimes a portion of Scripture always ready to do good & never to do evil, kind & good, if any one suffered from any nervious complaint she would order them to the sea side & tell them to touch the receding tide nine times & she gave them a little prayer to say as they were doing it & the[y] would often come home cured. I am hopeing to hear more about her soon, & also about about a Black Witch who lived at Black Rock, Crowan a woman promised to come here & let me know about them & their ways, as soon as I do hear I will let you know. I am also told that Tamey Blee was kind & good natured. I hope that you collected some good Folk lore up to the north. I am hopeing to see you when you come here to Camborne, because I am better at talking now then what I am at writing. I am sending you my notice card for our last evening Pilgrimage

                                                Yours Truly

                                                        J. Thomas

APPENDIX B:

CORNISH WITCHCRAFT QUERIES (1928)

1. JOBBER MAIL. During my visit to Trebarwith I collected some information concerning this strange individual. Can you tell me how long ago he lived and if he was considered a Witch or Wizard?

Jobber Mail was a cattle dealer noted for dishonesty. After his death, his spirit troubled the neighbourhood and the clergyman said he was earthbound, so 7 parsons assembled to exorcise the spirit and they drove it to Trebarwith Strand where he was bound to make beams of the sand. This was about 120 years ago. My informant's "Granny" is 78, and she was about 10 when Honor Miller was about 70, and told her how she saw the 7 Parsons driving the spirit with whips, when she was young.

2. ANN FRADD. I have some notes concerning Ann Fradd. According to an old lady now residing at Delabole, Ann lived at Rockhead and was noted for her charms & spells. On one occasion she charmed a donkey, which had been badly stung by an adder. Can you tell me how long ago she lived? The lady I went to see was too feeble to give me much information.

Ann Fradd lived at High Lane, Delabole. It was about 60 years ago. She never took money for her charms and was much respected. She was also a skilful midwife.

3. THE TINTAGEL WISE MAN. Can you give me any further information concerning him. His name, where he lived, etc.

Was known as Old Martin. He died in 1919. He lived at Tregatta, Tintagel. I knew him well, and he liked me, but some people were afraid of him for everyone believed in his power to "overlook."

4. HONOR MILLER. Was she a Witch? I am informed that about 40 to 50 years ago there lived an old Witch at Trewarmett, I wonder if this is the same person?

No, she was not a witch. I don't know who was the Trewarmett witch.

5. SAM BENNETT. Is he still alive? Was he the seventh son of a seventh daughter, if so, was he a Pellar?

Was our gardener here. He was the seventh son. He could do many charms and is said to have cured "King's Evil." I do not know about his mother but will ask his widow when she comes home.

6. MRS. CHILCOTT OF BOSINNEY. Can you give me any further particulars about this good lady?

She was certainly gifted with strange powers, and is said to have "overlooked" members of the Dangar family, as well as John Panter and others.

7. MR. SNOW, THE WHITE WITCH OF LAUNCESTON. I have some information concerning this "wise-man", I wonder if you can tell me any more about him?

Mr Snow died a few years ago (about 8 I think). He lived at Tregadellet near Launceston.

NOTES AND REFERENCES

INTRODUCTION

1. The modern scholarly literature on European and American witchcraft is vast. For a useful introduction see, for instance, Macfarlane, Alan., *Witchcraft in Tudor and Stuart England* (London: Routledge & Kegan Paul, 1970); Thomas, Keith., *Religion and the Decline of Magic* (London: Weidenfeld & Nicholson, 1971); Barry, Jonathan., Hester, Marianne. & Roberts, Gareth. (eds.), *Witchcraft in Early Modern Europe* (Cambridge: Cambridge University Press, 1996); Sharpe, James., *Instruments of Darkness* (London: Hamish Hamilton Ltd., 1996); Bostridge, Ian., *Witchcraft and its Transformations c.1650–c.1750* (Oxford: Clarendon Press, 1997); Clark, Stuart., *Thinking with Demons* (Oxford: Clarendon Press, 1997); Davies, Owen., *Witchcraft, Magic and Culture 1736–1951* (Manchester: Manchester University Press, 1999); Clarke, Stuart. (ed.), *Languages of Witchcraft* (Basingstoke: Macmillan Press Ltd., 2001); Maxwell-Stuart, P. G., *Witchcraft in Europe and the New World* (Basingstoke: Palgrave, 2001); Sharpe, James., *Witchcraft in Early Modern England* (Harrow: Pearson Education Ltd., 2001).
2. Deane, Tony. & Shaw, Tony., *The Folklore of Cornwall* (London: B. T. Batsford Ltd., 1975) p. 73; also Anonymous. [hereafter Anon.], *Cornish Charms and Witchcraft* (Truro: Tor Mark Press, n.d.) p. 3.
3. *Journal of the Royal Institution of Cornwall* 4 (1865) p. 93; for a discussion on nineteenth-century attitudes towards folklore see Hutton, Ronald., *The Triumph of the Moon—A History of Modern Pagan Witchcraft* (Oxford: Oxford University Press, 1999) pp. 112–131.
4. Simpson, Jacqueline. & Roud, Steve., *A Dictionary of English Folklore* (Oxford: Oxford University Press, 2000) pp. 283, 302, 363.
5. Anon., "Ways of Charming Warts Away." *Western Evening Herald* (6 May 1958) p. 7.
6. See, for instance, Russell, Jeffrey Burton., *Witchcraft in the Middle Ages* (Ithaca, NY: Cornell University Press, 1972) pp. 1–43, 199–264; Ginzburg, Carlo., *Ecstasies* (London: Hutchinson Radius, 1990) pp. 63–86; Broedel, Hans Peter., *The Malleus Maleficarum and*

the Construction of Witchcraft (Manchester: Manchester University Press, 2003) pp. 91–166.
7. L'Estrange Ewen, Cecil., *Witch Hunting and Witch Trials* (London: Kegan Paul, Trench, Trubner & Co. Ltd., 1929) pp. 13–21.
8. The surviving records for the Cornish Assize trials for witchcraft are detailed in L'Estrange Ewen, Cecil., *Witchcraft and Demonianism* (London: Heath Cranton, 1933) pp. 439–446.
9. For the most comprehensive recent treatment of cunning-folk, see Davies, Owen., *Cunning-folk—Popular Magic in English History* (London: Hambledon & London, 2003).
10. Anon., "Cornish Superstitions." *Cornish Times* (22 February 1929) p. 8.
11. Davies, Owen., *Witchcraft, Magic and Culture 1736–1951* (Manchester: Manchester University Press, 1999) pp. 271–293; Sharpe, James., *Instruments of Darkness* (London: Hamish Hamilton Ltd., 1996) pp. 276–302; By the middle years of the twentieth century surveys showed that some 3/5 of the British population actively disbelieved in the existence of the Devil, and that the remainder were split almost evenly between belief and uncertainty. Apparently belief in the Devil was "slight" amongst those under 34, and was mostly confined to the elderly in villages in the South West of England, see Gorer, Geoffrey., *Exploring English Character* (London: The Cresset Press, 1955) p. 252; also Gorer's *Death, Grief & Mourning in Contemporary Britain* (London: The Cresset Press, 1965) pp. 40, 166; Gorer suggested that the "sex and location of believers in the devil could perhaps be interpreted as a faint survival of the witch cult in the West country."
12. Davies, Owen., "Charmers and Charming in England and Wales from the Eighteenth to the Twentieth Century." *Folklore* 109 (1998) pp. 41–52.
13. Simpson, Jacqueline. & Roud, Steve., *A Dictionary of English Folklore* (Oxford: Oxford University Press, 2000) p. 36.
14. Anon., "Ways of Charming Warts Away." *Western Evening Herald* (6 May 1958) p. 7.
15. Hawke, Russell., "Bill doesn't Claim to be a Wizard despite all his Charms." *Sunday Independent* (18 March 1973) p. 9.
16. Davies, Owen., *Cunning-folk—Popular Magic in English History* (London: Hambledon & London, 2003) p. 188.

17. Paynter, William H., "Cornish Witchcraft." *The Cornish Review* 13 (1969) p. 70; While the notion of the maleficent witch and her benign counterpart the cunning-man gradually faded, ceremonial magic and simple sorcery proved more tenacious and both have enjoyed a revival in recent decades in the secular West, in part taken up and employed by the varieties of Neopagan practitioners, many of whom identify themselves as witches. Distinction must be made between the traditional witch, allegedly in league with the Devil and his hellish imps, and the modern Neopagan: see, for example, Russell, Jeffrey Burton. & Alexander, Brooks., *A New History of Witchcraft—Sorcerers, Heretics and Pagans* (London: Thames and Hudson, 2007) pp. 140, 145–163, 193–197.
18. Semmens, Jason., '"Whyler Pystry": A Breviate of the Life and Folklore-collecting Practices of William Henry Paynter (1901–1976) of Callington, Cornwall." *Folklore* 116 (2005) pp. 75–94.
19. Manuscript [Paynter Archive A].
20. Ibid.

CHAPTER 1: LIFE AND BACKGROUND

1. Per birth certificate.
2. See census returns—1871, R.G.10/2231/51 Schedule 38; 1881, R.G.11/2282/63; I am also grateful to Richard Paynter for his help with details of the Paynter family tree.
3. See census returns—1851, H.O.107/1914/391/122; 1861, R.G.9/1576/29/45; 1881, R.G.11/2283/19/170; 1891, RG12/1809/5/31; 1901, R.G.13/2191/35/99.
4. Press release for *Primitive Physic* (13 October 1958) pp. 2, 3 [Paynter Archive B].
5. See 1871 census return RG10/2233/11/62.
6. Lightbody, Sheila., *The Book of Callington* (Buckingham: Barracuda Books Ltd., 1982) pp. 47–55.
7. William Henry Paynter senior spent some years in his youth as a farm labourer, see 1891 census RG12/1809/44/32.
8. Callington Register of Electors 1924–1932, Cornwall Record Office (CRO.) RE1/1–9.
9. Press release for *Primitive Physic* (13 October 1958) pp. 2, 3 [Paynter Archive B]. Read was born at Devonport, Plymouth (1901 census, R.G.13/2191/35/99), and began teaching at

Callington in 1900. It was Read who also encouraged Paynter's interest in nature as she took her pupils on nature walks about the district. Paynter recorded 2 interviews with Read, by then Mrs. Giles, in 1970, recalling memories of her early life and career—Paynter/Tucker Collection, South West Film Archive, Plymouth.
10. Paynter recorded his scouting achievements in a scrapbook [Paynter Archive A]; See also Bishop, George., *A Parish Album of Callington* (Plymouth: The Colombian Press, 1988) pp. 88–91, 98.
11. Anon., "Callington Boy Scouts." *Cornish Times* (25 October 1929) p. 6.
12. Anon., "Looker-on." *Cornish Times* (13 May 1938) p. 2; also Scout scrapbook [Paynter Archive A].
13. For instance, Anon., "R.S.P.C.A. and Callington—Lack of Interest." *Cornish Times* (1 March 1929) p. 3.
14. Pers comm. Anne Tucker.
15. See bibliography, p. 255.
16. Anon., "The Passing of the Callington Urban Council." *Cornish Times* (6 April 1934) p. 4; also Bishop, George., *A Parish Album of Callington* (Plymouth: The Colombian Press, 1988) p. 109.
17. Anon., "To the Summit of Kit Hill—New Road Opened by Mayor of Plymouth." *Cornish Times* (14 September 1928) p. 3.
18. Anon., "Married or Single?—Callington Women's Institute Debate." *Cornish Times* (8 May 1931) p. 4.
19. Per marriage certificate; also Anon., "East Cornwall Weddings." *Cornish Times* (24 June 1932) p. 5.
20. Callington Register of Electors 1933–1939, CRO. RE1/10–16.
21. Pers comm. Anne Tucker; also press release for *Primitive Physic* (13 October 1958) p. 2 [Paynter Archive B]. Paynter enjoyed a lengthy career as a broadcaster on radio and television, both locally and nationally. He contributed items to numerous magazine programmes and was also featured on documentaries, including 'Power of the Witch,' broadcast nationally on 15 December 1971, in which Paynter was interviewed along with Keith Thomas, Theo Brown, Doreen Valiente and Alex Sanders.
22. Pers comm. Anne Tucker; also Paynter W. H., "Idle Thoughts from Kit Hill." *Cornish Times* (8 October 1939) p. 8.
23. Pers comm. Anne Tucker.

24. Anon., "Scouts' Greater Keenness." *Cornish Times* (2 February 1940) p. 3; Anon., "Callington Parish Affairs." *Cornish Times* (29 March 1940) p. 3.
25. Anon., "Callington Parish Council." *Cornish Times* (21 February 1940) p. 5.
26. See, for instance, Collins, Larry., *Cadets and the War 1939–1945* (Oldham: Jade Publishing, 2004).
27. Pers comm. Anne Tucker.
28. Ibid.
29. Colquhoun, Ithell., *The Living Stones: Cornwall* (London: Peter Owen Ltd., 1957) p. 178.
30. Allen, John. (Paynter, W. H. (ed.)), *The History of the Borough of Liskeard* (Marazion: Wordens of Cornwall Ltd., 1967) p. 62.
31. Press release for *Primitive Physic* (13 October 1958) p. 3 [Paynter Archive B]; There are a number of references and advertisements for productions in the Westcountry newspapers throughout the 1950s and 1960s, for instance see *Cornish Times* (1 March 1957) pp. 2, 6.
32. Paynter was Deputy Mayor between 1965 and 1969, and is mentioned as such on numerous occasions in the regional newspapers engaged on official business.
33. Pers comm. Anne Tucker; also correspondence Paynter–Colquhoun (21 September 1961) [Colquhoun Archive TGA929/1/1555, Tate Britain].
34. Correspondence Paynter–Caxton (24 May 1956) [Paynter Archive B]: "I have for the past three years been with Farquharson Bros, the makers of "Cyro" ribbons, carbons—Have a grand job covering the whole of Devon & Cornwall."
35. Pers comm. Anne Tucker.
36. For instance, see folders nos. 490 and 483 [Paynter Archive B]; Also *Cornish Times* (21 September 1973) p. 8.
37. Per death certificate.
38. Anon. "Cornish Bard and Witchcraft Expert." *West Briton* (10 June 1976) p. 26; Anon. "Wheler Pystry Dies Aged 75, Funeral Today." *Cornish Guardian* (10 June 1976) p. 6; Anon. "Former Liskeard Archivist Dies." *Cornish Times* (11 June 1976) p. 11.
39. Pers comm. Jeremy Tucker.

CHAPTER 2: "WHYLER PYSTRY"

1. Press release for *Primitive Physic* (13 October 1958) pp. 2, 3 [Paynter Archive B].
2. Ibid. pp. 3, 4.
3. Anon., "Witch Hunting in Cornwall—Mr. W. H. Paynter's Latest Investigations in the West." *Cornish Times* (13 September 1929) p. 2.
4. Hawke, Russell., "Bill doesn't Claim to be a Wizard despite all his Charms." *Sunday Independent* (18 March 1973) p. 9.
5. Paynter introduced his witchcraft lectures during the 1930s by recounting the activities of Matthew Hopkins during the 1640s before describing his own "witch hunt." Two versions of Paynter's notes for his "Witchcraft and the Black Arts in the Westcountry" lecture survive, one more detailed than the other, in folder 486.2 [Paynter Archive B]. Paynter owned a copy of the facsimile edition of Hopkins's 1647 pamphlet *The Discovery of Witches* (Norwich: H. W. Hunt, 1931) [Paynter Archive A]; Paynter also summarised his work to date in his letter "Belief in Witchcraft." *The Times* (25 September 1930) p. 8.
6. Vulliamy, Colwyn., *Unknown Cornwall* (London: John Lane The Bodley Head, 1925) pp. 226–228.
7. Paynter, William H., "A Cornish Bard—Appreciation of the Late Mr. F. J. Thomas." Newspaper clipping [Paynter Archive A], identified by Paynter as published in the *Western Morning News* (2 March 1934) though I have been unable to collate this with the actual publication.
8. For both conjurors see Semmens, Jason., *The Witch of the West: Or, The Strange and Wonderful History of Thomasine Blight* (Plymouth: Privately Printed, 2004).
9. Hunt, Robert., *Popular Romances of the West of England, Second Series* (London: John Cambden Hotten, 1865) p. 77, 78.
10. Anon., "The Case of Gross Superstition at Hayle." *West Briton* (11 December 1863) p. 5.
11. [Paynter Archive A]; see Semmens, Jason., "Tales of Cornish Witches." *Old Cornwall* 13, No. 7 (2006) pp. 22–27.
12. Paynter, William H., "Idle Thoughts from Kit Hill." *Cornish Times* (21 June 1929) p. 2.

13. Anon., "Belief in Witchcraft." *Cornish Times* (2 December 1932) p. 7.
14. Ibid; While he continued to mention fortune tellers and charmers in his later articles, 1932 was the last year in which Paynter mentioned the activities of figures recognizably identifiable as cunning-folk, before falling silent on such characters altogether. This is consistent with the findings of Owen Davies's survey of English cunning-folk, as he found the last references to practising conjurors dated from the mid 1930s, see Davies's *Cunning-Folk—Popular Magic in English History* (London: Hambledon & London, 2003) pp. 192, 193.
15. Ibid.
16. Anon., "Modern Survivals of Old Beliefs." *Cornish Times* (8 March 1929) p. 8.
17. Anon., "Belief in Witchcraft." *Cornish Times* (2 December 1932) p. 7.
18. Paynter, William H., "Witches and Witchcraft." *Western Morning News* (3 March 1932) p. 6.
19. Whitcomb, Noel., "Magic Leaves Me Spell-Bound." *Daily Mirror* (29 October 1960) p. 2.
20. Course notes for WEA lectures, folder 483 [Paynter Archive B]; Paynter also recorded a monologue on "Early Christianity and Witchcraft" about 1970 in which he described witchcraft as the remains of a prehistoric religion presided over by priestesses of the 'Dianic Cult,' whose descendents were the 'wise-women' and healers of more recent times—Paynter/Tucker Collection, South West Film Archive, Plymouth; much of Paynter's understanding of folklore and the roots of witchcraft seems to have been informed by Sir James Frazer's *Golden Bough* (1890).
21. Oates, Caroline. & Wood, Juliette., *A Coven of Scholars—Margaret Murray and her Working Methods* (London: The Folklore Society, 1998) pp. 12–17, 24–32; Hutton, Ronald., "Paganism and Polemic: The Debate over the Origins of Modern Pagan Witchcraft." *Folklore* 111 (2000) pp. 103–117; Murray has been characterised as the "Godmother" of modern pagan witchcraft on account of Gerald Gardner's enthusiastic uptake of her thesis of an underground pagan cult in his formulation of an 'Old Religion,' though Murray herself took a decidedly negative view of Gardner's 'Craft of the Wise.' Writing in a letter to Ithell

Colquhoun she noted, "As regards these modern "witches." It is an entirely modern sect, which has nothing to do with the old cult ... The modern imitation appeals to rather brainless young people who want to feel important ... To me the whole thing is absurd an[d] the performances rather ridiculous."—Correspondence Murray–Colquhoun (9 December 1960) [Colquhoun Archive TGA929/5/31/15, Tate Britain].

22. Paynter had acquired this nickname by the autumn of 1929, see Anon., "Witch Hunting in Cornwall." *Cornish Times* (13 September 1929) p. 2; also Anon., "Wanted: A Spell-Lifter." *Cornish Times* (13 December 1929) p. 2; Anon., "Appeals to "The Witch Finder"' *Cornish Times* (23 May 1930) p. 5; Anon., "Belief in Witchcraft." *Cornish Times* (2 December 1932) p. 7.

23. Hawke, Russell., "Bill doesn't Claim to be a Wizard despite all his Charms." *Sunday Independent* (18 March 1973) p. 9.

24. Anon., "Modern Survivals of Old Beliefs." *Cornish Times* (8 March 1929) p. 8; Paynter, William H., "Tales of Cornish Witches." *Old Cornwall* 1, No. 9 (1929) p. 33; the title was probably based on Harry Price's *Confessions of a Ghost Hunter* (1936), the title page is all that survives of the manuscript [Paynter Archive A].

25. Goad was born at Devonport, Plymouth. As well as a teacher she was also the author of several study guides for the Brodies' Notes series on English literature during the 1950s, and incumbent president of the Plymouth Shakespeare Society upon her death: Anon., "Tribute to Late President." *Western Evening Herald* (9 March 1966) p. 3.

26. Goad, Kathleen M., "Midsummer Magic—How the Flowers Kept Away Strange Evils." *Western Evening Herald* (22 June 1931) p. 6.

27. Correspondence Paynter–Colquhoun (9 February 1957) [Colquhoun Archive TGA929/5/31/17, Tate Britain]; Paynter–Kenneth Hudson (20 February 1957) and Paynter–Howard (23 August 1957) [Paynter Archive A].

28. Jenkin, A. K. Hamilton., *Cornwall and the Cornish* (London: J. M. Dent and Sons Ltd., 1933) pp. 263, 264, 269.

29. Anon., "Witch Hunting in Cornwall." *Cornish Times* (13 September 1929) p. 2.

30. Per photograph of 'Symbols of Cornish Witchcraft' in *The Cornish Review* 13 (1969) p. 45.

31. Colquhoun, Ithell., *The Living Stones: Cornwall* (London: Peter Owen Ltd., 1957) p. 182; the grimoire survives in Paynter Archive A and for many years was on display in Paynter's Cornish Museum.
32. Ibid.
33. Anon., "Ways of Charming Warts Away." *Western Evening Herald* (6 May 1958) p. 7; the object would appear to have been a black bag containing bats' wings— *The Cornish Review* 13 (1969) p. 45.
34. Correspondence Paynter–Howard (23 August 1957) [Paynter Archive A].
35. Anon., "Nobody Knew Words of Trad Song in Have-A-Go Work-out." *Cornish Times* (26 January 1962) p. 5; Anon., "Charms and Cures are in Demand." *Cornish Times* (2 February 1962) p. 7.
36. Semmens, Jason., '"Whyler Pystry": A Breviate of the Life and Folklore-collecting Practices of William Henry Paynter (1901–1976) of Callington, Cornwall." *Folklore* 116 (2005) p. 86.
37. Several of Paynter's preliminary sketches for the design of the talisman survive, see folder 486.2 [Paynter Archive B].
38. Colquhoun, Ithell., *The Living Stones: Cornwall* (London: Peter Owen Ltd., 1957) pp. 178–185; Colquhoun produced several pages of notes during her visit, most of which found their way into the relevant chapter on Paynter [Colquhoun Archive TGA929/2/1/35/1/22, Tate Britain].
39. Hawke, Russell., "Bill doesn't Claim to be a Wizard despite all his Charms." *Sunday Independent* (18 March 1973) p. 9; A quantity of Paynter's audio tape recordings are held at the South West Film Archive, Plymouth, which include various Cornish ghost and dialect stories, an introduction to folklore, a description of the Caradon meteorite, as well as the interview with Lillian Giles (formerly Read) and Paynter's reading of his *Old Cornwall* article "In Search of the Odd."

CHAPTER 3: "THINGS THAT GO BUMP IN THE NIGHT"

1. Anon., "Ghost Hunts in Cornwall." *Cornish Times* (6 April 1934) p. 9.
2. Anon., "Cornish Ghosts and Haunted Houses." *Cornish Guardian* (24 November 1949) p. 2.

3. In his survey during the early 1950s Geoffrey Gorer found that "A sixth of the population say that they believe in ghosts, just under a quarter are uncertain and two-thirds do not, gross figures which are almost identical with the belief in the Christian conception of Hell." *Exploring English Character* (London: The Cresset Press, 1955) p. 263; Asked in a similar survey "Do you believe in ghosts?," the British Institute of Public Opinion found in April 1950 that "8 per cent of the men and 12 per cent of the women replied in the affirmative; 84 per cent of the men and 75 per cent of the women in the negative; the remainder said they did not know. Two per cent of the men and 5 per cent of the women said they had seen a ghost." Ibid, p. 276.
4. Anon., "The Big Blackamoor Ghost of Stoke Climsland." *Tavistock Times* (11 September 1953) p. 2.
5. Paynter owned a copy of the ghost hunting magazine *Contact* 1, No.1 (1969) [Paynter Archive A].
6. Anon., "Cornish "Ghost" Dog." *Western Evening Herald* (18 February 1937) p. 5; Anon., "The Ghostly Dog." *Western Evening Herald* (19 February 1937) p. 7; Anon., "The Ghost of a Dog." *Cornish & Devon Post* (27 February 1937) p. 11.
7. Brown, Theo., "The Black Dog." *Folklore* 69 (1958) pp. 175–192; Brown, Theo., "The Black Dog in English Folklore." in Porter, J. R. & Russell, W. M. S. (eds.), *Animals in Folklore* (Ipswich: D. S. Brewer, 1978) pp. 45–58; Trubshawe, Bob. (ed.), *Explore Phantom Black Dogs* (Loughborough: Heart of Albion Press, 2005).
8. Anon., '"Phantom Dog" Reappears." *Daily Mail* (19 February 1937) p. 5; although anonymous this was by Paynter, as internal evidence demonstrates.
9. Anon., "Non-Appearance of Ghost Dog." *Western Morning News* (20 February 1937) p. 7.
10. Anon., "Ghost Dog Mystery." *Cornish & Devon Post* (27 February 1937) p. 7.
11. Pers comm. Anne Tucker; It seems likely that Paynter was familiar with the psychical investigations of Harry Price—compare Paynter's practices to Price's recommendations for ghost hunting in his *Confessions of a Ghost Hunter* (London: Putnam & Company, 1936) pp. 31, 165, 166.
12. Anon., "Ghost Hunts in Cornwall." *Cornish Times* (6 April 1934) p. 9.

13. Pers comm. Anne Tucker; on Prince Bira see Birabongse, Ceril., *The Prince & I: Life with the Motor Racing Prince of Siam* (Godmanstone: Veloce, 1992).
14. Anon., "The Big Blackamoor Ghost of Stoke Climsland." *Tavistock Times* (11 September 1953) p. 2.
15. Ibid; also Anon. "The Bloodstain that Appears on the Anniversary of a Dreadful Deed." *Tavistock Times* (18 September 1953) p. 3.
16. Anon., "Cornish Ghosts and Haunted Houses." *Cornish Guardian* (24 November 1949) p. 2; Anon., "The Haunted House was no More." *Cornish & Devon Post* (26 September 1953) p. 6.
17. Folder 469 (11) [Paynter Archive B].
18. It is noticeable that none of the sheets are individually paginated nor are there chapter page numbers in the contents list.
19. Braddock, Joseph., *Haunted Houses* (London: B. T. Batsford Ltd., 1956) p. 74.
20. Ibid. pp. 74, 76, 77; also Anon., "The Big Blackamoor Ghost of Stoke Climsland." *Tavistock Times* (11 September 1953) p. 2; a carbon copy of page 5 of a letter, apparently to Braddock, survives in folder 469 (11) [Paynter Archive B].
21. A manuscript typescript of Acts 1 and 2 survives in part, supplemented by handwritten notes [Paynter Archive A].
22. Thomas, Keith., *Religion and the Decline of Magic* (London: Weidenfeld & Nicolson, 1971) pp. 587–606; Brown, Theo,. *The Fate of the Dead—A Study in Folk Eschatology in the West Country after the Reformation* (Ipswich: D. S. Brewer Ltd., 1979) pp. 15–34.
23. For instance, see Rule, John., "Methodism, Popular Beliefs and Village Culture in Cornwall, 1800–1850." in Storch, R. (ed.), *Popular Culture and Custom in Nineteenth-Century England* (London, 1982) pp. 48–70; Davies, Owen., "Methodism, the Clergy, and Popular Belief in Witchcraft and Magic." *History* 82 (1997) pp. 252–265; Semmens, Jason., '"I will not go to the Devil for a Cure": Witchcraft, Demonic Possession and Spiritual Healing in Nineteenth-Century Devon." *Journal for the Academic Study of Magic* 2 (2004) pp. 132–155.

CHAPTER 4: OLD CORNWALL

1. Coombes, Brian., '"Gathering the Fragments...': Henry Jenner, the Old Cornwall Societies and Gorseth Kernow." in Williams, Derek

R. (ed.) *Henry and Katherine Jenner—A Celebration of Cornwall's Culture, Language and Identity* (London: Francis Boutle Publishers, 2004) pp. 161–164.

2. Stevens, Brian., "Gather ye the Fragments that are Left, that Nothing be Lost: The Origin of the Old Cornwall Societies." *Old Cornwall* 13, No. 6 (2006) pp. 2–11; see also Jenkin, A. K. Hamilton., "How it Started." *Old Cornwall* 7, No. 7 (1970) pp. 289–292.
3. Quoted in Stevens, Brian., "Gather ye the Fragments…" p. 6.
4. Nance, Robert Morton., "Old Cornwall Societies." *Old Cornwall* 1, No. 2 (1925) p. 41.
5. Hale, Amy., "A History of the Cornish Revival." in Saunders, Tim (ed.), *The Wheel: An Anthology of Modern Poetry in Cornish* (London: Francis Boutle Publishers, 1999) p. 20.
6. Coombes, Brian., "Gathering the Fragments…" p. 165.
7. Paynter, William H., "Seen by "Kit Hill."' *Cornish Times* (5 October 1928) p. 5.
8. Hale, Amy., "A History of the Cornish Revival…" p. 23.
9. Semmens, Jason., "Guising, Ritual and Revival: The Hobby Horse in Cornwall." *Old Cornwall* 13, No. 6 (2005) p. 43; Nance called the Penzance guisers' horse *Penglaze*, and devoted an entry to this supposed Celtic beast in his *New Cornish–English Dictionary* (1938) p. 128, believing it to be a genuine Celtic noun for 'hobby horse'; however 'Old Penglaze' was a human character, accompanied by a nameless hobby horse, see Sandys, William., *Christmas Carols, Ancient and Modern* (London: Beckley, 1833) p. cxiii.
10. Anon., "Old Cornwall." *Western Weekly News* (12 January 1929) p. 8.
11. Anon., "Bonfires—Chain of Flame through Cornwall." *Cornish Times* (28 June 1929) p. 6.
12. "J.F.", "Midsummer—Customs Observed at the Summer Solstice." *Western Evening Herald* (24 June 1930) p. 4.
13. Anon., "Cornish Gorsedd at The Hurlers." *Cornish Times* (5 September 1930) p. 2.
14. Paynter, William H., "Idle Thoughts from "Kit Hill."' *Cornish Times* (20 January 1933) p. 2.
15. Paynter, William H., "Idle Thoughts from "Kit Hill."' *Cornish Times* (26 May 1933) p. 8.
16. Anon., "Ancient Callington." *Cornish Times* (5 July 1935) p. 6.
17. The 1927 *Cornish Times* article on St. Mary's Church, Callington, resulted in the Church Guide of 1933; similarly articles published

in 1932 and 1963 were republished as *Daniel Gumb—The Cornish Cave-man Mathematician* (1946) and *Our East Cornwall Mines* (1964) respectively. The manuscript notes concerning St. Mary's, Callington, were donated by Paynter to the Royal Institution of Cornwall in December 1956. A similar collection concerning Kit Hill was donated on 1 September 1957.

18. One of the Cornish 'characters' Paynter had a particular interest in was the unfortunate Charlotte Dymond of Bodmin Moor. Paynter was the first modern writer to take an interest in her murder, in 1844, enlivened by his grandfather's account of a sighting of Dymond's ghost by the Rifle Volunteers in the late nineteenth century, and again by another sighting reported by a visitor to Tredethy House in the 1940s. Paynter was contacted in 1973 by Pat Munn of Bodmin who was keen to write a history of the affair. Paynter provided Munn with source materials and directed her to several others. Munn's *The Charlotte Dymond Murder: Cornwall, 1844* was published in 1978 and acknowledged Paynter's contribution. Paynter's interest was also the inspiration behind Charles Causley's *Ballad of Charlotte Dymond* (1958), and he was presented with a signed copy upon publication [Paynter Archive A]. For subsequent use of Paynter's research see also Turner, James., *Ghosts in the West Country* (Newton Abbot: David and Charles, 1973) pp. 12–19.

19. Paynter never applied for membership to The Folklore Society, London, nor ever apparently submitted a paper for publication in its journal. Pers comm. Caroline Oates.

20. Several manuscript versions and printers' proofs of Paynter's pamphlets survive in both archives, confirming costs, quantities and to whom Paynter sent review copies and suggestions for distribution. They are *Looe—A History and Guide* [Paynter Archive A], *Trelawne and Bishop Trelawny* (folders 475 and 477) and *Primitive Physic* (folder 485) [Paynter Archive B].

21. Paynter's interest in Wesley's work and his edition of *Primitive Physic* was profiled in Truen, David., "Take Live Spider, Cover in Breadcrumbs and … Swallow!" *Cornish Guardian* (16 January 1975) p. 26.

22. Allen, John. (Paynter, William H. (ed.)), *The History and Borough of Liskeard* (Marazion: Wordens of Cornwall Ltd., 1967) p. 7.

23. Anon., "The Cornish Moors." *Cornish Times* (13 May 1932) p. 7; Regarding Paynter's interest in the antiquities of East Cornwall, he compiled a notebook entitled THE CHEESEWRING & CARADON / ANTIQUITIES / NOTES & REFERENCES which contained notes on Daniel Gumb (including photographs of his house), the Cheesewring, the Hurlers, Trethevy Quoit, Doniert's Stone, Dosmary Pool, Minions Mound, Manor Pound, 'The Prehistoric Burial Place,' and George Barrow [Paynter Archive A]; Following their meeting in 1955, Paynter proposed Ithell Colquhoun for bardship of the Gorsedd to Nance. The process progressed smoothly before grinding to a halt, apparently stopped due to unease concerning Colquhoun's involvement with several esoteric movements and her work on the occult (pers comm. Amy Hale); For a discussion concerning the Cornish Gorsedd and modern esotericism see Hale, Amy., '"In the Eye of the Sun': The Relationship between the Gorseth and Esoteric Druidry." *Cornish Studies* 8 (2000) pp. 182–196.
24. Anon., "Display of Cornish Antiquities." *Cornish Guardian* (23 January 1969) p. 11; Anon., "Treasures and Antiquities on Display." *Cornish Guardian* (27 February 1969) p. 3.
25. Correspondence Paynter–Munn (11 February 1974) and (2 April 1974) [Paynter Archive A].
26. Anon., "Round about Liskeard." *Cornish Guardian* (12 December 1965) p. 3.
27. Anon., "Cornish 'Exiles' Gathered at Cirencester." *Cornish Guardian* (25 April 1968) p. 13; By 1959 Paynter offered 12 different lectures, including: "Witch-hunting in Cornwall," "Cornish Charms and Charmers," "Cornish Ghosts and Haunted Houses," "Tales of Mystery and Imagination," "An Evening with the Tinder Box," "Cornish Humour," "While I Remember," "In Search of the Odd," "An Evening with the Birds," "Ask Me Another," "A Cornish Quiz" and "This & That." [Author's Collection].
28. Anon., "Week at Looe—Cornish Museum Opened." *Cornish Times* (19 June 1959) p. 5; Paynter noted that he had been collecting objects relating to the history of Cornwall for much of his life and recalled the encouragement given by his teacher Lilian Read, in whose classroom was a cupboard for the collection of curiosities

known as "The Museum"—Paynter/Tucker Collection, South West Film Archive, Plymouth.

29. Perry, Ronald., "The Changing Face of Celtic Tourism in Cornwall, 1875–1975." *Cornish Studies* 7 (1999) pp. 94–106.

30. Stevens, Brian J., "Gather Ye the Fragments that are Left, that Nothing be Lost: The Origins of the Old Cornwall Societies." *Old Cornwall* 13, No. 6 (2006) p. 7.

31. Truen, David., "Whyler Pystry—or Bill Paynter to his Friends." *Cornish Guardian* (16 January 1975) p. 29; for another contemporary reaction see Hogg, Garry., *Museums of England* (Newton Abbot: David & Charles, 1973) pp. 50, 51; also Anon., "New Book features Looe's Museum." *Cornish Times* (2 November 1973) p. 6.

32. Anon., "Week at Looe—Cornish Museum Opened." *Cornish Times* (19 June 1959) p. 5; the artefact is now at the Guildhall Museum, East Looe.

33. Pers comm. Jeremy Tucker.

34. Paynter was filmed at the Cornish Museum during 1968, and again in May 1969 and August 1969, talking about 'Cornish' mementos manufactured in the Far East, and recounting several Cornish stories. These are now at the South West Film Archive, Plymouth.

35. Coombes, Brian., "Keeping Cornwall Cornish: Robert Morton Nance and the Federation of Old Cornwall Societies." in Thomas, Peter W. & Williams, Derek R. (eds.), *Setting Cornwall on its Feet: Robert Morton Nance, 1873–1959* (London: Francis Boutle Publishers, 2007) pp. 227, 228.

CHAPTER 5: WITCH-HUNTING IN CORNWALL

1. *Cornish Times* (9 March 1928) p. 7; the "little Devon town" in question was Lifton, see Anon., "Mystery of Lifton—Queer Happenings in a Cottage." *Western Morning News and Mercury* (15 February 1928) p. 5; also Anon., "Mystery of Lifton Cottage—Sir A. Conan Doyle's Explanation." *Western Morning News and Mercury* (18 February 1928) p. 5.

2. *Western Morning News and Mercury* (26 April 1928) pp. 3, 10.

3. *Western Morning News and Mercury* (4 June 1928) pp. 6, 10.

4. *Old Cornwall* 1, No. 9 (1929) pp. 28–33; Here Paynter misread the seventeenth-century divine Joseph Glanvill's (1636–1680) work, confusing the Wiltshire haunting of the 'Demon of Tedworth' in 1661/62 with the examinations taken by the Somerset J.P. Robert Hunt in 1657 and printed in *Saducismus Triumphatus* (1681) pp. 270–289.
5. *Cornish Times* (23 August 1929) p. 2; The Westcountry case alluded to was probably that heard in a Somerset court, see Anon., "Witchcraft Fears." *Western Weekly News* (15 June 1929) p. 5.
6. *Western Morning News and Mercury* (3 March 1932) p. 6; For details of the Wolverhampton case see Anon., "Witches—Secret "Spells" in the Night." *Daily Mail* (14 January 1932) p. 7; also Anon., "Witchcraft in Midlands." *Sunday Times* (17 January 1932) p. 16; Many of the letters Paynter received are contained in Paynter Archives A and B; An 'emmenagogue' is a substance derived from plants used to excite menstrual discharge.
7. *Cornish Times* (2 November 1934) p. 8.
8. *Cornish Times* (1 February 1935) p. 7.
9. *The Cornish Review* 13 (1969) pp. 69–73.

CHAPTER 6: CORNISH CHARMS AND CURES

1. *Old Cornwall* 1, No, 9 (1929) pp. 41, 42.
2. *Old Cornwall* 1, No, 9 (1929) p. 42.
3. *Old Cornwall* 1, No, 9 (1929) p. 43.
4. *Old Cornwall* 1, No, 9 (1929) p. 44.
5. *Western Weekly News* (31 August 1929) p. 4.
6. *Western Evening Herald* (24 July 1931) p. 7.
7. *Western Evening Herald* (11 September 1931) p. 7.
8. *Cornish Times* (8 April 1932) p. 2.
9. *Western Evening Herald* (16 February 1933) p. 6.
10. *Western Evening Herald* (3 March 1933) p. 4.
11. *Cornish Times* (14 April 1933) p. 7.
12. *Cornish Times* (7 July 1933) p. 2.
13. *Cornish Times* (1 June 1934) p. 8; Paynter took the 'Babylonian incantation' from Thompson, Charles., *Mysteries and Secrets of Magic* (London: John Lane, 1927) p. 38, where an "hulduppi" would appear to be a transliteration of the cuneiform for an otherwise untranslatable word.

14. *Cornish Times* (4 October 1935) p. 7.
15. *Old Cornwall* 6, No. 11 (1966) pp. 483–488; the dating of Paynter's ramble on the coast to 1965 is confirmed by one of his surviving tape recordings, in which he read aloud his *Old Cornwall* article with several additions not found in the printed version—Paynter/Tucker Collection, South West Film Archive, Plymouth.

CHAPTER 7: CORNISH GHOSTS AND HAUNTED HOUSES

1. Manuscript (1949), [Paynter Archive B].
2. Manuscript (1953), [Paynter Archive B]. The article was submitted to the editor of *The Sunday Pictorial* on 17 October 1953 for inclusion in a series the magazine was running on ghosts. It was rejected in a letter dated 15 November 1953; for further details of Paynter's investigations into the Stoke Climsland Negro haunting see Anon., "The Big Blackamoor Ghost of Stoke Climsland." *Tavistock Times* (11 September 1953) p. 2; Madford House was demolished in September 1953 after being condemned by the local council as dangerous. By chance Paynter was on business in the area on 25 September 1953 and was presented with the carved oak head of the banister by the foreman overseeing the demolition—see Anon., "The Haunted House was no More." *Cornish and Devon Post* (26 September 1953) p. 6. The artefact is now in the Guildhall Museum, Looe.
3. Manuscript draft script (February 1956), [Paynter Archive A].
4. Transcript from 'Cornish Ghosts and Haunted Houses' lecture (c. 1969), Paynter/Tucker Collection, South West Film Archive, Plymouth.
5. Manuscript (1 July 1969), [Paynter Archive A]; Beatrice Chase was the pen name of the writer Olive Katharine Parr (1874–1955), descended from William Parr, brother of Catherine the sixth wife of Henry VIII. Born at Harrow, Middlesex, Chase settled in the Westcountry, at first at Looe, later at Widecombe-in-the-Moor. Owing to her many Dartmoor-based novels, including *The Ghost of the Moor*, she was popularly referred to as "The Lady of the Moor."

6. Transcript of "Black Cockerel Ghost Story" (10 December 1969), Paynter/Tucker Collection, South West Film Archive, Plymouth. The inn in question was the Punch Bowl Inn, Lanreath.

CHAPTER 8: CORNISH HUGGER MUGGER

1. Manuscript of talk broadcast on the B.B.C. *West of England* programme (20 January 1939), 6.30–7.00 p.m. [Paynter Archive B]; the bottle that Paynter was to be heard blowing into was not the original "Tammy Blee's Scent Bottle," but rather a reproduction; he is shown holding such in Hogg, Garry., *Museums of England* (Newton Abbot: David & Charles, 1973) p. 51.
2. Manuscript (June 1948), [Paynter Archive A].
3. Manuscript draft script (June 1956), [Paynter Archive A].
4. Manuscript draft script (February 1957), [Paynter Archive A].
5. Text from the booklet accompanying the "Hap Da" Talisman, (1959) [Paynter Archive A].

CHAPTER 9: TALES OF MYSTERY AND IMAGINATION

1. *Cornish Times* (1 January 1937) p. 6.
2. Uncollated newspaper clipping [Paynter Archive A], provenanced by Paynter as *Cornish Times* (21 January 1942).
3. Uncollated newspaper clipping [Paynter Archive A], provenanced by Paynter as *Cornish Times* (23 May 1950).
4. *Cornish Times* (29 December 1950) p. 2.
5. *Cornish Times* (4 January 1952) p. 6.
6. *Cornish Times* (26 December 1952) p. 4.

WILLIAM H. PAYNTER
Select Bibliography

Some difficulty attends the compilation of a complete bibliography of Paynter's published works, which would be a labour of considerable persistence with diminishing returns. Paynter produced articles from 1924 until at least 1968—a period of 44 years or more, and while the *Cornish Times* was Paynter's main outlet, especially during his most active period as a folklore fieldworker, the *Cornish and Devon Post*, the *East Cornwall Times*, *Old Cornwall*, *The Cornish Review*, the *Western Evening Herald*, the *Western Morning News*, and the *Western Weekly News* also published his articles regionally, and he is known to have submitted occasional articles to various London papers and journals, including the *Daily Mail*. Paynter was in the habit of keeping his printed articles in scrapbooks and generally annotated them with publication provenance, though oftentimes this bibliographic information was added later and Paynter was occasionally at fault with the details.

The cuttings scrapbooks and the British Library catalogue have been the basis of the following select bibliography, which incorporates Paynter's monographs, articles, weekly columns and letters, arranged thematically and chronologically. Each article has been collated with the relevant newspaper and the several articles provenanced but not collated are appended at the end. The *Cornish Times* and *Old Cornwall* have been read systematically from 1926 to 1970, the other papers only partially. While the list of monographs and weekly columns is complete, it seems likely that there are further articles and an abundance of letters still to index.

Monographs

Kit Hill—A Souvenir (Callington, 1928).

Callington: The Official Guide (Callington: Callington Urban District Council, 1930).

A Short Guide to the Church of St. Mary (the Blessed Virgin), Callington (Plymouth: Underhills, 1933) Second Edition 1967.

Daniel Gumb: The Cornish Cave-man Mathematician (Liskeard: Privately Printed, 1946).

Trelawne and Bishop Trelawny (Wadebridge: Quintrell & Co., 1962).

Our Old Cornish Mines: East Cornwall (Liskeard: Privately Printed, 1964).

The Parish Church of St. Martin, Liskeard (Liskeard: Parochial Church Council, 1966).

Liskeard and District Official Guide (London: Directory Publications, 1967).

Looe—A History and Guide (East Looe: The Cornish Museum, 1970).

Monographs Edited

Wesley, John., *Primitive Physic—John Wesley's Book of Old fashioned Cures and Remedies* (Plymouth: Underhills, 1958) Subsequent reprints.

Allen, John., *The History of the Borough of Liskeard* (Marazion: Wordens of Cornwall Ltd., 1967).

Articles

"Rowdyism." *East Cornwall Times* (7 November 1924) p. 8.

"A Westcountry Anecdote." *East Cornwall Times* (27 August 1926) p. 2.

"Arrival of Woodcock." *East Cornwall Times* (5 November 1926) p. 7.

"Stoke Climsland Nature Story—A Strange Visitor to Stoke Climsland Farm." *Cornish Times* (5 November 1926) p. 8.

"Linkinhorne Badger Club—Unusual Experience with a Badger." *Cornish Times* (19 November 1926) p. 3.

"Fox Fights Dog—Unusual Incident in Valley near Callington." *Western Morning News* (23 November 1926) p. 9.

"Bird Life on the North Coast of Cornwall." *Cornish and Devon Post* (6 August 1927) p. 7.

"Saint Mary's Church, Callington—Its History and Unique Monuments." *Cornish and Devon Post* (3 September 1927) p. 6.

"The Knight and the Lady—Romantic Story of an Old Cornish Well." *Western Morning News* (3 August 1927) p. 4.

"A Cheesewring Grave—Ancient Man's Burial Place." *Cornish Times* (26 August 1927) p. 8.

"Cornish Superstitions and Omens." *Cornish and Devon Post* (1 October 1927) p. 8.

"Rush Lights in Cornwall—Story of an Old Industry." *Cornish Times* (30 December 1927) p. 3.

"Witchcraft—A Glance into the Past." *Cornish Times* (9 March 1928) p. 7.

"Witch of the West—Tammy Blee and her Scent Bottle." *Western Morning News and Mercury* (26 April 1928) pp. 3, 10.

"A Helston Witch." *Western Morning News and Mercury* (4 June 1928) pp. 6, 10.

"Historical Note." *Cornish Times* (14 September 1928) p. 3.

"Candlemas—The Festival and its Customs." *Cornish Times* (1 February 1929) p. 3.

"Peace with France Celebrations in Devon and Cornwall." *Western Weekly News* (18 May 1929) p. 4.

"Tales of Cornish Witches." *Old Cornwall* 1, No. 9 (1929) pp. 28–33.

"East Cornwall Baby Lore." *Old Cornwall* 1, No. 9 (1929) pp. 41, 42.

"Curious East Cornwall Cures." *Old Cornwall* 1, No. 9 (1929) p. 42.

"Rattle-Bones and Pancakes." *Old Cornwall* 1, No. 9 (1929) pp. 42, 43.

"King's Evil." *Old Cornwall* 1, No. 9 (1929) p. 43.

"A Ringworm Cure." *Old Cornwall* 1, No. 9 (1929) p. 44.

"The Evil Eye." *Cornish Times* (23 August 1929) p. 2.

"West Country Folk Medicine." *Western Weekly News* (31 August 1929) p. 4.

"Samuel Drew, M.A." *Cornish Times* (8 November 1929) p. 8.

"Old Time Items." *Cornish Times* (20 December 1929) p. 10.

"Some Curious Westcountry Epitaphs." *Western Weekly News* (4 January 1930) p. 4.

"Old Time Notes." *Cornish Times* (17 January 1930) p. 2.

"The Well—Its History and Legends." *Cornish Times* (24 January 1930) p. 2.

"Old Time Notes—Mother Shipton's Prophesies." *Cornish Times* (14 February 1930) p. 8.

"Old Times Notes." *Cornish Times* (14 March 1930) p. 2.

"A Story of Cotehele—Doctor and Nocturnal Ghost." *Cornish Times* (11 April 1930) p. 8.

"A Pessimist at Callington—Interview by "Kit Hill."" *Cornish Times* (25 April 1930) p. 7.

"Old May-day Celebrations." *Western Evening Herald* (29 April 1930) p. 4.

"Old Joe Wilton's Lodging House." *Old Cornwall* 1, No. 11 (1930) p. 37.

"Football at Callington—"Kit Hill" Interviews Our Correspondent." *Cornish Times* (9 May 1930) p. 7.

"Traditions and Legends of Saint Neot." *Western Evening Herald* (13 May 1930) p. 4.

"Politeness—A Literary Curiosity Found in East Cornwall." *Cornish Times* (25 July 1930) p. 3.

"What is a Gorsedd?" *Cornish Times* (15 August 1930) p. 2.

"Memories of the Great Plague—North Devon Experiences." *Cornish Times* (26 September 1930) p. 6.

"The Piskies." *Old Cornwall* 1, No. 12 (1930) p. 12.

"St. Germans, Looe and Polperro—A Tramp's Experiences." *Cornish Times* (6 February 1931) p. 3.

"Curios of Cornish Churches—Epitaphs and Admonitions." *Cornish Times* (6 March 1931) p. 8.

"The Commandments—Century-old Charm Found at Callington." *Cornish Times* (10 April 1931) p. 3.

"Lighting in Other Days—The Innovation of Gas." *Cornish Times* (8 May 1931) p. 6.

"Balloon Adventure of 1837." *Cornish Times* (22 May 1931) p. 6.

"Extraordinary Human Ingenuity—Performing Fleas and Other Novelties of 353 Years Ago." *Cornish Times* (29 May 1931) p. 7.

"Curious Westcountry Cures." *Western Evening Herald* (24 July 1931) p. 7.

"Joanna Southcott." *Cornish Times* (14 August 1931) p. 2.

"Cornish Charms and Cures." *Western Evening Herald* (11 September 1931) p. 7.

"Mysterious and Unlucky Rings." *Cornish Times* (27 November 1931) p. 7.

"Trials by Ordeal." *Cornish Times* (1 January 1932) p. 6.

"Witches and Witchcraft." *Western Morning News* (3 March 1932) p. 6.

"Cures for Toothache." *Cornish Times* (8 April 1932) p. 2.

"Daniel Gumb—The Cornish Cave-Man Mathematician." *Old Cornwall* 2, No. 4 (1932) pp. 1–4.

"The Living Spirit in Cornwall." *Cornish Times* (28 July 1932) p. 8.

"Yuletide Lore." *Cornish Times* (23 December 1932) p. 2.

"Westcountry Bird Lore." *Western Evening Herald* (16 February 1933) p. 6.

"Tales and Superstitions About the Cuckoo." *Western Evening Herald* (3 March 1933) p. 4.

"Love and Magic—Some Curious Superstitions and their Origin." *Cornish Times* (14 April 1933) p. 7.

"Most Common Superstitions." *Cornish Times* (7 July 1933) p. 2.

"Callington Church—To-day's Need Recalls Fire of 1895." *Cornish Times* (18 August 1933) p. 3.

"A Flourishing Industry in Bygone Days." *Western Evening Herald* (21 March 1934) p. 4.

"Witchcraft Trees and Flowers." *Cornish Times* (1 June 1934) p. 8.

"At Kit Hill." *Cornish Times* (29 June 1934) p. 4.

"Clocks—Old and New." *Cornish Times* (13 July 1934) p. 2.

"'Kit Hill" Recalls Some Early Newspapers." *Cornish Times* (18 September 1934) p. 8.

"I Have My Fortune Told." *Cornish Times* (2 November 1934) p. 8.

"The Tinder Box." *Cornish Times* (21 December 1934) p. 4.

"The Horse Shoe." *Cornish Times* (1 February 1935) p. 7.

"Callington." *Cornish Times* (10 May 1935) p. 3.

"For "Whoopen Cough,"—"Witch Remedies" of Our Forefathers." *Cornish Times* (4 October 1935) p. 7.

"A Tragi-Comedy of Linkinhorne—Who Killed Poor Betsy." *Supplement to the Cornish Times* (20 December 1935) p. v.

"Origin of Nursery Rhymes." *Cornish Times* (8 May 1936) p. 3.

"The Picture of "The Lady"—A Weird but True Story." *Cornish Times* (1 January 1937) p. 6.

"The Mysterious Visitor." *Cornish Times* (24 December 1937) p. 8.

"The March of 47 Years Ago." *Cornish Times* (1 April 1938) p. 8.

"Some Little-Known Facts." *Cornish Times* (23 September 1938) p. 3.

"Old Cornwall Yarns." *Cornish Times* (6 January 1939) p. 3

"The Mysterious Visitor—The True Story of a Midnight Apparition." *Cornish Times* (23 December 1949) p. 8.

"Two Strange Stories." *Cornish Times* (29 December 1950) p. 2.

"Murder Will Out—Strange Westcountry Story." *Cornish Times* (4 January 1952) p. 6.

"A Strange Dream." *Cornish Times* (26 December 1952) p. 4.

"Wind-Engine once Feature on Summit of Historic Kit Hill." *Western Morning News* (16 March 1953) p. 4.

"Old Callington—Looking Back 90 Years." *Cornish Times* (3 April 1953) p. 2.

"A Cornish Pasty." *Cornish Times* (23 July 1954) p. 7.

"Old Liskeard—Jottings by Borough Archivist." *Cornish Times* (23 September 1956) p. 8.

"The Pipe Well's Water is Contaminated." *Cornish Times* (14 June 1963) p. 5.

"They Three Choughs." *Cornish Times* (9 August 1963) p. 8.

"The Cornish Chough." *Cornish Times* (30 August 1963) p. 2.

"The Mines About Callington." *Cornish Times* (30 August 1963) p. 3.

"The Mines About Callington." *Cornish Times* (6 September 1963) p. 5.

"The Mines About Callington." *Cornish Times* (27 September 1963) p. 4.

"The Mines About Callington." *Cornish Times* (11 October 1963) p. 5.

"The Caradon Miners' Friendly Society." *Cornish Times* (6 December 1963) p. 5.

"The Mines About Liskeard." *Cornish Times* (13 December 1963) p. 5.

"About Our Old Mines." *Cornish Times* (17 January 1964) p. 3.

"In Search of the Odd on the North Cornish Coast." *Old Cornwall* 6, No. 11 (1966) pp. 483–488.

"The Moorland Murder—A Cornish Romance Which Ended in Tragedy." *Old Cornwall* 6, No. 12 (1967) pp. 532–536.

"19th Century Justifications of the Ancient Sport of Cock-fighting." *Western Morning News* (20 March 1968) p. 4.

"Gleaning from an Old Cornish Guide." *Old Cornwall* 8, No. 12 (1979) pp. 608–611.

Correspondence

"New Year Folk-Lore." *Western Morning News* (6 January 1927) p. 8.

"Cleet Wine." *Western Morning News* (12 May 1927) p. 3.

"Our Songsters." *Western Morning News* (20 May 1927) p. 2.

"Oil Pollution and Birds." *Western Morning News* (29 July 1927) p. 2.

"Remember the Birds." *Western Morning News* (21 December 1927) p. 3.

"Disappearance of Swallows." *Western Morning News* (15 May 1928) p. 3.

"Insect Mimicry." *Western Morning News* (2 September 1929) p. 2.

"Sherborne Men." *Western Morning News* (2 November 1929) p. 9.

"The Old Volunteers." *Western Morning News* (10 February 1930) p. 3.

"Homing Pigeon Enemies." *Western Morning News* (15 April 1930) p. 3.

"Candle-Jumping." *Western Morning News* (5 June 1930) p. 3.

"Belief in Witchcraft." *The Times* (25 September 1930) p. 8.

"Innovation of Gas." *Western Morning News* (19 May 1931) p. 3.

"High Tide at Plymouth." *Western Morning News* (20 May 1931) p. 3.

"Robert Jeffrey." *Cornish Times* (11 March 1938) p. 5.

Columns

"The Scout Corner." *East Cornwall Times* (28 March 1924–26 September 1924).

"Nature Story." *Western Morning News* (14 April 1924–1929).

"The Scout Corner." *Deanery of East Magazine* (1927).

"Seen by "Kit Hill."—Callington Notes & News." *Cornish Times* (28 October 1928–31 October 1930).

"Here and There—Notes by "Kit Hill."'" *Cornish Times* (5 December 1930–20 February 1931).

"Idle Thoughts from "Kit Hill."'" *Cornish Times* (15 January 1932–22 March 1940).

"West in the Past." *Western Morning News* (1 February 1934–31 July 1935).

Articles Provenanced by Paynter but Uncollated

"A Cornish Moorland Romance Which Ended in Tragedy." *Western Evening Herald* (1930s) [Paynter Archive A].

"A Cornish Eccentric—Sir James Tillie and Pentillie Castle." *Cornish Guardian* (24 December 1929) [Paynter Archive B].

"Songs a Century Ago—Weird Words for Children's Tongues." *Cornish Times* (26 May 1931) [Paynter Archive B].

"Personages of Old Callington." *Cornish Times* (23 February 1938) [Paynter Archive A].

"Westcountry Children's Rhymes & Games." *Western Evening Herald* (3 July 1939) [Paynter Archive B].

"A Weird Christmas Eve—Wine and Cards at a Cornish Inn." *Cornish Times* (21 January 1942) [Paynter Archive A].

"Call from the Dead—A True Telephone Story." *Cornish Times* (23 May 1950) [Paynter Archive A].

Correspondence

"Notes and Queries 469.—Daniel Gumb." *Western Morning News* (1925) [Paynter Archive A].

"Desecration of the Countryside." *Western Morning News* (February 1927) [Paynter Archive A].

"The Protection of Birds." *Western Morning News* (4 May 1927) [Paynter Archive A].

"Cornish Choughs." *Western Morning News* (4 September 1927) [Paynter Archive A].

"Cornish Witches and Charms." *Cornish Times* (12 October 1930) [Paynter Archive A].

"Mother Shipton—Did She Make a Compact with the Devil?" *Western Morning News* (19 December 1930) [Paynter Archive B].

"Honest and Faithful Servant." *Western Morning News* (20 December 1930) [Paynter Archive B].

"Westcountry Folk Medicine." *Cornish Times* (23 May) [Paynter Archive B].

"A Cornish Bard—Appreciation of the Late Mr. F. J. Thomas." *Western Morning News* (2 March 1934) [Paynter Archive A].